ANDRÉ
CITROËN

André Citroën, 1878–1935

ANDRÉ CITROËN

The Man and the Motor Cars

JOHN REYNOLDS

Foreword by Chris Goffey

ALAN SUTTON PUBLISHING LIMITED

First published in 1996 by
Alan Sutton Publishing Limited • Phoenix Mill
Thrupp • Stroud • Gloucestershire • GL5 2BU

British Library Cataloguing in Publication Data
A catalogue record for this book is available from the British Library

ISBN 0 7509 1258 8

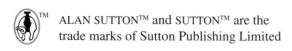

TM   ALAN SUTTON™ and SUTTON™ are the
trade marks of Sutton Publishing Limited

Typeset in 10/13pt New Baskerville
Typesetting and origination by
Alan Sutton Publishing Limited
Printed in Great Britain by
Butler & Tanner, Frome, Somerset.

Contents

Acknowledgements   vii

Picture Credits   viii

Foreword   ix

A Brief Chronology   xi

Introduction   1

Part 1: The Engineer

1. The Discovery of the Double Chevron   6

2. Citroën Goes to War   23

3. The Henry Ford of France   49

4. The Talk of London and Paris   67

Part 2: The Explorer

5. Caterpillars that Crossed the Sahara   85

6. An African Adventure   102

7. An Eastern Odyssey   116

8. The Lord of the Ice   135

Part 3: The Entrepreneur

9. Boom Turns to Bust   142

10. The Final Gamble   166

11. Citroën Pressé   189

12. Citroën sans Citroën   207

Appendices

The Cars of the André Citroën Era   218

Other Citroën Models Available between 1935 and 1939   219

European Car Production – Major Manufacturers 1919–35   219

Sources and Bibliography   234

Index   236

Citroën nous fait du bien; il nous
empêche de nous endormir
Louis Renault

(Citroen does us all good; he
prevents us from lulling ourselves
to sleep)

Acknowledgements

While this book cannot claim to be an official, authorised biography, since its production was in no way commissioned, sponsored or supported by either Automobiles Citroën or the Citroën family, in compiling it I was privileged to have been offered a considerable amount of unofficial help from within the Citroën organisation and, particularly, from certain *anciens* or ex-employees. The number of surviving Citroën personnel or associates who actually worked face to face with André Citroën, over sixty-five years ago, can now be counted on the fingers of one hand. Fortunately, I was able to speak to a couple of this tiny band, one of whom died within weeks of our discussions, at the age of ninety.

Of the other notable 'old boys' among my collaborators and contributors (whose service, though long and distinguished, does not actually extend quite as far back as the André Citroën era), two in particular deserve special mention. Firstly, I must pay tribute to M. Jacques Wolgensinger (Automobiles Citroën's former Director of Public Relations and himself a biographer of André Citroën) for his work in establishing the details of Citroën's early life, information which he has kindly allowed me to draw upon here. And secondly, grateful thanks are due, as ever, to Mr Ken Smith (former Chief Engineer of Citroën UK Ltd) for his unstinting support and encouragement throughout the very long and difficult process involved in turning this project from an idea into a reality.

I am also grateful to the following individuals for their contributions in providing advice, information, illustrations or support in research matters: Fred Annells, Sylvie Bader, Eric Bailey, Christopher Balfour, Gilles Blanchet, Malcolm Bobbitt, David Burgess-Wise, Jean Daninos, Bob Date, John Dodson, David Fletcher, Nick Georgano, Peter Hall, Gro Hoeg, Mike Ibbett, Wouter Jansen, Julian Leyton, Gerri Noone, the late Jack Pitchford, Mary Reynolds, Fabien Sabates, Tony Searle, Olivier de Serres, Eric Verhaest, John Walker, Malcolm Wright and Michael Wright (Assistant Curator of Mechanical Engineering, The Science Museum)

And finally, I must also acknowledge the very great debt I owe to my wife and family, including my parents. Without their patience, interest and understanding, this book could never have been produced.

John Reynolds, 1996

Picture Credits

Foreword

You never, so it is said, forget your first car. Now that's certainly true of me, because today I'm driving around in a rather better example of the model I first bought as a seventeen year old, more years ago than I care to remember. I was living in a North London bedsit at the time, impoverished, and desperate for my first set of 'wheels'.

I should have bought something sensible, economical and durable. Instead, I saw an advert in a newsagents' window. 'Citroen Light 15,' it said, 'good runner, £50.' Hardly the most inspiring invitation to trade I've ever come across. Nevertheless I shot round to the address, and in less time than it takes to say 'Here comes another mug' I was the proud possessor of a bright blue 1949 Citroën Traction Avant, with equally bright yellow wheels, and best of all a 15 ft ex-army whip aerial mounted on the back bumper.

Did I notice the rust holes in the floor through which you could see the road, listen to the ominous bearing rumble from deep in the crankcase, smell the oil fumes from the rocker cover and exhaust, or feel the tug at the steering as failing constant velocity joints jerked and snatched? Of course I didn't. I was in love, intoxicated with the rakish lines and inimitable style of a car which at its launch in 1934 had taken the motoring world by storm, and was destined to remain in production for twenty-three years, until its foibles and delights were known literally all over the world.

My love affair did not last long. I drove down to see my parents, then living at the other end of England. As dawn broke over the wild and beautiful vistas of Bodmin Moor, the oil smoke which tended to hang in layers inside the passenger compartment suddenly cleared. The old car bounded forward into the sunrise better than it had ever gone before. I touched a giddy 55 miles an hour before a fearsome bang and clatter proclaimed a broken con rod and a wrecked engine. The smoke had cleared, of course, because the entire contents of the sump had been used up in the 200 mile journey. I sadly sold the wreck for £5 to a dealer who said he might need a couple of parts off it, and went home on the train. But despite the experience, I remained an enthusiast for the marque.

My fascination with all things Citroën had its roots in a much earlier experience: as a schoolboy in the 1950s I had been given a lift in a shining black Citroën DS after the family MG Magnette had broken down in Spain. It was like being picked up in a space ship – the styling, the ride, the controls were so different to anything we had thus far experienced. That half-hour journey created a deep respect for the company and its products. So when, in the late '60s, I started writing the motoring page on various local and regional newspapers, and subsequently joined *The Autocar* magazine, I always made a point of road testing the latest models from the company. I drove the last of the incomparable DS range, the 23 EFi, looked after a long term GS, tested that memorable road rocket the Ami-Super, raced a 2CV, coveted and drove whenever I could the Citroen Maserati SM that belonged to the Sports Editor, and road tested the first CX. When television beckoned in the shape of BBC2's 'Top Gear', I made sure my name was against tests of the BX in various guises, the AX, XM and Xantia. I've just finished a happy week with the Xantia Activa, the first mass production car with active ride – an achievement of which I'm sure André Citroën, the founder of the company, would have approved.

Over the years I've read a great deal of material about the cars, but little about the man himself. John Reynolds' book has put that omission to rights. It's a perceptive insight into a versatile, contradictory and perhaps overambitious man, but above all an individualist, who put an indelible stamp upon his cars and his company.

Today's cars are designed by committee, hidebound by safety and emission laws, styled by computer, and market researched in clinics to the point of blandness and anonymity. That was something you could never say about Citroën; the cars that resulted from André Citroën's revolutionary thinking were, and sometimes remain, quirky, odd-ball and idiosyncratic in both design and execution. You either loved or loathed them; there could be no halfway house. But for me the love-hate affair goes on. Eight years ago I was driving home to Oxford when I saw a familiar tail sticking out of a garage. The foreman showed me round a very tidy 'Onze Normale' Traction Avant, built in Paris in 1949, but restored in Switzerland in the early 1980s. I contacted the owner, a delightful lady, who much against her will was being forced to sell because her new husband said they needed the garage space for his Aston. Money changed hands, and I drove away in my new possession. And I love it still. It's painted a two-tone creme caramel, trimmed in beige cloth with brown carpets. It will cruise all day at 60 miles an hour, and can exceed 70 mph with ease, though things get a bit noisy at that velocity. It possesses superb steering, precise to the inch, the ride is supple and the cornering and roadholding absolutely astonishing, even by modern standards. It is low and wide, and with big Michelin X tyres (still in production in the right sizes) it handles like a competition car. There's a huge amount of leg and headroom, especially in the back where three people sit at ease on a sort of great sofa. The floor of course is completely flat, no prop shaft tunnel to take up room. We've travelled all day across France, and stepped out at our destination free from stiffness, aches and pains. And the car raises interest and a smile wherever it goes.

It's fascinating to drive something that was the expression of one man's extraordinary vision. You can feel the force of personality behind the flow of a line and the turn of a wheel. It's a privilege to be allowed to share in the master's work. André Citroën deserves a far more prominent place in automotive history, and I hope that John Reynolds' book will go some way towards achieving that end.

In the meantime those of us who are lucky enough to enjoy the cars that bene-fited from his touch, as well as drivers of modern Citroën products, can now reflect upon the enterprise, foresight and ingenuity behind this famous name.

Chris Goffey, 1996

The Citroën Traction Avant, 1934–57, the world's first mass-produced front-wheel-drive car.

A Brief Chronology of the Life of André Citroën

1878   5 February André Citroën (AC) is born at 44 rue Lafitte, Paris IX.

1885   AC enters the Lycée Condorcet, Paris.

1898   AC enters the Ecole Polytechnique, Paris.

1900   April: AC visits Poland and acquires rights to manufacture double heli-cal gearwheels.
        July: graduates from Ecole Polytechnique.

1901   AC undergoes national service in an artillery regiment of the French army.

1902   AC opens a workshop to produce gearwheels, trading under the name of André Citroën et Cie.

1907   An office of André Citroën & Company is opened in the City of London, at 19/21 Queen Victoria Street.

1908   AC assumes responsibility for the management of Automobiles Mors.

1912   AC makes first visit to the USA and meets Henry Ford in Detroit.

1913   His gearwheel company, now known as Engrenages Citroën, Hinstin et Cie, is incorporated as a société anonyme or limited liability company.

1914   27 May: AC marries Giorgina Bingen.
        1 August: AC is mobilised as a reservist on the outbreak of the First World War.

1915   17 March: begins construction of a munitions factory on the Quai de Javel in Paris. By 15 June the factory is in full production.

1917   AC made responsible for organising a ration-card system to feed the people of Paris. Becomes a founder member of the Cercle de l'Union Interalliée.

1918   AC reorganises the affairs of the French Government's arsenal at Roanne.

1919   The Quai de Javel factory is adapted to manufacture Citroën's first auto-mobile, the Type A, Europe's first mass-produced, mass-marketed car.

1920   October: the first examples of the Citroën-Kegresse half-track vehicles are demonstrated at Saint-Denis. The Société Citroën-Kegresse-Hinstin is formed to manufacture these autochenilles. A Citroen Type A wins the French fuel-economy trials at le Mans and is acclaimed as the world's most economical car.

1921   October: the B2 is announced in conventional and half-tracked form at the Paris Salon motorshow.

1922   June: launch of the C3 (5CV) baby car.

July: AC attends demonstration of Citroën-Kegresse vehicles at Slough.

21 August: a branch of the Citroën-Kegresse company is established in London.

October: Citroën's name is sky-written in vapour trail letters by an aircraft flying over Paris.

1923   January: a convoy of Citroën B2 caterpillar cars arrives in Timbuktu, the first motor vehicles to cross the Sahara desert.

23 July: Citroën Cars Ltd is founded in the United Kingdom, as Automobiles Citroën's first foreign filiale or subsidiary.

November: AC hosts British premiere of *Raid Sahara* film at Victoria Palace Theatre, in presence of Queen Mary.

1924   March: AC makes second visit to the USA.

28 July: establishment of Automobiles Citroën as a limited company or Société anonyme. Creation of filiale companies in Italy, Belgium, Switzerland, Spain, Denmark and the Netherlands. Rate of construction at the Quai de Javel factory exceeds 260 vehicles a day.

September: creation of the Compagnie des Taxis Citroën based at Levallois in Paris.

October: Croisière Noire trans-African expedition sets out from Colombe Bechar.

All-steel bodywork is introduced on the B10 at the Paris Motor Show.

AC is made a Chevalier of the Legion d'Honneur.

1925   July: the Eiffel Tower is illuminated with the name Citroën, displayed by thousands of electric light bulbs visible for sixty miles in all directions.

October: the B12 is presented at the Paris Salon.

1926   Citroën production reaches 400 vehicles per day.

18 February: AC opens his British factory at Slough, the first of his factories outside France.

25–28 October: AC revisits London to open his showrooms at Devonshire House, Piccadilly and attend the Motor Show at Olympia.

October: at the Paris Salon, the B14 replaces the B12.

AC is promoted Officier de la Legion d'Honneur.

1927   May: AC receives the Prince of Wales at the Quai de Javel factory.

21 May: AC entertains Charles Lindbergh on the completion of the first solo trans-Atlantic flight.

July: representatives of the merchant bankers Lazard Frères join the board of directors of Automobiles Citroën.

1928   Total production of Citroën vehicles to date reaches 400,000 vehicles – 5 per cent of current production is exported.

16 January: AC visits London to attend gala performance of Croisière Noire film, preceded by a dinner party given by the Prince of Wales

at which the future King George VI and Queen Elizabeth are present.

October: the new AC4 and AC6 models are launched at the Paris Salon.

1929   AC is responsible for organising the French pavilion at the Barcelona International Exhibition.

The Arc de Triomphe, the Place de la Concorde, the Madeleine and the Chambre des Deputes are floodlit at Citroën's expense, as a gift to the citizens of Paris.

AC is promoted Commander of the Legion d'Honneur.

1930   Following a divergence of views, the representatives of Lazard Frères resign from the board of Automobiles Citroën.

1931   April: the Citroën Central Asian Expedition (Croisière Jaune) leaves its starting points in Beirut and Peking.

October: inauguration of the Magasin d'Europe in Paris.

AC sails for the USA to address the 8th Congress of American Heavy Industries in New York.

Foundation of the Société des Transports Citroën, a bus network covering metropolitan France.

1932   January: creation of the Citroën motor insurance company.

12 February: the Croisière Jaune arrives in Peking.

5 March–29 April: at Montlhery Rosalie II covers 36,000 kilometres in 54 days at an average speed of 104 kph, a new world record for distance and speed.

15 March: death of the Croisière Jaune's leader, G.-M. Haardt, in Hong Kong.

October: the new 8, 10 and 15 models are displayed at the Paris Salon.

30 November: a reception is held at the Sorbonne for the survivors of the Citroën Central Asian Expedition. AC is presented with the gold medal of the French geographical society by President Lebrun.

AC is promoted Grand Officier de la Legion d'Honneur.

1933   10 March–10 August: the Quai de Javel factory is reconstructed.

15 March–27 July: Rosalie III ('Petite Rosalie') covers 300,000 km in 133 days to smash 106 world endurance records.

8 October: the rebuilt factory is reopened with a banquet for 6,000 guests.

18 October: AC visits Sir Harry Ricardo in England to discuss joint diesel engine venture.

November: three Citroën caterpillar tracked lorries are despatched to the Antarctic, to participate in the US expedition led by Admiral Richard E. Byrd.

1934   28 February: Certain financial bills, interest payments and trade accounts due cannot be settled, because of the refusal of the Bank of France to extend further short-term credit. An appeal to the Citroën dealer network raises the funds required. André Citroën appeals to the Michelin family for further assistance.

18 April: The new Traction Avant (Citroën 7CV) model is officially unveiled at the Magasin d'Europe.

October: Francoise Lecot drives a Traction Avant from Paris to Moscow and back, non-stop. The Traction Avant range is the sensation of the Paris Motor Show.

November: a minor creditor opens default proceedings against Automobiles Citroën SA in the commercial court of Paris.

21 December: unable to prove its solvency, the company is placed under financial administration.

1935   3 January: the Citroën factories are closed while an inventory is made by the administrators.

18 January: André Citroën enters the Georges Bizet Clinic.

3 July: he dies from cancer of the stomach.

5 July: AC is buried at the Montparnasse cemetery.

31 July: An agreement between Automobiles Citroën and its creditors is formally ratified by the court. The Michelin firm assumes full control of Automobiles Citroën.

Introduction

The world's most famous unknown man?

Considering the thousands of makes that have arrived on the market over the past one hundred years since the automobile was invented, only to vanish almost as rapidly as they appeared, very few men indeed have been fortunate enough to lend their names to an enduring motor car marque, much less an immortal one.

Even fewer have had the strengths of talent and character to stamp on their creation not just their name but also their entire personality; and to do so with such forcefulness that their influence lived on in the vehicles produced by their successors, long after they themselves had departed from the scene.

André Citroën was just such a man. Along with such notables as Henry Ford, Vincenzo Lancia, Ettore Bugatti and Frederick Royce, he ranks as one of that tiny handful of pioneering engineer-entrepreneurs who created the very pattern of the motor car and the motor industry as we know them today, and whose names have survived to be associated forever with the achievement of excellence in automobile engineering.

Certainly, it is a matter of historical fact that many of the ideas and principles that now seem fundamental to car design and construction were first developed and put into practice by Automobiles Citroën, under his guidance and leadership. When he died in 1935, in its obituary the *Daily Telegraph* described him as 'a man whose business achievements were astonishing. By sheer ability, he succeeded in making his previously unknown name almost as famous as any in Europe . . . No enterprise was too great for André Citroën.'

Yet although today his name continues to be a familar (if unpronounceable) household word to countless millions of Anglo-Saxon motorists, displayed on almost every street of Europe beneath his ubiquitous double chevron badge, the man behind that name has somehow been lost. Indeed, only sixty years after his death, the character, personality and achievements of André Citroën himself have sadly been forgotten by succeeding generations, at least in America and Great Britain, and the enormous worldwide fame that he enjoyed during his short, active lifetime is now entirely overlooked.

Why should this be so? One reason, perhaps, is that since his demise, the Citroën firm has seen two far-reaching changes of ownership and management, the most recent owners – Peugeot – being a former rival. Another is that, quite inexplicably, no book has ever been written in English to record Citroën's life

André Citroën's first car, the Type A,
introduced in 1919, photographed at the
entrance to the Quai de Javel factory. At
the wheel is Citroën's first customer,
M. Testomolle of Beaulieu-sur-Dordogne.

and work and provide a memorial to his remarkable achievements, which were by no means confined to France.

For although he was often called 'the Henry Ford of France', André Citroën was very much more than just a motor magnate. Gifted with extraordinary talent, flair and creative energy, like Ford, he pioneered the manufacturing technology that made the mass-produced popular motor car a reality in France, England, Italy, Germany and the rest of Europe during the boom years that followed the First World War. And in doing so, he also created, almost single-handedly, the mass-market culture of car distribution and advertising that has surrounded this ultimate consumer product ever since.

Indeed, it can be claimed that, by stamping so many novel ideas and products with his double chevron badge, Citroën created a company with a distinctly individualistic corporate culture or identity. The yellow-painted Petite Citron 5CV car, the Croisières expeditions, the Eiffel Tower illuminations and the Traction Avant – all these achievements were utterly original and unique.

But in sharp contrast to Henry Ford (and also to his own great French rival Louis Renault), André Citroën was not by nature a conventional, conservative businessman. Neither orthodox in his methods and mentality nor entirely prudent in his financial dealings, he was far from being the kind of narrow-minded, hard-nosed capitalist motivated only by the bottom line on a balance sheet. On the contrary, his attitude to money was cavalier in the extreme. His famous saying, '*Dès l'instant où une idée est bonne, le prix n'a pas d'importance*' ('a good idea is beyond price') was characteristic of his brave but incautious response to commercial challenges.

Again, as the son of a Jewish diamond merchant with international business and family connections, André Citroën came from the affluent, sophisticated *haute bourgeoisie*, rather than the provincial farming or bicycle-making background that produced so many other notable motoring pioneers such as Ford. Urbane, intelligent and highly educated, as a graduate of the celebrated Ecole Polytechnique in Paris (the technical academy of the French Army), he ranked as a leading member of his country's scientific, commercial and cultural elite. But although his network of influential business, political and military contacts extended to the very highest levels of French, British and American society, he himself was somehow classless and cosmopolitan, preferring the company of artists, musicians, music hall singers and film stars to that of his fellow industrialists and businessmen. One such friend was Charlie Chaplin, perhaps an unlikely relationship in view of the caustic way that Chaplin caricatured Citroën's industrial methods in his film *Modern Times*.

However, despite this association with the bohemian milieu of showbusiness and popular entertainment, André Citroën was a man of high moral principles. A progressive, democratic, socially responsible employer who paid generous wages and was rewarded by the deep affection and loyalty of his workforce, his remarkable commercial acumen was combined with a profound social awareness. He foresaw that, if the ideal of emancipation was ever to be achieved by all

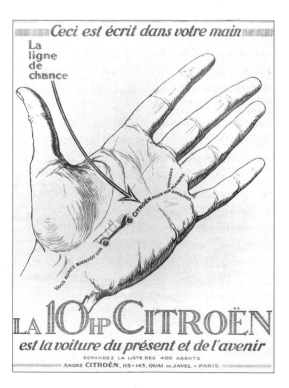

Nothing gives a better clue to André Citroën's methods and mentality than this extraordinary advertisement published in 1922. His optimistic disposition and his love of risk-taking and gambling are both revealed here by palmistry. 'The line of chance' appears to point directly towards health and happiness for his customers and great wealth for the motor-magnate himself. But, unfortunately, fate held a tragic destiny in store for Citroën.

classes, the key to future economic prosperity and political stability lay in finding ways to make the motor car available to the masses. The social mobility afforded by the car, he believed, could help bring liberty and self-fulfilment for all. By introducing the economies of large-scale production to automobile manufacture in Europe, as in America, he could bring down prices and increase output and so contribute to a technological and a sociological revolution simultaneously.

In all things, Citroën was an iconoclast, and as an engineer, industrialist and social reformer he played a significant part in shaping the course of world events during the First World War, the twenties and the thirties. On one hand, his dedication to technological and social progress provided a major driving force behind the early development of the motor car and road transportation in Europe, Africa, Asia and even North and South America. On the other, his profound creative energy and gift for innovation also influenced improvements or stimulated discoveries in a wide variety of other fields, ranging from military science and munitions production through matters of politics, business administration, industrial organisation and social welfare, and even extending to the worlds of cinema, journalism, fashion, commercial art and geographical exploration.

But as a personality, his immediate impact on current world events was greater still. Throughout his career, his face, words and deeds were familiar to millions on both sides of the Atlantic, thanks to his constant appearances on the cinema newsreels. No other industrialist before or after has ever achieved such status as

Citroën's final – and finest – creation, the Traction Avant, introduced in 1934, a mere fourteen years after the Type A. In celebrating a love of natural, human and mechanical beauty, this sunny photograph by Pierre Louys captures the spirit of Citroën the man, as well the essence of his most famous machine.

an international media celebrity – a tycoon whose flamboyant behaviour and free-spending lifestyle consistently made headline news around the globe. A legend in his own short lifetime, his activities were constantly reported by the gossip columnists of the day, while his own mastery of publicity and media relations consistently made headline news for his company in the international business, financial and motoring press.

At the height of his fame and fortune, he became a gregarious socialite who enjoyed to the full an extravagant lifestyle, dining with royalty or dancing with the aristocracy of the entertainment world. Constantly visible at the fashionable restaurants, racecourses and casinos of Paris, Deauville, Biarritz, Monte-Carlo or Saint-Moritz, he behaved 'like an emperor', playing baccarat for huge stakes and entertaining lavishly in a continual round of festivities.

The aim of this book is merely to set the record straight by restoring a recognisable human face to the familiar brand-name of Citroën, and so to help rehabilitate the reputation of the man who has often been described in his native land as '*un grand disparu*' ('a great departed') and '*le plus illustre inconnu de notre siècle*' ('the most famous unknown man of our century'). Besides telling the life story of this remarkable character, it also aims to explain, from an Anglo-Saxon perspective, the circumstances in which the earliest Citroën products were created and to account for the spectacular rise and fall of André Citroën's business empire.

By portraying the fascinating contrast between Citroën the progressive, innovative industrialist and social reformer and Citroën the capricious socialite, it also attempts to shed some light on another great historical paradox – the contrasting currents of gravity and frivolity that powered the age in which he lived and which created the tensions that energised and motivated his career.

The car that made Citroën's name – the 5CV Type C two-seater, introduced in 1922. Normally painted lemon-yellow, it was nicknamed the Petite Citron. Its low price and running costs combined with its ease of handling and simplicity of maintenance made it the first real woman's car.

PART 1: THE ENGINEER

The Discovery of the Double Chevron

Just as the word 'Camembert' conveys the pungent character of French cheeses, and 'Gitanes' the powerful aroma of French tobacco, so the word 'Citroën' has come to symbolise the distinctive flavour of French motor cars. Yet despite the fact that his name will always be associated with Gallic individuality and creativity in automobile design, André Citroën was neither a motor car engineer, an enthusiastic motorist or even, strictly speaking, a Frenchman, at least by descent. Although born and educated in France and therefore undeniably '*un vrai Français*' ('a true Frenchman'), he came from a family background more Dutch and Jewish than French.

André Citroën was born in Paris at exactly thirty minutes past midnight on the morning of 5 February 1878. The fifth and youngest child of Levie Citroen, a Jewish diamond merchant from Amsterdam who, in 1871, had adopted French nationality and settled in France with his Polish-Jewish wife Masza Kleinmann, the infant André joined two brothers and two sisters in the family. His earliest years were spent at the family home at 44 rue Lafitte, in the 9th arrondissement of the French capital, a street of small shops and apartments leading off the Boulevard Haussmann and lying, both geographically and sociologically, roughly midway between the Opera and the *Folies Bergère*. Then, as now, the 9th arrondissement was a cosmopolitan commercial quarter, a place of business and pleasure rather than a purely residential district, with its many flats and workrooms situated above shops and inhabited on short leases by a constant procession of busy working people, making their way either up or down in the world. In the lives of those who occupied these huge, seven-storey Parisian apartment buildings, 'down' meant 'up', since the middle classes resided on the lower floors and the poor lived in the rooftop attics and garrets.

The business fortunes of the Citroen family were most definitely in the ascendant. With the upheavals of the Franco–Prussian War and the even more unfortunate events of the Siege of Paris and the Commune in 1870–1 now a fading memory, under the administration of the Third Republic the French capital was enjoying an economic boom and fast becoming the centre not just of the world of fine art and high fashion but also of the infant European motor industry. As a successful dealer in diamonds, precious stones and jewellery and a respectable and respected member of the capital's business community, Citroen *père* had already built up a wealthy clientele and had no cause to regret his move to France.

But, in truth, he had never really moved away from home. Having risen from humble beginnings as fruit merchants and market traders in Amsterdam by following the familiar Jewish path of enterprise, effort and shrewd marital alliances, the Citroen family was already established as a veritable commercial dynasty, with a network of family branches extending right across Europe.

Levie Citroen was the eighth of fourteen siblings, twelve of whom survived, prospered and married, thus providing the young André Citroën with a collection of no less than eighty-seven first cousins on his father's side alone. So although he was the sole member of his family living in Paris, Levie was no more isolated from the support and affection of his close relations than would be the ambassador of a foreign power with important interests in France or the resident French representative of a rich and influential multinational business organisation.

At the time of André's birth, the far-flung Citroen family could already trace its ancestry back with certainty for almost a hundred and fifty years, to the birth of André Citroën's great-great-grandfather Jacob in 1750. But the family history really began with the arrival of Jacob's son Roelof thirty years later, in 1780. Roelof was known to have been a costermonger or itinerant fruit-seller who toured the streets of Amsterdam pushing a barrow full with oranges, lemons and other exotic citrus fruits imported from the Dutch colonies. Roelof died young in 1814, but not before he had bestowed upon his descendants a priceless legacy in the form of its unusual surname. At that point in its history, Holland was ruled directly by France, having been annexed in 1810 by the Emperor Napoleon I, who made his brother Louis King of the Netherlands. Under the Napoleonic legal code, it was required that all Dutch citizens should adopt a patronym, and naturally, in recognition of his trade, Roelof chose the soubriquet or nickname by which he was already well known among his customers in Amsterdam – Limoenman ('Lemon man').

Roelof's only son Barend (André's grandfather), who lived and worked in the Jewish quarter of Amsterdam from 1808 to 1895, did not follow in his father's footsteps behind a fruiterer's barrow but instead became a trinket-seller and jeweller, thus beginning the Citroen family's long connection with that ancient and traditional Jewish activity. Ever since the Middle Ages, through alternate periods of religious tolerance and persecution, the Jews of Europe had engaged in gold- and silversmithing and moneylending. Settling in every capital and major city across the continent to form a closely-knit and intercommunicating business and information network, by the seventeenth century they had won the trust of royalty and the nobility and were established as court paymasters and moneylenders to most of the ruling houses of Central Europe, Catholic and Protestant alike, financing wars and providing loans for the building of palaces and churches. From this network, over the next two centuries a number of important and powerful Jewish families such as the Rothschilds ultimately emerged. Eventually, these clans became more than just Europe's principal goldsmiths and jewellers but also its leading bankers and financiers, serving the administrative needs of governments rather than the intrigues of individual monarchs and the avarice of the aristocracy and the Church.

In little more than a hundred years, the Rothschild family had prospered to become the pre-eminent banking dynasty of Europe. Founded during the second half of the eighteenth century by a penniless orphan, Meyer Amschel (1744–1812), who carried out his business as a coin-dealer and moneychanger at his residence, Das Haus des Rotes Schildt ('The House of the Red Shield') in the Jewish ghetto of Frankfurt, it was now the model for all aspiring upper-middle-class Jewish families such as the Citroens. In fact, the Rothschilds were not just plutocrats but aristocrats in their own right, for within the space of just three generations they had amassed a fortune far greater than that of most of the ancient royal houses whose financial affairs they controlled, and consequently had been admitted to the nobility.

Amschel's first major client was the immensely rich ruler of the Frankfurt region, the Landgrave of Hesse-Cassel. A grandson of George II of England, who was also related to the Kings of Denmark and Sweden, the Landgrave's wealth arose from hiring out his male subjects as mercenaries. These Hessian troops not only fought throughout Europe for whoever could raise sufficient funds to pay their master, but they also served in the redcoat uniforms of the British Crown throughout the American colonies, and particularly during the Wars of Independence. It was Meyer Amschel who was responsible for collecting payment from the British government and investing the proceeds on behalf of the Landgrave, earning handsome commissions in the process.

Amschel had ten children, three of whom were sent out to establish branches of the Rothschild banking enterprise in the great European capitals: Salomon in Vienna, Nathan in London and Jacob (James) in Paris. The events of the Napoleonic era further increased their wealth and influence as military paymasters, so much so that the entire family was enobled by the Austrian emperor, who in his gratitude bestowed the title of baron upon all the Rothschilds *en bloc*. Later, in 1885, Nathan's grandson Nathaniel was raised to the British peerage in his own right, as a baron, in recognition of the family's assistance in affairs of State.

Ten years earlier, at very short notice, the Rothschilds had provided a loan of 100 million francs to enable the British government, then led by Benjamin Disraeli (born a Jew, but baptised a Christian at the age of thirteen), to purchase a controlling interest in the Suez Canal from the near-bankrupt Ottoman ruler of Eygpt, thus frustrating at a stroke the expansionist colonial ambitions of the French who had built the canal. Fifty years later, this financial manoeuvre was still remembered among certain circles in France as an act of treachery on the part of the Rothschilds, and further evidence of, as these conservatives believed, the unreliability and cupidity of '*la haute juiverie*' ('high Jewry').

The Citroen dynasty developed in a similar way, albeit on a rather more modest scale. In 1813, Barend married a Dutchwoman, Netje Rooseboom, who bore him no less than fourteen children. The twelve survivors of this brood intermarried with other prominent Jewish jewelsmith, goldsmith and merchant banking families to spread the Citroen family's interests and activities right across Northern Europe, encompassing Holland, France, Germany, Poland and Russia – and, ultimately, Great Britain as well.

As more and more diamond mines were discovered in South America and South Africa during the nineteenth century, the world trade in precious stones – controlled by Jewish interests – expanded enormously. Barend Citroen and his brothers and sisters and their respective wives and husbands in the Dutch jewellery trade prospered accordingly as Amsterdam became a world centre for diamond-dealing and cutting. Perhaps to indicate his family's new middle-class status as merchants rather than mere market traders, Barend began to refer to himself in the French form, using the Flemish word for 'lemon', Citron, so that the original Dutch Limoenman surname gradually became transmuted into Limoenman-Citron. By the end of his life in 1895, he was known as Bernard Citroen – yet to young André, he would have remained, quite simply, 'Grandpapa', a distant, patriarchal figure who, though rarely seen, was somehow ever-present in the household.

All the events of this long family history would doubtless have been related in detail to the young André Citroën and his brothers and sisters, by now installed with their proud parents in a larger, far grander apartment just around the corner in the rue Châteaudun, where they were attended by a nursemaid and several other house-servants. Yet in these long discussions of their Jewish heritage, there seems to have been none of the introverted, defensive rhetoric so often adopted by strangers in a foreign land. Levie Citroen was unblinkered by the ghetto mentality that affected Jews elsewhere. Having been readily accepted into French bourgeois life, enjoying its benefits and comforts and encountering relatively little prejudice or hostility among his Parisian neighbours and business colleagues, Levie was determined that his children should be raised and educated in the French way, to take their rightful place as loyal French citizens.

André Citroën's upbringing as a true Frenchman began with his very first steps on the rue Châteaudun, as, accompanied by his nursemaid, he began to explore the streets and boulevards of Paris. At first, he became acquainted with the little shops of the neighbourhood that catered for the basic essentials of French domestic life – *la boulangerie* (the baker's), *l'épicerie* (the grocer's), *la quincaillerie* (the ironmonger) and so forth, and then later, the *grands magasins* (department stores) of the Boulevard Haussmann, where more frivolous, luxurious and expensive merchandise was on display. As he grew older and stronger, these sightseeing tours increased in length and intellectual scope to include visits to the great public buildings and cultural institutions that lay outside the 9th arrondissement – historic places like the Louvre, les Invalides and the Place des Vosges, visited by tourists today. Somehow combining the sordid with the sublime, the Paris of André Citroën's childhood was the same serenely beautiful city painted by the Impressionists. On his daily walks, he would have seen identical street scenes to those so vividly captured in the works of Monet, Manet, Renoir and Pissarro. As he passed the countless cafés, bars, brasseries and dance halls that lined the streets, doubtless he would also have caught a disturbing glimpse of the mysterious sexuality of the adult underworld, as portrayed by Degas and Toulouse-Lautrec.

The Paris of the late 1880s was a city poised excitingly and precariously between the new world and the old. Its *grands boulevards*, so recently laid out by Baron Haussmann, were thronged by thousands of horse-drawn carriages, cabs and wagons as the streets of the capital had been for centuries past, and as yet there were no motor cars to be seen. But, behind the scenes, the revolution in public and private transport that André Citroën himself was destined to lead had already begun. The first internal combustion-engined car to run on the streets of Paris (a vehicle powered by coal-gas, designed and built by Jean-Joseph Etienne Lenoir) had done so almost thirty years earlier, in 1860. And by now, the experiments of Daimler, Benz and Otto in Germany and de Dion-Bouton in France that would make the petrol-engined car a commercial reality were already in progress. Exactly when the young André saw a motor car for the first time is unrecorded by any family legend, but by 1897, when he was nineteen, the concept of the horseless carriage would surely have been a familiar, understandable and desirable idea to all teenage boys in France, no matter how mechanically-minded. By the time that André Citroën was in his twenties, the experiments were over; the automobile had adopted its final, familiar technical form and was becoming a common sight on the streets of Paris, albeit owned only by rich and progressively-minded people.

In short, André Citroën's childhood coincided with a period of rapid industrial and technological advancement in France. As legitimate members of the bourgeoisie, isolated from the social unrest increasingly evident among the emerging industrial proletariat, at first the prosperous Citroen family participated fully in the optimistic sense of material and intellectual progress that pervaded Paris at the onset of this golden age, *la Belle Epoque*.

But sadly, their good fortune was not to last. In the autumn of 1884, when little André was aged six, Madame Citroen took her five children on holiday to the seaside resort of Trouville, on the coast of Normandy. One day – Sunday 14 September, to be precise – the children returned to their hotel from the beach to find their mother in a state of shock; from her face, it was clear that she had been crying bitterly. Nothing was said, however, and the children watched in silence as their beloved mama packed her case for an immediate return by train to Paris. Obviously, something terrible had happened at home – but exactly what?

A few days later, she returned to collect them, with the explanation that their father had left their apartment to go on a long journey, and that it would be some time before the family could be reunited again. Only much later was André Citroën given an explanation of his father's sudden and permanent disappearance. Flushed with optimism for the future, Citroen *père* had acted without his usual prudence and probity and had speculated unwisely in a South African diamond-mining venture. The certain, risk-free investment had failed to produce the promised results, and now the shares were worthless. Even so, despite being the victims of a ruthless swindle, the family was far from ruined. Yet, given by his temperament to wild swings of mood between euphoria and depression, in a fit of panic and remorse, Louis-Bernard Citroen (as he now styled himself) had decided that the stigma of bankruptcy was unavoidable. There was only one honourable course of action left open to him; he dressed in his finest clothes and threw himself out of the window of the rue Châteaudun apartment onto the stone-paved courtyard several floors below. His death – at the age of only forty-two – was instantaneous.

Surprisingly, the traumatic events surrounding his father's tragic death do not appear to have affected André Citroën's academic progress. In fact, they may have enhanced his capacity for study, for evidently the boy retreated into another world of his own imagination, reading the books of Jules Verne, Fenimore Cooper, Walter Scott and Charles Dickens and re-living in his imagination the adventures of the characters he met between their covers. This constant reading, often late into the night by the dim light of a spirit lamp, worsened the myopia that had afflicted him since birth, and the young André was soon obliged to begin wearing the rimless pince-nez spectacles that formed an essential part of his persona for the rest of his life.

On the advice of his uncle Roelof (the eldest of Barend Limoenman's sons), who swiftly arrived from Amsterdam to supervise the funeral arrangements, the family moved to a smaller apartment at 62 rue la Fayette, once again in the 9th arrondissement. Here, Madame Citroen took over her late husband's business affairs, dealing with customers and supervising the cutting and mounting of stones, while still finding time to teach her youngest child the rudiments of mathematics, science, geography, history, Latin and Greek in preparation for his first attendance at school. French, English, German and Dutch, it seems, he had already mastered!

On 1 October 1885, aged seven, André Citroën was duly enrolled as a pupil at the local Lycée Condorcet, a school still fashionable today among the Jewish community of Paris (during the 1930s, Jean-Paul Sartre was employed as a teacher there). In the Lycée's archives, the entry recording his admission can still be seen, with the name Citroën bearing, for the very first time, an *accent tréma* (diaeresis) over the 'e', indicating that the two vowels of the last syllable of the family name were henceforth to be pronounced separately, an eloquent testimony to the fact that the immigrant Jewish family was now emancipated from its past and fully integrated into French life and culture. Another of the fascinating twists of motoring history is that it was here at the Lycée Condorcet that André Citroën first met Louis Renault, who at Billancourt in 1899, at the age of twenty, founded that other famous French car firm, and who was consequently destined to become his greatest rival. Indeed, it is more than likely that the long and bitter commercial battle between these two great automobile marques began here with a juvenile playground quarrel between the two fellow schoolboys.

André-Gustave Citroën proved to be an able, intelligent and popular pupil, an all-round scholar capable of winning prizes in whatever subjects he studied – the Classics, mathematics, chemistry, German and English. Later, in his Baccalaureat exams, he was to achieve the highest marks of any candidate in

France for that academic year. But even at that early age, what really interested him most was the world of engineering, science and technology. Machinery fascinated him, and often he would sneak off to watch the steam locomotives arriving and departing at the nearby Gare Saint-Lazare, just as Claude Monet, one of the greatest of all the Impressionists, had done eight years earlier. The sights and sounds of nineteenth-century railway travel that so excited the young André Citroën would have been the same in every detail as those depicted in Monet's famous paintings of the station. When his older fellow pupil Louis Renault stowed away in the coal tender of one of these hissing, smoking engines and got as far as Rouen before being discovered, he was mightily impressed, although he did not attempt to repeat the adventure himself.

But then, in 1887, an even more exciting engineering spectacle began to command his attention. That year, on a site beside the River Seine, the construction of the Eiffel Tower commenced. As the giant structure rose slowly, stage by stage, into the sky, its looming silhouette obsessed his thoughts, exerting a powerful formative influence. The sudden arrival of the Eiffel Tower in the centre of Paris caused a schism among the city's two million inhabitants. Progressives welcomed its appearance as an expression of modernity and of the boundless opportunities of technology, but traditionalists considered it to be an ugly, vulgar intrusion, out of scale with its surroundings and out of tune with the architectural character of the capital. André Citroën was far too young to get involved in the subtleties of this debate. For him and his schoolfriends, the tower was a toy construction set on a monumental scale.

André Citroën grew up with the Eiffel Tower. He was only nine when work began on its foundations, but by the time construction had reached the level of the first viewing platform, he was ten. When the third and final stage was completed and the whole complex structure comprising twelve thousand steel girders held together by seven million rivets was opened to the public in 1889, he was eleven. During that two-year building period, he had studied every tiny detail of its design and construction, observing the work in progress with a telescope. He knew that a mere two hundred men had been engaged in assembling it. And that, despite its weight of 7,000 tons, it was actually an amazingly light structure, exerting proportionally no more pressure on the ground beneath it than a man sitting in an armchair. Like its designer, he knew that the structure was massively over-engineered and that, being anchored by four huge concrete blocks, each 46 feet deep, there was no danger whatsoever of it being toppled over by the wind; actually, Eiffel had included four superfluous supporting arches to give an impression of solidity and stability, and thus reassure the public of its strength. The young Citroën was also well aware that the Eiffel Tower had not been built merely as a tourist attraction, to adorn picture-postcards of Paris and provide a novel knick-knack for sale in souvenir shops. Rather, it was intended as a symbol of all that could be achieved by the application of science and technology, and as it soared towards the clouds, it showed that the sky was the limit. But did he have any foreknowledge of the influence that it would have on his own ambitions and aspirations? Could he

André Citroën grew up alongside the Eiffel Tower. Aged nine when its foundations were laid, he was eleven by the time it was opened to the public, during the Grande Exposition Universelle de Paris in 1889.

have dreamed that, forty years on, the giant tower would carry his own name in letters of light, in a bold and brilliant electrical advertisement visible for 60 miles all round?

Certainly, there can be no doubt that, accompanied by his older brothers Hugues and Bernard, André would have made his first ascent to the top of the 300 metre-high tower that year, while visiting the Grande Exposition Universelle which it had been built to crown. Staged in 1889 to mark the first centenary of the French Revolution, the lavish exhibition commemorated the achievements of French science and technology, and notwithstanding its earnest purpose and serious subject matter, it attracted fifteen million visitors within six months. By displaying the French Republic's manufacturing abilities, acclaiming its recent colonial conquests and celebrating its acquisition of new markets and sources of raw materials overseas in Africa and the Far East, the exhibition's organisers aimed to encourage a marriage between art and industry that would guarantee the country's prosperity over the next hundred years.

The Paris Exhibition was undoubtedly a crucial event in the story of the motor car. Its Gold Medal was won by the German firm of Otto and Langen, who exhibited a low-speed, stationary, four-stroke internal combustion engine designed for power-production duties by Nicholas Otto (1832–92) and built at

Citroën's birth coincided with that of the automobile and he belonged to the first generation of Frenchmen accustomed to the motor car from their earliest years. As a boy he would have been familiar with sights like this early Serpollet vehicle, photographed in the Bois de Boulogne in about 1898.

the Deutz Motorenwerk near Cologne. This engine and the many other impressive engineering exhibits in the Galerie des Machines and the Palais des Industries that the young Citroën inspected must surely have had a profound influence on the future course of his life. Quite possibly, it was here that his mind first turned towards the motor car, for several primitive examples were shown there by firms such as Peugeot (then a bicycle-maker), Serpollet, de Dion, de Dietrich and even Benz. Indeed, Karl Benz might never have found commercial success had he not exhibited at the Exposition. Here, he attracted the interest of Emile Roger, who signed an agreement to become his French concessionaire and placed an order for several vehicles. The Exposition also resulted in the meeting of Gottlieb Daimler (Otto and Langen's technical director) and Emile Levassor, who, when Daimler left Otto to found his own firm with Maybach, arranged for Daimler's new high-speed engine (the first engine really suited for mobile use in propelling a car) to be manufactured by Levassor's engineering firm, thus founding another pioneering automobile marque, Panhard and Levassor. It has often been said that while Germany fathered the motor car, France was its mother country. If so, then it was at the Grande Exposition Universelle of 1889 that this fruitful union was consummated.

But the lives of adolescent boys rarely move in a straight line towards a pre-ordained destination. Instead, they find their early path in a more circuitous way as they explore the limits of a series of concentric circles – their family, their schoolfriends, their hobbies and, of course, the territorial boundaries of the

As a teenager, Citroën followed progress in the great international motor car races of the Belle Epoque, in which pioneers such as Peugeot, Panhard and Renault fought for supremacy in the emerging automobile industry. Yet at that point in his life he could have had no inkling that his name would eventually be ranked with these illustrious marques. Here, Edouard and André Michelin take part in the 1895 Paris–Bordeaux race in the 'l'Eclair', a vehicle built to demonstrate their new Michelin pneumatic tyres.

Unlike his fellow school-boy Louis Renault, André Citroën took no practical interest in motor-racing, or even in building cars. In this photograph taken in about 1889, Renault is at the wheel of a voiturette which he designed and constructed himself. Renault actually competed in numerous races such as the 1902 Paris–Vienna event in this and other equally primitive vehicles.

place in which they live. Only in later life do their careers assume a linear trajectory towards some far-off goal – and even then, these ambitions are likely to be deflected off-target by force of circumstances, causing them to travel in quite unexpected directions. André Citroën was no exception to this rule!

On being asked by an uncle, at the age of sixteen, what he planned to do for a living, he replied that he hadn't yet made up his mind, except that he would prefer to start his own business and be his own boss. When it was pointed out that this required capital, he replied that money was always available for entrepreneurs with a sound business proposition. To make his way in the world, what he needed was a new idea – an original and innovative product to make and sell. Already, he had decided that he would prefer to be a manufacturer rather than a merchant – and anyway, his elder brother Hugues had long since taken over the running of the diamond business. But in which field of engineering would he make his fortune?

As it happened, the agonising choice could be postponed for several years, for it was decided that, thanks to the family's much improved financial situation, André could stay on at school and study for entrance into one of the *grandes écoles* (technical universities). For this, however, academic qualifications alone were not enough. Under French law at that time, to be eligible for university, candidates had to possess full French nationality. Thus on 30 April 1896, at a short ceremony held before a justice of the peace in the 9th arrondissement of Paris, the eighteen-year-old André Citroën was received as a citizen of the République Française. At that time, there were roughly eighty thousand Jews living in France out of a total population of 39 million, although that number was shortly to double with an influx of refugees from central Europe fleeing the pogroms carried out by the Tsar in Russia and Poland.

So it was that two years later, in October 1898, he took up his place at the celebrated Ecole Polytechnique in Paris, founded in 1794, shortly after the French Revolution, by the Directoire (revolutionary council). As the engineering academy of the French Army, '*l'X*' had long been recognised as the key entry point into a far-reaching and highly influential career network. For ambitious high-flyers from humble backgrounds seeking careers in the technical branches of the French military and civil services, attendance there was the essential qualification for a successful future. Indeed, despite the vast scientific and technological changes that have occurred since André Citroën's time, *polytechniciens* continue to dominate France's scientific and technical elite, proof not merely of the rigorously exacting formal education they receive there but also of the powerful and enduring *esprit de corps* that it fosters among its alumni. In Citroën's day, the Ecole Polytechnique was run on authoritarian lines, following a regime even more spartan than that of a Victorian English public school and similarly intended to encourage unquestioning loyalty and obedience.

For the eighteen-year-old Citroën, ranked number 62 of the 201 entrants in order of merit that year, as determined by the entrance examinations, the mental effort demanded by the course was strenuous enough. But the physical exercise was far more taxing still. In fact, the entire routine was exhausting and

The Ecole Polytechnique in Paris, in about 1900, when André Citroën was a cadet there. Founded in 1794, the original building was demolished shortly after this picture was taken.

unremitting, with little spare time allowed for relaxation. His day began at 6 a.m. with reveille sounded on bugles and drums. Roll-call was at 6.30 a.m., followed by two hours of study, then after breakfast, at 9 a.m. exactly, the cadets assembled on the parade ground for rifle drill. Next, it was back into the classrooms for lectures until 2 p.m., when there was a half-hour lunch break. The afternoon was devoted to physical exercise and sport – gymnastics, riding, fencing and so forth – but at 5 p.m., studies recommenced for a further four hours until supper at 9 p.m. Lights out in the sparsely-furnished dormitories was at 10 p.m. sharp. Only on Sundays did the routine change, when the cadets were allowed out between the hours of 10 a.m. and 10 p.m., to amuse themselves in the town. Even then, they were still obliged to wear their distinctive uniforms – dark-blue jackets with two rows of silver buttons, red trousers with a broad blue stripe down the legs and, on their close-cropped heads, the famous *frégate*, a shiny, black leather bicorn hat with a tricolour cockade.

On these occasions, André Citroën usually went home to see his mother, who had now moved once again to an apartment in the rue Taitbout, just around the corner from the family's previous abode. Here he could enjoy a proper meal and all the other familiar domestic comforts so lacking at the Ecole Polytechnique, and afterwards join in the games of chance or fortune that play a traditional part in Jewish family life. Already, the notion that the difference between success and failure in life could be settled by the toss of a dice, the fall of a card or the spin of a wheel or coin, and that human existence itself was a

André Citroën, aged twenty, wearing the uniform of the prestigious Ecole Polytechnique, the technical academy of the French army.

thrilling gamble in which the greatest rewards went to those who took the highest risks, had begun to fascinate him.

Naturally, Madame Citroën took a maternal pride in her youngest son's appearance, resplendent in his prestigious uniform. In her fond eyes, at least, he was beginning to cut an attractive figure, especially as he had taken to wearing pointed, waxed moustachios, upturned in the military manner. Already, there was something about him that marked him out from the other cadets – a formidable intelligence and determination that made him seem much larger and stronger than his actual physique. Although small in stature (barely 5 ft 4 in) and slightly built, his forceful but unaggressive personality overcame this lack of size and gave him an attractively confident presence that impressed much older and larger men and intrigued women of all ages. Blessed with a genial disposition and a jovial countenance, the young André Citroën was certainly an unusually engaging character – but at that point in his life, few of even his greatest admirers suspected just how great were the talents hidden within his expansive but diminutive figure.

Incessantly, throughout his two-year course, one topic of conversation came up over and over again among both Citroën's family and his fellow cadets at the

Ecole Polytechnique: the Dreyfus affair. Indeed, the matter was discussed ad infinitum in bars and salons across the whole of France at that time. The events and issues of this much-prolonged court case so scandalised the nation and polarised popular opinion that it became a *cause célèbre* deeply and permanently etched in the national consciousness, creating an enduring divide between conservatives and radicals. In the cafés of Paris, the Dreyfusards and their opponents, the Nationalists, sat at opposite sides of the room, left or right according to their views on the debate, copying the seating arrangements in the French parliament, the Chamber of Deputies. In truth, echoes of the Dreyfus affair continue to reverberate in France today.

Born in Mülhausen in Alsace of a rich Jewish family, Captain Alfred Dreyfus was an army officer and former *polytechnicien* serving in the Ministry of War. When, in 1894, the French intelligence service discovered that certain secret military documents had got into the hands of the German military attaché in Paris, Dreyfus was accused of being the source of the leak and was arrested on charges of treason. Found guilty by a military tribunal, he was stripped of his rank and sentenced to be deported and imprisoned for life on Devil's Island. In 1896, however, a counter-espionage investigation revealed that the informant was actually a fellow officer, Major Esterhazy, but to maintain the status quo, the High Command attempted to suppress this new evidence, even to the extent of forging letters in Dreyfus's handwriting to strengthen its case. The security of the State was at stake, and '*pour encourager les autres*', the proud military tradition of France could not be allowed to be further discredited. Eventually, after a series of newspaper articles written by the radical politician Clemenceau and the crusading journalist and author Emile Zola had publicised this injustice, the case was re-opened. In 1899, a re-trial was held and Dreyfus was again found guilty, but with extenuating circumstances. Although he was subsequently pardoned, it was not until 1906 that the Court of Appeal declared him completely innocent and he was reinstated in his military rank and awarded the Legion of Honour.

The Dreyfus scandal provoked a long and virulent controversy throughout France, forcing its citizens to pass judgement on the ever-increasing influence and importance of international Jewry in their national life. To the deeply Catholic and conservatively-minded population of provincial and rural France, the Dreyfus affair symbolised all that was corrupt and repugnant about the regime in Paris. Hostile feelings were further aroused by xenophobic pamphlets and anti-Semitic comment about cosmopolitan Jewish capitalists and intellectuals in the press, and immigrant Jewish families began to experience racial prejudice and persecution from reactionary elements at both ends of the social spectrum, accusing them of presenting a threat to traditional French values and even to the political stability of the Republic. Anti-Semitic riots broke out in many of the major provincial cities, causing considerable alarm among France's Jewish community.

Since the Revolution, there had been a consensus among educated Jews that France had done more for the Jewish cause than most other nations, but this view was shattered by the Dreyfus affair. Consequently, the case caused the members of emancipated immigrant Jewish families such as the Citroëns to reconsider their position. For their part, however, the Citroëns no longer thought of themselves as Jews except by the accident of birth. Although they still celebrated the traditional Jewish festivals, they had renounced the old Orthodox doctrines long ago. Now they worshipped the new, universal, secular religion of material progress and prosperity. They worked on Saturdays, ignored the dietary laws, rarely attended the synagogue and made no attempt to follow all 630 precepts of the Torah.

Apart from maintaining the essential ceremonies of circumcision and burial, being Jewish was for them mostly a social and commercial matter, and certainly not a religious or racial issue. They now considered themselves to be French citizens, first and foremost. How could they be involved in a sinister plot against the Republic? How could this be happening to them in the land of 'Liberty, Equality and Fraternity'? 'Can you tell me the essential difference between the Jews and the Gentiles? What exactly is it, to be a Jew?' André Citroën is said to have asked his brother Bernard at a family reunion. 'Being Jewish is when other people call you a Jew,' was the wise reply.

In fact, these regular family gatherings were the one aspect of traditional Jewish life that the Citroën tribe preserved and cherished. But on one of his Sunday visits in May 1899, André noticed that his mother seemed tired, withdrawn and unwell, so much so that during the afternoon she excused herself from the party and retired to bed. The following Wednesday, he was called from his classes to the office of the Commandant of the Ecole, General Toulza. Unexpectedly, his brother Bernard was also in the room. His ashen face presaged dreadful news. Their beloved mother had died suddenly during the night, aged only forty-six.

That day marked the watershed between boyhood and manhood in the life of André Citroën. Completely unprepared for this terrible stroke of fate, he was devastated by grief. As with his father's untimely death, the bereavement was swift and totally unexpected. He had been too young to know – and miss – his father, of course. But the loss of his mother left a terrible void in his life. For as long as he could remember, she had been his guiding light, providing encouragement and inspiration when things went well, and reassurance and comfort when they did not. No other woman, wife or mistress, would ever replace her in his estimation and affections. Later, it would be upon his factories and his cars that he bestowed his deepest love and devotion.

By now, both his sisters were married: Fernande to Alfred Lindon, a jeweller and *negociant* in diamonds and pearls living in Paris, and Jeanne to Bronislaus Goldfeder, a wealthy Polish banker residing in Warsaw. So, in April 1900, André spent his Easter holidays on a visit to Poland to stay with Jeanne, her husband and children, and to visit numerous members of his mother's family, the Kleinmanns, most of whom he had never previously met.

One day while in Poland (a day he would never forget), he made the discovery that was to bring a new sense of purpose to his life – the long-hoped-for mechanism that would provide the motive power to drive his intended career as an industrialist forwards at full speed. Ironically, it was a gearwheel.

On an excursion to Glowno, a small industrial town on the road between Warsaw and Lodz, he was introduced to a distant relation who managed a small engineering factory. Here, there was a foundry where gears and other specialist mechanical parts were cast by the sandbox method from patterns carved in wood. While being shown around the premises, he noticed a set of reduction gearwheels with a design quite unlike anything he had ever seen before. Instead of having simple, straight, cross-cut teeth, these had a complicated arrangement of V-shaped teeth, shaped like corporal's stripes, set around the circumference of both wheels, which could also be bevelled so as to run together at an angle. In theory, this made them ideally suited for transmitting heavy power loads through 90° while at the same time increasing or decreasing the turning speed of the output shaft. By virtue of the way that they meshed with precision, these helical gears were much more efficient than conventional straight-cut gears, and therefore capable of withstanding far greater loads. Silent-running, they generated no axial thrust, which meant that more power could be transmitted through them with minimal loss of efficiency due to friction.

However, in practice, it had so far proved difficult to realise the advantages promised by this design. As his hosts explained, the difficulty lay in manufacturing the gearwheels to the very high standard of dimensional accuracy essential to ensure a perfect mesh. This precision could simply not be achieved by their normal process of casting and fettling; the only answer was to cut the teeth from a solid blank of high-quality cast or forged steel by removing the metal from the grooves, a machining operation that was well beyond the skills and capacities of most of the major mechanical engineering companies in Europe. Yet this small Polish factory had found a way.

As an engineering student, André Citroën was already well aware of the exciting developments in metallurgy and machine-tool design that were then taking place in the USA and which were already transforming the capacity of heavy industry to produce complex, high-precision metal components for industrial machinery and military equipment. Certainly, he would have known about the experiments carried out by Frederick Winslow Taylor of the Bethlehem Steel Works in Pennsylvania, since Taylor's experimental fast-cutting lathe, equipped with chrome-tungsten tools that could rapidly cut through case-hardened steel, had caused a sensation when demonstrated at an exhibition in Paris that very year. Combined with the Polish discovery, this new metalworking technology from America would provide him with a highly profitable business, he anticipated. So, with characteristic speed and decisiveness, he made an offer to purchase the Russian patent and licensing rights on the spot, with money provided by Bronislaus Goldfeder, Poland then being under Russian control. The deal accomplished, he bade farewell to his Polish friends and hurried back to Paris by the very next train, his mind already racing with ideas on how these gears could be manufactured and employed.

Just like his hero Henry Ford, André Citroën combined an ingenious, inventive, creative mind with great commercial astuteness. But unlike Ford, he was not truly a 'hands-on' inventor or designer, and could never lay claim to producing personally, from a bare sheet of paper or a virgin blank of steel, the devices and machines that made his name famous. However, just as Ford and other American motor-manufacturing pioneers (whose products were soon to appear on the streets of Paris – the first Ford arrived there in 1904) had taken the concept of the automobile from Europe, Citroën repaid the compliment by borrowing back Ford's volume-production manufacturing technology and marketing methods from America.

As we shall see, Citroën was a technocrat rather than a tinkerer. Although he was far from untrained or unskilled in engineering matters, his flair and creativity as an entrepreneur lay in recognising and exploiting the talents of other creative individuals. Rather than designing cars and machinery or inventing new products and processes himself, his life's work was to be concerned with devising ever more brilliant ways of manufacturing and marketing the ideas generated by the many other gifted engineers and designers that he employed and supported. Thus, on returning to Paris he drew up detailed plans to exploit the idea that he had discovered in Poland, by establishing, two years later, a small workshop and laboratory in association with two friends from his days at the Lycée Condorcet, André Boas and Jacques Hinstin, with the aim of perfecting the double-helical gear principle and developing its industrial applications.

From these small beginnings, located in the Faubourg Saint-Denis near the Gare du Nord, a giant industrial empire was destined to grow. Indeed, the Citroën company's origins as a manufacturer of double-helical gears is still commemorated today in its famous double chevron badge, which André Citroën himself devised.

CHAPTER TWO

Citroën Goes to War

As the nineteenth century drew to its close, André Citroën and the automobile came of age together. Fittingly, the celebrations that marked, in effect, the twenty-first birthday of the motor car were held in Paris, since the people of France – unlike their Anglo-Saxon neighbours across the Channel – had welcomed its arrival unreservedly from the very start.

In 1894, the world's first motor car time trial took place along a 78 mile route between Paris and Rouen. This event was followed in 1895 by the first actual motor race, from Paris to Bordeaux and back. Three years later, the first Paris motor show, a rudimentary affair, occurred in the Jardin des Tuileries, right in the centre of Paris, where no less than 269 different examples of the horseless carriage were exhibited. Then, in 1901, the first large-scale Salon des Automobiles was held in the Grand Palais, attracting over 200,000 visitors, only an infinitesimal minority of whom could have had any immediate prospect of becoming motorists.

As a direct consequence of the public interest in the horseless carriage aroused by these events, by 1905 or thereabouts, a sizeable number of bona fide car manufacturers had been established in France – marques such as Peugeot and Renault which remain on the roads today, and others like Panhard, Brasier, Mors and Delaunay-Belleville which were destined sooner or later to vanish from the scene, replaced by relative latecomers to the market such as Automobiles Citroën. The Renault factory at Billancourt had been opened in 1899 by Citroën's former fellow pupil at the Lycée Condorcet in partnership with his two brothers, thus giving Renault a two-decade head start over his upstart Jewish rival. A practical mechanic and inventor, Louis Renault built his first car with his own hands at the age of twenty-one.

However, it is doubtful that, as he daydreamed away the long hours on the train returning to Paris from Warsaw in the spring of 1900, André Citroën would ever have envisaged that his name, like Renault's, would one day appear on the front of a car. The nineteenth century had seen enormous changes in transport by sea and by railway due to the perfection of steam power that had taken place, and it was clear that the arrival of the internal combustion engine now promised similar advances in travel by road, and even by air. But at that early stage in his career, the young Citroën could never have suspected that he would become so closely involved in, or identified with, the motorisation of Europe. At that time, his ambition was solely and simply to establish his gearwheel-manufacturing business. He had estimated that achieving this objective alone would demand all his efforts for the next five years at least, and he was well content to apply himself single-mindedly to the task of refining and perfecting this gear-cutting technique, and to confine himself to making and supplying the vital component parts that would improve the machines designed and built by other men.

But before he could get on with the job, there was a certain amount of unfinished business to attend to. First, he had to finish his studies at the Ecole Polytechnique and sit the final examinations. Second, he had to complete the one-year period of military service which was then compulsory for all young Frenchmen, as it was until the end of 1996.

Accordingly, in July 1900, he passed out from '*l'X*', ranking 160th among 201 cadets, perhaps a disappointing result considering the very high hopes that his tutors had held for him at the start of the course. This meant that, even if he had wanted to do so, he would no longer be eligible to join that exclusive band of ex-*polytechniciens* who would automatically go on to enjoy preferred status and rapid promotion in the French civil service for the rest of their lives. But Citroën was not unduly upset at the thought of renouncing a career as a government official or military officer. He already considered himself temperamentally unsuited to a career in a bureaucracy where a rigid, unwavering adherence to the rules of protocol was the paramount qualification. He had far too much drive, initiative and individualism for that. Instead of being a military man, he was happy to become a captain of industry and to fight for the rapid industrialisation of France!

That autumn, André Citroën was posted to the 31st Regiment of Artillery stationed at le Mans, with the rank of sous-lieutenant. However, the prospects of having to delay his plans while carrying out his national service duties in the army may well have been far less dull and irksome than it would seem at first sight. At the turn of the century, artillery and ordnance – like missile and aerospace warfare today – lay at the leading edge of technological progress. Naval and military gunnery employed the most advanced scientific knowledge of the day, involving not just the physics of ballistics and the chemistry of explosives but also the metallurgy of gun and ammunition manufacture. Then, as now, the armaments industry called for the most refined and accurate metalworking techniques and the most sophisticated and expensive machine tools, an aspect of industry that already interested him greatly. While stationed at le Mans, Citroën made frequent visits to the factory founded by the prolific inventor and steam-car pioneer, Amédée Bollée, in partnership with his two sons. It was here in 1907 that Bollée produced his famous six-cylinder Type 30/40 petrol-engined luxury car, which later came to be regarded as a serious rival to the Rolls-Royce.

Ever since the events of the Franco–Prussian War of 1870, in which the machine gun made its first appearance on the battlefield, it had been obvious to all but the most blinkered military minds that the outcome of any future conflict would be decided not so much by the leadership of generals or the heroism of ordinary rank-and-file soldiers, as by the firepower of the terrible new weapons that were presently being devised. Henceforth, wars would be mechanised and motorised, requiring that a national war-machine involving every available citizen be welded together and pitted against the enemy in a trial of industrial strength. No longer confined to the troops in the field, the battles of the future would be won or lost on the home front, in a struggle between the manufacturing capacities of the combatant nations. In short, in this new age of technological warfare, victory would go to those with the power not just to construct these new weapons in sufficient numbers but also to supply them continually with ammunition. The victor would be decided as much by the mobilisation of resources and raw materials as by military strength and expertise.

On manoeuvres with his unit, seeing the guns and ammunition wagons being towed by teams of heavy horses in a way unchanged since Napoleonic times, André Citroën's thoughts must also have turned to these questions of military tactics and logistics and have reached the same conclusion: steeped in tradition and essentially backward-looking, the French Army was ill prepared for war. Although the British and Germans had long ago adopted camouflaged khaki or field-grey uniforms, the French infantryman still marched proudly into battle wearing the customary baggy, bright-red pantaloons. Yet, for all his insight and perceptiveness, Citroën was not an intellectual or a theorist. His was a practical, pragmatic intelligence, concerned with solving the difficulties of the present and not the hypothetical problems of the future. When his military service was over, he put these apocalyptic forebodings to the back of his mind.

For the next ten years or so, as he passed between the ages of twenty-five and thirty-five, André Citroën was to be occupied entirely with establishing his gearwheel business and securing his financial independence. In 1902, trading under the name of André Citroën & Cie, he opened a small engineering workshop in the rue Saint-Denis near the Gare du Nord, employing the minimum of staff – just ten workers – with the express intention of developing a technique for cutting helical and double-helical gears.

There was nothing new in the idea, of course. The mechanical principles of such gears had first been set down on paper over two hundred years earlier by the English inventor and experimental physicist Robert Hooke (1635–1703), who demonstrated, in theory at least, their advantages over ordinary straight-cut gears. By virtue of the way they ran in constant mesh with no free play between the driving and driven wheels, they eliminated both backlash and side-thrust, and thus avoided the shock-loads, stress, vibration, friction and noise inevitably encountered in conventional gears. Silent-running, they were especially suited to all those applications where high-speed running and reversing were required, and particularly where large velocity ratios, either in the reduction or stepping up of operating speeds, were involved. Such applications included fast-running power-transmission work in factories and generating stations, heavy-duty power-transmission duties in the milling, mining and metalworking industries, and in other situations where great exactitude of operation was essential, for instance in printing and textile machinery or in steering and winding gear.

But as the Polish factory had found to its cost, in practice, the helical gear had so far proved an extremely difficult device to manufacture. Indeed, the very high degree of precision required had eluded every other engineering company that had attempted the task. Without the very low manufacturing clearances upon which accurate engagement between wheel and bevel depended, all advantages over spur-cut gears were lost, of course. When simply cast or moulded, helical gears could never achieve this essential accuracy of interplay – only if the gears were machined from high-quality cast or forged steel could the inherent precision and durability be achieved. But at that time, no manufacturer anywhere in the world had succeeded in solving the technical problems inherent in cutting a run of true, V-shaped, helical gear teeth from a block of solid steel with one continuous, uninterrupted stroke of the cutting tool. All previous attempts had involved two cutting strokes per tooth, which left a groove running up the centre of the V pattern, thus seriously compromising the strength and accuracy of the mesh.

As Citroën had shrewdly foreseen in Poland two years earlier, recent developments in American machine-tool technology had brought this complex machining task within the bounds of possibility. Within a few months, he had developed an end-milling machine to his own specification. Using special revolving cutting tools supplied from the USA, this was capable of achieving the required dimensional accuracy, forming the teeth by cutting out a series of perfectly-profiled grooves in the blank, each groove being fashioned in a single, uninterrupted pass of the tool. Soon, his publicity material was proudly

An official Citroën publicity picture taken in the workshops of the Société des Engrenages Citroën, showing an example of the massive double-helical gears that provided the driving force behind the establishment of André Citroën's industrial empire. The ghost-like figure to the right appears to have been added later by a re-toucher, to give the picture human scale!

Citroën Gears at the South Essex Waterworks, supplied to the order of Messrs. Hunter & English, Ltd., Pumpmakers, London.

Another illustration from a brochure published by André Citroën & Co. in London before the First World War shows a typical industrial application for his products. Citroën gears imported from Paris saw widespread use throughout the United Kingdom and the British Commonwealth at that time.

proclaiming that the Citroën helical and double-helical gears were 'the first genuine machine-cut helical gears, having continuous teeth automatically cut with one tool in one single operation in the solid', a state of affairs that continued for many years. So accurately were they made that an efficiency of 98 per cent was guaranteed.

Fortunately for Citroën, his mastery of the principle of helical gears was very well timed, for it coincided with the almost universal adoption of electric motors as the preferred power source throughout industry and commerce. All over Europe and the USA, the traditional motive-power method, in which a factory's machines were collectively propelled by a system of belts and chains coupled to one large, central, stationary steam or gas engine, gave way to the concept of individual power sources, supplied by electricity. But for this to take place, the existence of highly-efficient, quiet-running gear systems was also required, so as to reduce the high rotational speed of electric motors to fit the requirements of industrial machinery.

Undoubtedly, Citroën rode to fame and fortune on the back of this revolution; his first recorded patent application covering an innovation of his own devising, taken out in Paris in October 1910, was for a speed-reduction gearbox. But although it represented the state of the art in motive-power technology at the turn of the century, unlike his later manufacturing activities, this gear-cutting business always remained a small-scale, highly-specialised enterprise. The precision machining of these large, complex gears was a slow and expensive process, and there was no mass production for stock. Normally, each item was custom built to order, to fit a specific machine or purpose, and therefore the greater part of Citroën's work involved finding potential customers and persuading them of the advantages of his products, a task that called on his talents as a publicist and marketing man. Moreover, since his two partners in the venture (his friends Messieurs Boas and Hinstin) had other interests and employment, at first he was obliged to do almost everything himself, acting as chief engineer, production manager, office manager and sales manager, visiting customers to demonstrate his wares.

By 1905, the business had expanded and prospered sufficiently for its activities to have been moved to bigger and better premises located at the Quai de Grenelle, a new industrial development area on the left bank of the Seine. Eventually, in 1913, the firm was incorporated as a limited company, the Société des Engrenages Citroën, with André and Hugues Citroën, André Boas, and Jacques Schwob de Héricourt (a friend of Jacques Hinstin, who was by then a fully-fledged industrialist on his own account, involved with the Sizaire and Naudin car firm) as its principal directors and shareholders. Indeed, its successor still exists today as a subsidiary of the Peugeot-Citroën industrial group, manufacturing large industrial gearwheels weighing as much as 180 tons.

By 1907, the firm's reputation for high-quality engineering had travelled beyond the borders of France, and sales offices had been opened in Moscow, Brussels and London, where the firm occupied premises at Queen Victoria Street in the City. Here, following the established practice of keeping things within the family, Citroën's British affairs were managed by his Dutch first cousin, Daniel Metz, one of six children born to Barend Citroen's eleventh child, Abigail. The Anglophile Daniel Metz remained a Londoner all his life, living there in retirement until his death in 1961, long after retiring from the company in 1935.

Thanks to Dan Metz's efforts, large numbers of these gearwheels bearing the distinctive double chevron trademark were imported by leading British heavy-engineering companies during the Edwardian era. Incorporated in the products of Armstrong-Whitworth and others, these saw service throughout the United Kingdom and the British Empire. An example is believed to have been fitted in the steering mechanism of the ill-fated British White Star liner *Titanic*, launched in 1911 and sunk by collision with an iceberg on its maiden voyage across the Atlantic the following year, with the loss of 1,513 lives. Steering gear failure was not the cause of this disaster, needless to say.

During this fools' golden age before the outbreak of the First World War, André Citroën lived to the full the free and easy life of a wealthy Parisian bachelor or *célibataire*, sharing a flat with his brother Bernard at 21 rue d'Aumal, as ever, in the 9th arrondissement. From here, on moonlit nights, the shining white dome of the newly-completed Basilica of Sacré Coeur could be seen above the rooftops, shimmering like a ghostly sepulchre on the hilltop of Montmartre a mile or so to the north. It was said that this church had been built by the

The Place de l'Opéra in about 1910. Already the motor car had begun to usurp the role of the horse and carriage on the streets of Paris, with numerous Renault taxis and buses appearing from 1905 onwards. André Citroën was born just a few streets away from the Opéra and lived in this 9th arrondissement until his marriage in 1914.

Bishop of Paris specifically to expiate the past sins of his flock and, by acting as an architectural counter-force to the temple of depravity represented by the Paris Opéra, to atone for the manifold wickednesses of the splendid but sordid city spread out beneath it.

There is no reason to suppose that either of the Citroën brothers actually led a celibate existence, however. Bernard was the artistic member of the family; or rather the one with artistic inclinations. A talented amateur musician, he cultivated the company of other gifted and amusing dilettantes, surrounding himself with a retinue of friends and acquaintances, and staging parties and entertainments for their diversion in the way that an actor-manager organises a play. So, as a member of his brother's bohemian circle, André never lacked female company nor was short of invitations to interesting places.

In 1906, Bernard opened just such a place himself – le Sans Souci, a tearoom-cum-café-bar located in the rue Caumartin near the Opéra, and the first such establishment in the capital to cater for the new rage of '*thé dancing à l'anglaise*' that was sweeping through fashionable circles. Its opening was one of the great social events of the year in Paris, attracting a host of celebrities from both high society and the *demi-mondaine* world of the theatre and the arts. The American actress and dancer Isadora Duncan was rumoured to be an *habituée*. As its name suggests, the Sans Souci was a place of introduction and assignation where affluent couples could meet discreetly in civilised surroundings to pursue their casual extramarital affairs.

After the death of the staunchly pro-German Queen Victoria in 1901, the British and French called a truce in their long colonial rivalry and embarked on a more amicable diplomatic relationship, encouraged by the new King Edward VII, who greatly preferred the French way of life to that of his German relations. As Prince of Wales, he had been a frequent visitor to France and had acquired a taste for the decadent delights of Paris. This new spirit of understanding and cooperation, the *entente cordiale*, was cemented by a very successful State visit which King Edward made in 1903, during which he charmed his hosts by publicly praising a beautiful actress for personifying 'all the grace and *esprit* of France'. In the enthusiastic atmosphere of mutual admiration and respect between the two nations that resulted from this fortuitous royal remark, all things English – including the drinking of tea – quickly became the height of fashion in Paris. Thus, the Sans Souci aimed to reproduce a decorous Edwardian English atmosphere of gracious living and good form, as an alternative to the cheerful, alcoholic ambience of the more typically Parisian cafés, brasseries and nightclubs of the neighbourhood.

This was surely the time when Citroën acquired his taste for gambling and the good life, a liking which was to grow even stronger in later years. By offering an intoxicating, over-stimulating mixture of sophistication and seaminess, the indulgent city of Paris spoiled its young men with a generous choice of pleasures, mainly of the flesh. From 1905 onwards, large numbers of motor cabs, mostly made by Renault and Unic, began to appear on its streets. By hailing one outside his apartment, within a five-minute ride, Citroën could find himself enjoying the very best and the very worst distractions that the capital had to offer. It can be safely assumed that many convivial evenings were spent applauding Sarah Bernhardt at the Comédie-Française, listening to Caruso at the Opera, watching Mistinguette and the young Maurice Chevalier at the *Folies Bergère* or witnessing the wonder of Nijinksky dancing with the Ballet Russe at the Châtelet Theatre. In these lavish theatrical productions, the sets and costumes were designed by the Russian Jew Leon Rosenberg, whose stage name was Leon Bakst. Elaborate, exotic, erotic and extraordinarily expensive, they set the opulent, sensual decorative taste of the era and must surely have greatly impressed André Citroën and his companions. These outings were followed, of course, by gastronomic dinners at celebrated restaurants such as La Tour d'Argent, le Vefour and Maxims, which further sharpened his taste for glamour and luxury. However, these late nights did not blunt his appetite for hard work, for this was a highly productive period in his life, and one in which his career took off in new and unexpected directions.

In 1904, André Citroën joined a lodge of the influential masonic order, the Grand Orient of France, but left it in 1919. Exactly what benefits he derived from membership is unknown. However, in France, Freemasonry plays a minor role compared to Great Britain, where it assumes a central and scarcely clandestine part in respectable business and public life. In 1926, there were only 583 lodges with a total membership of 52,000 in the whole of France, and thus the French masonic movement was plainly little more than an employment agency or business contact network. So it could well be that Citroën's membership of the secret society lapsed when he realised that, in a predominantly Catholic country, to be both a Jew and a Freemason was more of a hindrance than a help in his ambitions.

What is known for certain, however, is that André Citroën's first involvement with the automobile industry occurred as early as 1905, when his engineering company, André Citroën & Cie, built 500 engines for the Paris-based car-makers Sizair and Naudin, then being run by his old friend Jacques Hinstin. But in 1908, he actually became personally involved in the making and marketing of cars, as a consultant to the Mors company, the makers of one of France's oldest and most distinguished marques, founded in 1895. As a result of its earlier grand prix racing successes, Mors's luxurious touring and sporting cars had once been the height of fashion – but by then, the firm was experiencing severe financial difficulties as a result of dwindling sales and the defection of its chief designer, Henri Brasier. By advising on the complete re-organisation of all aspects of its business, including the improvement of its products, the modernisation of its machinery and the provision of fresh working capital, André was able to transform the company's affairs. Within five years, output had increased tenfold, from 120 to 1,200 vehicles per year, and the company was saved, although after the First World War its factory in the rue du Théâtre in Paris became caught up in, and absorbed by, the growth of his own company, and the Mors name was discontinued in 1925.

André Citroën entered the motor industry in 1908, taking over the management of the old-established Mors firm. This example of a Mors tourer, photographed in London, was built in 1913 under his regime.

Typically, this development came about through family connections. In August 1900, his elder brother Hugues (now established as a highly successful diamond merchant and recently elected president of the professional association of dealers in diamonds, pearls and precious stones in France) had married Suzanne Harbleicher, the pretty and vivacious daughter of André Harbleicher, a merchant banker. As his bank was one of the Mors firm's principal creditors, Harbleicher was immediately interested when his son-in-law suggested that brother André might have some ideas for resurrecting the firm's sales and preventing its otherwise unavoidable liquidation. It was a challenge that André Citroën was unable to resist.

His plans for solving Mors's problems also relied on family influence and connections, albeit indirectly. It so happened that another member of the Citroën clan – David Citroën, one of his uncle Roelof's sixteen grandchildren – had preceded him in joining the motor trade and was now a director of the Belgian Minerva company, another much respected maker of luxury cars based near Antwerp. Originally a bicycle-maker, Minerva had switched to motor cars in 1899 with some success, for its products were favoured by the Kings of Belgium, Sweden and Norway and distributed in England by no less a personage than the Hon. C.S. Rolls. In 1909, Minerva surprised the automobile world by adopting the novel, smooth and silent-running engines designed by the American Charles Knight, which it built in Belgium under licence. In these engines, the noisy, conventional poppet induction and exhaust valves used in other types were replaced by a pair of concentric, cylindrical sleeve-valves located between the piston and the cylinder walls. Despite involving extremely delicate, precision-made components, these Silent Knight engines had the advantage of being especially quiet and clatter-free in operation, And although they were expensive to produce, since their valves required no frequent re-grinding they were particularly durable as well.

Right from the start, it was always typical of Citroën's talent that he could judge at a glance if an unfamiliar technical innovation was right or wrong for his purposes. In this case, the Knight sleeve-valve engine – also employed by Daimler – was exactly the new dimension he was seeking to revitalise the appeal of the by now old-fashioned Mors and thus revive interest in one of France's most prestigious marques. After visiting his cousin David Citroën (who lived in London), André struck a deal whereby Minerva would build and supply Knight's engines for Mors as well. The result was a completely new range of 2, 3, 4 and 6 litre Mors cars, which Citroën christened the SSS series ('Sans Soupape Sport'), and by 1912 sales of these cars had reached a level sufficient for the business to be saved. This trip to London, made in 1909, was probably the first time that Citroën set foot on British soil. Thereafter, he was to be a frequent and enthusiastic visitor. In Edwardian England, wealthy Jewish industrialists were always made welcome in high society, especially if they were as charming and personable as André Citroën. Indeed, they were particularly popular in royal circles, at the court of King Edward VII, who had succeeded to the throne on the death of Queen Victoria in 1901.

Three years later, in connection with his work for Mors, André Citroën made his first visit to the United States, a trip that was to have a profound impact on his life. As a man who always refused to take no for an answer, he was bowled over by the vitality and inventiveness of this great but youthful nation, where nothing seemed to be held impossible or unachievable, and where the power of positive thinking was venerated like a religion. In America, drive, ability and ambition were all that were necessary to succeed in life – inherited wealth and social position were unimportant, it seemed. Indeed, the passion to produce – and even more importantly, to sell – appeared to André Citroën to be the impelling energy behind every aspect of American life, providing the irresistable force for change and progress that was transforming the prospects of every American citizen, rich and poor alike.

So it was that in 1912, at the Highland Park factory at Dearborn near Detroit, Citroën met the man that the whole industrial and automotive world was talking about – Henry Ford, creator of the Model T, the world's first standardised, mass-produced vehicle. Thanks to its rock-bottom price and robust, almost indestructable reliability, an incredible total of almost 160,000 units of this pioneering 'people's car' had already been sold since its arrival in October 1908. Throughout the United States, the Model T Ford was already replacing the horse, cart and carriage, and thus transforming American rural and city life.

The experience clearly made an enormous impact on Citroën, for it gave him a glimpse not just of the industrial methods of the future, but also an insight into the political and economic significance of America's fast-developing industrial superiority. At Highland Park, already recognised as the world's largest ever factory complex, he was one of the first Europeans to be shown the advanced machine tools and the sequential moving-chain production-line assembly methods that the American industrialist was on the point of introducing in order to increase output and bring down the prices of his product further still. Impressed with the vigour and enterprise of Ford's operations, Citroën realised immediately that if, like their American counterparts, European motorists of all classes and incomes were also to enjoy the freedom, mobility and material wellbeing provided by automobile ownership, these techniques of mass production had to be brought across the Atlantic at the earliest opportunity, since cars in Europe remained the exclusive property of the rich and privileged. But as Mors itself was solely a maker of luxury cars, this development would have to wait for a while, at least in France.

These seven years at Mors between 1907 and 1914 provided André Citroën with his first experience of running a large-scale industrial enterprise. With over a thousand workers, Mors was a much bigger company than his own gearwheel business, and so, given the harsh working conditions of the time, he found himself increasingly concerned with labour relations and social questions at the factory. The normal shopfloor working day for men in France was then no less than twelve hours long, six days a week, with no paid annual holiday; women and children were expected to toil for ten hours a day, although this was cut by an hour a day in 1909. In 1912, however, the Mors workers went on strike, demanding the introduction of the five-day week, known in France as '*la semaine anglaise*', together with the right to join a trade union. Unlike many other bosses in his position, Citroën proved to be a progressive and sympathetic employer. Without hesitation, he opened negotiations with the strikers and avoided a confrontation. These talks led to the Mors workers being granted big concessions, resulting in considerable improvements in their working terms and conditions, a development that did little to improve Citroën's standing among fellow employers. Already, his arrival in the French auto industry was being perceived as a threat to the established order by men such as Louis Renault.

It was through his work for Mors that Citroën built up the team of experts that assisted his affairs with their loyalty, friendship and professional advice throughout his career; men like the millionaire Armenian diamond merchant and racehorse owner Atanik Eknayan, a friend of both Hugues and André Harbleicher. The sixty-year-old Eknayan was a fervent Mors enthusiast who had found a new lease of life in the arrival of the motor car. He delighted in driving his huge six-seater Triple Phaeton at top speed, and was unstinting in his financial support of Citroën's rescue scheme. Later, he was to provide funds for other ventures. Also joining his entourage around this time were Mattern, the production expert; Manheimer, the administrator; Fauchier and Guillot, the engineers and technical experts; Pommier, the dynamic salesman who later built up Citroën's network of dealers in France, and the multilingual Felix Schwab, who had begun his career as a furrier. Possessing a shrewd commercial brain and a pleasant, diplomatic manner, Schwab eventually became director of the export department at Automobiles Citroën.

But the most important recruit by far was Georges-Marie Haardt, then aged only twenty-six. A naturalised Frenchman born in Italy of Belgian parents, Haardt soon became André Citroën's right-hand man, and remained his closest business confidant for over fifteen years. Tall, thin and languid in demeanour, the suave, elegant Haardt was a natural salesman of luxury goods, having grown up in this milieu – his parents owned a business in Naples making and selling chocolates of the most elaborate and extravagant kind. Being an aristocrat in all but birth, and endowed with all the social graces, he had long since found that touring the continent to demonstrate expensive motor cars to the rich and the nobility provided a most congenial and lucrative occupation.

Haardt was more than just a dandy, however. Having joined the Mors company as its sales supremo, it soon became clear that he possessed a flair for organisation and an eye for administrative detail that matched Citroën's own. Yet in personality and physique, the two men were completely opposite in type, so that Haardt's phlegmatic temperament and cool business judgement perfectly complemented Citroën's impetuous, energetic drive. Although six years younger than his boss, Haardt was reputedly the only man to whom *le patron* would ever listen, and undoubtedly, his advice and influence was to have a profound effect in restraining some of Citroën's wilder ideas and in keeping the business on an even keel. In 1913, the two men launched a company to exploit a new carburettor patent, opening a factory on the Quai de Javel, not far from where the gearwheel company was located. This venture marked Citroën's first connection with the site where, a few years later, his great car factory was to spring up.

Having achieved a certain status in the world, Citroën's enjoyment of the high life was now unbridled, and the downside of his impulsive, excitable personality had begun to take hold; far from diminishing his desire for further adventure, his success increased his urge to take risks; to push things to their limits; to test his fortune; to try his luck. As he grew ever wealthier, this penchant for dangerous living began to affect his life at play as well as at work, and he soon became an inveterate gambler, taking to the fashionable racecourses and casinos of Europe like a fish to water. No matter if it were Longchamps, Chantilly, le Touquet, Biarritz or Monte-Carlo, Citroën would invariably be there, in his element, enjoying a flutter in convivial company. And win or lose, he always had the same cheerful, optimistic smile on his face. Later, at the height of his fame and fortune, Citroën was repeatedly criticised by his fellow directors, who, fearful of the harm it was causing to his reputation as a sound businessman, became increasingly alarmed at the publicity given to his gambling exploits in the popular press. To these remonstrances, he always gave the same irrefutable reply: 'If I were not a gambler, I would not be where I am today.'

It was while on such an excursion to the casino at le Touquet in the autumn of 1913 that Citroën met the attractive young woman who was to become his wife. The daughter of an Italian Jewish banker, Giorgina Bingen was only twenty-one, not far short of half his age, a slim, *soignée* brunette who dressed with sophistication in the informal, liberated clothes then being brought into vogue by the milliner Gabrielle Chanel. 'Coco' had recently opened her first boutique at Deauville, further down the coast, backed by her boyfriend, the rich English coal baron Arthur 'Boy' Capel, one of Citroën's business associates. Giorgina's youthful vivacity, refreshingly spontaneous but by no means naïve, captivated Citroën immediately, and he became her devoted sugar daddy.

Evidently, it was a *coup de foudre* – love at first sight. On returning to Paris, they continued to meet frequently, and before long their holiday romance had developed into a committed relationship. They must have made an intriguing couple; the chic Giorgina, her striking, intelligent face peeping gaily from beneath her Chanel cloche hat, and the jovial, rotund André, looking every inch the successful industrialist, bowler-hatted as usual (now aged thirty-five, he was already quite bald), with his moustache now clipped close to his upper lip, and his dark eyes twinkling behind his pince-nez spectacles.

Often, the pair would go for long drives through the surrounding countryside in Citroën's splendid Mors, but with Giorgina at the wheel. Strangely, for a man who was to have such an enormous impact on the development of the popular car, André Citroën was a very reluctant motorist, perhaps on account of his poor eyesight. He rarely drove, and he had little interest in practical mechanics or motor sport. He was a technocrat, not a technician, and was never to be seen dressed in overalls, tinkering beneath the bonnet or putting his cars through their paces on the racing track, like so many other famous automobile pioneers.

At a civil ceremony held on 26 May 1914 – less than ten months after their first meeting – André and Giorgina were united in marriage, signing a contract of property in the traditional Jewish way. They began their married life in an agreeable apartment at 5 Chaussée de la Mouette in the fashionable 16th arrondissement of Passy, a residential district of smart mansions and villas lying south-west of the Place de l'Etoile; Citroën had not only abandoned bachelorhood but he had forsaken also his customary territory in Paris near the opera!

For prosperous, cosmopolitan couples such as André Citroën and his bride, it must have been an idyllic time. At the height of that gilded age before the outbreak of the First World War, Western civilisation had reached its zenith. Never before had a culture offered such opulence, luxury and refinement. Never before had optimism in the future been greater or more unqualified. Civilisation seemed not just to be an illusory condition enjoyed only by the privileged, moneyed classes but an absolute human reality and moral right, the benefits of which would, in time, be cascaded down to the less fortunate throughout the world through the mechanisms of international trade and travel. Medicine, science, technology and education flourished, and a complacent sense of order, stability and wellbeing prevailed. A fervent, unquestioning belief in the bounties of progress held sway, constituting the dominant religion of the era, and in every sphere of human endeavour it was considered that things could only get better still.

But the Golden Age was an illusion after all. Scarcely two months later, the Citroëns' honeymoon was rudely and brutally interrupted by an official proclamation posted on the streets of Paris. On 1 August 1914, France declared a state of general mobilisation in anticipation of the formal declaration of war issued by Germany two days later. The Belle Epoque was over. As a reservist, André Citroën was summoned to report immediately for military duty. Soon, all three Citroën brothers would be under arms in defence of the Republic.

On 15 August, having previously overrun Belgium, the German Army invaded France, bringing with it the greatest catastrophe ever to befall the French nation. Over the next four years, almost five million Frenchmen were to be killed or wounded in the mud and blood of the trenches. Total French losses in the First World War exceeded 1,385,000 men reported dead or missing – more than 10 per cent of its active adult male population and almost twice the level of casualties sustained by British and Commonwealth troops. Over two million more French veterans were demobilised maimed and unemployable, fit only to wander the streets of the large cities. Today, eighty years later, French public life and the French national consciousness bear the scars of this massacre still.

By 2 September, the vanguard of the German Army had thrust south from Belgium as far as Senlis, less than 20 miles from Paris, causing the French government to flee to Bordeaux. But then, instead of wheeling west to encircle the city as had been anticipated in the Kaiser's master plan, his troops were forced south-east along a different axis of advance by the intervention of the British Expeditionary Force based near the coast, which threatened their right flank. As the Germans began to cross the River Marne, a gap in their front was opened up, an opportunity quickly spotted and exploited by the French, thanks mainly to the vital intelligence gained by a vast superiority in reconnaissance aircraft. To reinforce the counter-attack, the military governor of Paris, General Galliéni, mobilised the garrison, requisitioning all the taxis and private motor cars that he could find on the streets of the city to transport over six thousand soldiers to the battle of the Marne, in groups of five or six per vehicle. For the first time in history, the automobile – like the aeroplane – had become an effective instrument of war.

Finding himself in danger of being outmanoeuvred by the French and British counter-attacks, on 10 September the German commander-in-chief von Moltke ordered a retreat back across the rivers Aisne and Somme to the higher ground of Artois, Picardie and the Champagne. Here, the Germans dug into defensive positions protected by machine gun nests and barriers of barbed wire. Unable to dislodge their enemy in the face of such withering fire, the French and their ally, the British Expeditionary Force, followed suit, and soon a double line of opposing trenches stretched along a 400 mile front from the Belgian coast to the Swiss Alps. Despite the Kaiser's predictions of a swift victory based on tactical surprise, speed and manoeuvrability, the war then settled down into a demoralising slogging match, as each side attempted to smash its rival's defences by artillery fire. But even with the aid of these devastating barrages, in which over 1,000 guns would often fire non-stop for a week, discharging several million shells onto a few square miles of ground, the attacking infantry could rarely capture more than a hundred yards of territory without sustaining appalling casualties, and thus it was never possible for them to open up a gap through which the cavalry could make a breakthrough and attack.

Mobilised as a lieutenant in the 2nd Regiment of Heavy Artillery (a new unit formed by amalgamation with his old regiment at le Mans) and now stationed in the Argonne area on France's eastern border, André Citroën witnessed the effects of this stalemate with despair. As his particular responsibility involved the resupply of ammunition for the guns, he saw at first hand that a shortage of shells – and, indeed, of artillery itself – was already having a serious effect on the fighting efficiency of the French Army. In contrast to the 500 German heavy guns ranged against it in his sector of the battlefield, the IVth Army to which he belonged had only 300 of comparable calibre with which to return fire. But worse than that, it was estimated that given the present furious rate of consumption, within a few weeks its stocks of shells would be completely exhausted. As Citroën had foreseen fourteen years earlier, guns were useless without the means to feed their insatiable appetites for ammunition. The war would be won or lost in the munitions factories.

Already, it was obvious that the production rate of the government-owned arsenals alone would never be sufficient to satisfy the demands of all 170 divisions of the French Army, in which over 5,600,000 men were now enlisted. Consequently, a number of France's largest industrial companies, including André Citroën's own gear company and the Renault car firm, had been organised into regional groups, and their factories hastily converted to produce shells. Even so, being critically short of workers due to the call-up (the Citroën firm's own labour force was down to twenty men too old to fight), this Paris group was having difficulty sustaining the modest production rate of 10,000 shells a day. In contrast to industrial giants like the USA, Great Britain and Germany, France was still an agrarian country, with half of its labour force engaged in agriculture and half of its population – some 18 million souls – living and working in rural communities of less than 2,000 inhabitants. Nearly 40 per cent of the 5½ million farms were less than 2½ acres in size, and industry was organised in similarly small-scale units. Out of 1,100,000 manufacturing enterprises, 1,000,000 had fewer than five employees and only 600 employed over 500 workers. Moreover, the quality of the small and quite inadequate quantity of shells that French industry was able to produce was uneven, to say the least, and a high percentage failed to explode. The whole situation, reeking of unpreparedness, inefficiency and even corruption, amounted to a national emergency.

Meanwhile, the artillery duel continued day after day, and casualties mounted horrifically on either side. Then on 15 October, André Citroën received an official letter of the kind already dreaded by millions of families throughout England and France: six days earlier, his brother Bernard, fighting as a volunteer with the infantry a few miles further along the front had been killed in action while attempting to rescue a wounded comrade under fire. Although half-expected, the news came as a terrible blow to Citroën, recently promoted to captain. Bernard was not just his brother, but also his best friend; the fact that he had been posthumously awarded the Croix de Guerre for his bravery was no consolation. From that point onwards, Citroën abandoned any reservations he might have had about the killing going on around him. It was now not just a question of doing his duty to defend his homeland, or of fighting to uphold certain moral and cultural values – it was simply a matter of personal revenge, and he vowed to do all in his power to hit back harder at the enemy and return its aggression in kind.

Within two months, he had formulated a plan of action. Thanks to a letter of introduction provided by Louis Loucheur, his mentor at the Ecole Polytechnique, in early January 1915 he was able to present his ideas in person to General Bacquet, the Under-Secretary of State for Munitions at the Ministry of War in Paris. General Bacquet was an artillery expert who needed little in the way of explanation or persuasion, but when he heard what the captain was proposing he could hardly believe his ears! The plan was that, given government backing, over the next four months Citroën would build and equip a new munitions factory from scratch, to manufacture shrapnel shells for the army's standard 75 mm field gun, one of France's most successful weapons. By June, he calmly promised, this factory would be capable of producing 10,000 shells per day, as many as were presently being produced by all the Paris munitions factories combined. But by the end of the year, its daily rate of production would be at least double that.

On 9 February 1915, an order for the purchase of a million such shells at a price of 24 francs each was signed by the authorities and, having been given leave of absence from the army, André Citroën got his scheme under way. His first act was to recruit his two old friends and partners from the Mors car company, Haardt and Eknayan, to be his principal lieutenants and fellow directors in the venture. Eknayan was put in charge of raising the finance, Haardt in charge of obtaining the necessary plant and machine tools for the new factory (from the USA), while Citroën concentrated on the construction of the building itself, which he designed, drawing on his lessons in architecture at the Ecole Polytechnique.

From beginning to end, the whole operation was meticulously planned and carried out, forming an object lesson in the rational, scientific organisation of industrial activity. As already noted, during his visits to the USA, Citroën had become an ardent disciple of the American engineer and metallurgist Frederick Winslow Taylor (1856–1915), who, while working at the Bethlehem Steel Company, had developed the principles of scientific management and made himself a name as the father of time and motion studies. In his books *Shop Management* (1903) and *Principles of Scientific Management* (1911), Taylor had demonstrated that the key to efficiency and productivity lay in analysing the sequence of events in a job of work, reducing every single task and operation to its smallest component part, and then rearranging methods so that this sequence of events could be performed with the minimum of effort by the minimum number of operatives, thus saving time and money. In short, it was Taylor's thinking that lay behind the success of Henry Ford's assembly-line methods, in which a single product was produced in very great numbers from standardised components and then sold at a very low price to encourage further demand.

The façade of the munitions factory that Citroën established at the Quai de Javel during the First World War. By the end of the conflict it was producing over 15,000 shells a day.

Faced with a similar objective, André Citroën had no hesitation in following similar methods. In setting up his munitions factory, he copied Ford's example by applying the principles of Taylorism thoroughly from start to finish, firstly in organising the construction of the factory itself, and secondly, in organising the work that actually took place within its walls. The site chosen was a 30 acre plot of open ground at the Quai de Javel on the left bank of the River Seine, just 2¼ km downstream from the Eiffel Tower. Previously devoted to market gardens and allotments, the site was purchased on 17 March 1915, and construction work commenced immediately. Within two months, the first stage had been completed, so that the production of the lead shrapnel pellets could begin – the factory had its own foundry and even produced the special quick-cutting tool steel (*Acier à Coupe Rapide Citroën*) with which the shell cases were machined. In fact, it was completely self-sufficient in all respects, producing its own light, heat and power – electric, hydraulic and steam – and buying in only the basic raw materials. It even had a laboratory to check and control the quality of supplies and finished products, plus its own electric railway to transport them both about the site.

By 15 June, the whole factory complex was completed, with its machinery installed and working, and the assembly of shells in progress in the vast assembly

The Quai de Javel factory used the latest American machines and methods. Note the use of individual electric motors to drive the lathes in contrast to the centralised motive power system of overhead belts normally found in factories of that era.

shed, 400 metres long and 100 metres wide. By 16 August, production was running at the rate of 1,500 units per day. By 11 September, it had reached 5,000 a day, exactly as Citroën had predicted. One year later, that daily figure had doubled to 10,000 shells; two years later, in 1917, it was 15,000. By the end of the war, Citroën's factory had produced a staggering total of 23 million shells.

Over the three-year duration of the First World War, production capacity at the Quai de Javel was trebled – and so was the labour force, and to a size previously unheard of in France. At the start of operations in 1915, 3,500 employees were involved, 750 (21 per cent) of them female. But so enormous was the demand for fresh supplies of ammunition that, by the time of the Armistice in 1918, this total had risen to 11,700 workers, no less than 6,000 (50 per cent) of whom were women (or *munitionettes*). To control and administer this multitude of workers – greater in numerical strength than two full army divisions – Citroën's elder brother Hugues was released from military duties to act as personnel manager. In fact, to keep the war-machine going, over 300,000 skilled workers and managers from among the conscript troops had to be returned to industrial work, and between 1915 and 1918 the munitions workforce in France expanded from 50,000 to 1,780,000 people, mainly at the expense of agricultural production.

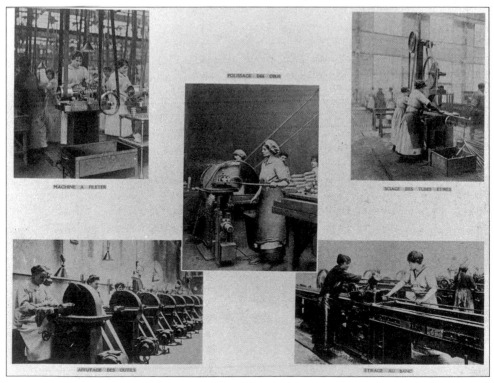

A page from the souvenir brochure that André Citroën published for visitors to his munitions factory in 1918. The predominance of female workers is clearly visible.

The factory worked night and day, seven days a week. The day shift clocked on at 7 a.m. and finished at 6 p.m., and the night shift started at 7 p.m. and worked until 6 a.m. One hour's meal break only was allowed per shift, and there were no rest days or holidays, except on Christmas Day. Towards the end of the war, however, this exhausting regime was relaxed slightly, and the working day was reduced to ten hours only, with one day off allowed per fortnight. Clearly, although they may not actually have been called upon to die for the Republic, these fighters in the munitions factories were subjected to a discipline no less rigorous than that imposed on the troops in the field. For the first time in history, the common civilian workforce of France – like that of Germany and Great Britain – had become servants of the State, organised and regimented as cogs in the war-machine or as components of the great apparatus of bureaucratic administration. Composed principally of women, this army of supply and munitions workers was subject to the same restrictions on individual freedom as applied to those citizens who wore its military uniform. Although conscription had long been enforced in France, unlike Great Britain, this curtailment of civil rights was particularly severe and deeply resented. By the winter of 1916/17, Paris was more or less a city under siege, bombarded by German long-range guns and Zeppelins, and subject to severe shortages of food and fuel. When the temperature fell to minus 14°C in February 1917, it was not even possible to turn to the traditional means of keeping warm. The production of absinthe – the Parisian's gin – had been outlawed, and the sale of wine and other alcoholic beverages was restricted to mealtimes. Entertainment, especially of the type available in brothels, was the one solace that was not rationed, and the cinemas, theatres, dance halls, cabarets and bordellos of Paris did a roaring trade.

In this state of total war, the authority exercised over civilian employees by industrial generals such as André Citroën fell little short of the medieval right of *droit de seigneur*. But although the working regime imposed at the Quai de Javel was both arduous and tedious in the extreme, Citroën used his lawful powers with enlightenment, so much so that he created at the Quai de Javel a model factory that set an example by its progressive social welfare provisions as well as its advanced industrial practices. Following Taylor's doctrine, Citroën had calculated that there were exactly thirty-nine separate operations to be performed in the manufacture of a 75 mm shrapnel shell, from the pressing and drawing of the shell case out of a solid billet of metal through to the final assembly of the explosive charge, fuse and shrapnel pellets in the projectile. Each worker carried out his or her own appointed task and nothing more, performing one simple movement or action over and over again, like a machine, perhaps as many as 5,000 times a day. Taylor claimed that his ideas would replace authoritarianism and anarchy on the shopfloor and lead to the elimination of almost all the causes of dispute and disagreement between workers and managers. But in recent years, his thinking has been severely criticised for degrading the dignity of human work, alienating the labour force, creating a socially divisive gap between employers and employees, and encouraging exploitative, entrepreneurial dictatorships. But if André Citroën

The output of Citroën's munitions factory was directed solely at supplying the French army's famous 75 mm field gun. Here this weapon is being towed on trials by a Citroën–Kegresse caterpillar car, sometime in the early twenties.

was a dictator, he was certainly a benevolent one, for notwithstanding the boredom of this repetitive toil, the overall working environment in which it was performed was greatly superior to that generally prevailing in France at that time, and most certainly so far as Citroën's female employees were concerned.

In common with many other Jewish and Quaker industrialists at the turn of the century, Citroën was a paternalistic but progressive employer who provided the very best wages and working conditions that he could afford. Clean, light, airy and hygienic, the factory boasted extensive washing, lavatory and bathing facilities, and an infirmary with a doctor in attendance full-time. A motor ambulance stood by round the clock to transport serious accident cases to hospital, and dental facilities were also on hand. At the works canteen, employees could eat well at subsidised prices – and at its various shops (including a butcher, a baker and a dairy), they could buy food, clothing, footwear, and even toys, far cheaper than anywhere else in Paris. With so great a number of female workers on the shopfloor, maternity and childcare arrangements also had a high priority, and the factory was surely the first in the world to provide a nursery and a crèche. And, finally, to entertain the workers during the very few leisure hours available, free band concerts and silent movie shows were staged. Among the most popular of these were the comedies starring Charlie Chaplin, who, known to them as 'Charlot', had as great a following among French film fans as among British and American cinemagoers. Much later on, André Citroën and Charlie Chaplin became great friends, even to the extent of sharing family holidays together in Switzerland. Later still, long after Citroën's death, Chaplin poked fun at Citroën's industrial methods in his film *Modern Times*. It could be said that the joke was on Chaplin, however, for after the Second World War, while living in Switzerland, the comedian proudly owned an example of Citroën's greatest car – a Traction Avant.

A model of organisational efficiency and social responsibility, André Citroën's shell factory was considered to be one of the great industrial wonders of the world, exceeded in its size and scale of operations only by Henry Ford's factory at Detroit. Consequently, many of the world's greatest military, industrial and political leaders came to the Quai de Javel to look, to learn and to listen to its remarkable creator and animator. From France came Generals Foch, Pétain and Gourard, the car-maker Louis Renault and countless politicians and government officials, too numerous to mention. From Great Britain came, among many others, Field Marshal Sir Douglas Haig (later Earl Haig), commander-in-chief of British troops in France, the successive Ministers of Munitions David Lloyd George and Winston Churchill, and also Sir Percival Perry (later Lord Perry), Henry Ford's right-hand man in Britain and subsequently the creator of Ford's Dagenham factory. Visitors from the USA included General Pershing, commander of the American Expeditionary Corps in France, and Herbert Hoover, later President of the USA but then serving as Minister of Supply in the US government. It seems that Henry Ford never made the journey to the Quai de Javel. Intending to tour France on a peace-making mission during the First World War, he got as far as Oslo, Norway, on board his 'peace ship' in December 1915, but feeling unwell as a result of the stormy crossing, he promptly turned back. Later, he visited Europe incognito on a couple of occasions, travelling under an assumed name. But there is no record in the Ford archives of him ever visiting André Citroën in Paris.

The following year, the slaughter in the trenches reached catastrophic proportions. From the outset, civilian journalists were banned from the war zone, and the military authorities controlled the news. The casualty figures could not be censored, however, and were recorded by the press as bleak statistics of the carnage. When the truth about the appalling conditions at the front began at last to get through to the civilian population, a wave of revulsion and pacifism spread throughout France and beyond, a sentiment for which the 'cosmopolitan Jewish-Bolshevik intelligentsia' was partly blamed, of course. Following the battles of Verdun and Passchendaele, in which a total of over a million Allied soldiers were killed within a month, French troops mutinied, and strikes broke out in the munitions factories of Paris. In June 1917, this industrial unrest reached the Quai de Javel, where the female workers (but not the men) came out on strike, demanding better pay and shorter working hours, and singing the '*Internationale*' with a revolutionary fervour that anticipated the events of the Russian Revolution three months later. As he had done before at Mors, André Citroën defused a dangerous situation with tact and discretion. By listening immediately to the *munitionettes*' grievances and then referring the dispute to arbitration by a conciliation council presided over by the Socialist Minister of Armaments Albert Thomas, a fair settlement and return to work was soon arranged. Meanwhile, the arrival on the scene of a new premier and War Minister, the radical, reformist Georges Clémenceau, and also a new Commander-in-Chief, Maréchal Pétain, served to restore order among the troops and stiffen the resolve of the French nation and its army to fight on.

In the spring of 1918, the Americans entered the conflict and sent troops to France. Even so, having recently concluded a peace treaty with the Bolshevik Russians which stopped the fighting on the eastern front and released troops for the west, the Germans revived their offensive with renewed vigour. By September, they had broken out from their defensive lines to advance once more within striking distance of Paris, and had recaptured most of the territory originally gained in 1914. But then, with their supply lines over-extended and their troops exhausted by this final desperate effort, the morale of the German Army suddenly collapsed before an Allied counter-offensive. Pushed back to its own borders and fearing mutiny or even revolution at home, the German High Command chose to surrender rather than to continue the fight on German soil, and on 11 November 1918, an armistice was signed in a special railway carriage in the middle of the Forest of Compiègne. The long, bitter war of attrition that the generals had predicted would be no more than a short, swift textbook manoeuvre was over at last. The final, sombre reckoning was that 1,357,800 Frenchmen had been killed in action and 4,266,000 wounded, of which 1,500,000 were permanently maimed, so that French casualties alone totalled a horrific 73 per cent of the 8,410,000 men mobilised – 3 out of 10 French males between the ages of eighteen and twenty-eight had been wiped out. In addition, 1,800,000 German and 908,000 British and Empire troops had also been killed, plus an estimated 9,000,000 Americans, Russians, Austrians, Italians, Turks and other nationalities, making a grand world total of 13,000,000 deaths. Nobody had won, except perhaps the suppliers of weapons and munitions.

Certainly, Citroën's reputation as an industrialist had not been harmed by the war, for in addition to his activities at the Quai de Javel, he had undertaken several other important tasks for the French government, with considerable success. Apart from re-organising the affairs of the State-owned arsenal at Roanne, he had also been made responsible for organising food supplies to factories working on defence contracts and also for creating an organisation to supply coal to these factories, plus the nation's gasworks and electric power stations as well. Ultimately, he was also asked to organise the feeding of the civilian population, by devising and introducing a ration-card scheme. As a result of this work, much later, in 1926, he was invited to take charge of the re-organisation of the government tobacco monopoly, by setting up the Régie France Tabac and re-establishing the famous Gitanes and Gauloise brands still smoked today.

After the Armistice, there was much talk of profiteering on the part of men like André Citroën. Clearly, by providing the French artillery with shells and supplying its officer corps with large numbers of Mors staff-cars, Citroën had done well out of the war, enhancing both the finances of his various companies and his own personal prestige. But quite how much money he, Haardt and Eknayan made from their munitions venture will never be known, as the exact capital and operating costs of the factory were never disclosed. All that can be said in defence of the accusation is that, well before the war had ended, Citroën was already making plans to put these profits to good use by investing them in a new and socially beneficial enterprise. Now that the need for shells had ended as abruptly as it had begun, there could be no return to vegetable-growing at the Quai de Javel – another purpose would have to be found for the factory and its huge labour force. That task would be the construction of the means of transport that had proved its worth so powerfully in the war – the automobile – and indeed, well before the ending of hostilities, permission had already been obtained from the authorities for work to commence on the development of a car at the Citroën premises. Throughout the war, a constant procession of foreign delegations passed through the Citroën factory to inspect its facilities. This gave André Citroën the thought of setting up an international forum for the exchange of information and ideas; and so, with ten others of like mind, after the Armistice, he founded the Inter-Allied Union (l'Union Interalliée, a Gallic version of the Anglo-Saxon League of Nations), with the object of

An advertisement published by the Citroën gear company in 1918, clearly directed at the motor industry and highlighting transmission applications.

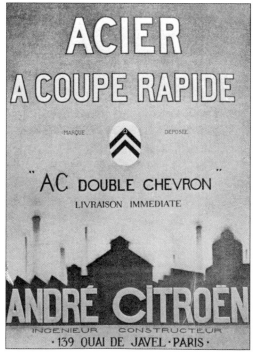

Also published in 1918 was this advertisement for Citroën's quick-cutting tool steel, produced in the foundry he had established at the Quai de Javel.

André Citroën in 1918, aged forty. Even before the first cars bearing his name appeared on the roads of Europe he was well established as an engineer and industrialist of international repute.

'contributing towards the creation of a spirit of understanding and cooperation between the peoples of Europe so as to maintain peace and develop civilisation'. This society, which met regularly at the Hotel le Vieux in the Faubourg Saint-Honoré for many years after the First World War, was the only club of its era which admitted women on equal terms to men. In 1920, Maréchal Foch, the Allied Supreme Commander during the closing stages of the war, became its president. This unending flow of visitors also gave Citroën the idea of providing a brochure describing the past and present activities of his factory. On the last page of this brochure, produced in November 1918, there appears the following passage which *le patron* wrote himself:

At present we are preparing here the transformations necessary to ensure that our 12,000 workers continue in useful and remunerative employment and that the creative forces assembled in this establishment remain active in the national interest. Where visitors now see shells being made, in a short time cars will be constructed.

The machine tools employed will be different but, as in the past, the objective will be to achieve the highest degree of quality and productivity. The method of working will continue to be scientific, and the amenities of the factory will once again signal the care devoted to the physical and moral welfare of all those who work in it. Having contributed so greatly to the victory of the French armed forces, the Citroën factory will continue to devote itself to the economic greatness of France by every means at its disposal.

André Citroën, whose personal contribution to the war effort had played such an important part in achieving victory, was ready to fight the new but no less arduous peacetime battles that lay ahead. Moreover, now that he was the doting father of three children (Jacqueline, born in 1915, Bernard, born in 1917 and Maxime, born in 1919), he intended to do so with redoubled energy and optimism.

CHAPTER THREE

The Henry Ford of France

With hindsight, it is easy to see how the decade known as the 'Roaring Twenties' got its name. No sooner had the guns of the First World War fallen silent than the air was torn by rumblings of a different kind – the roar of the ever-increasing torrent of motor traffic that began to pour onto the streets of Europe and America.

Nowhere in Europe was this boom more audible and visible than in France, for although the motor car may not actually have been invented there, it was certainly the French who first discovered popular motoring as we know it today. By the turn of the century, they were already turning out more examples of this new contraption than the Americans, Germans and British put together, and Paris was well established as the capital of the automotive world. The problems caused by the wholesale slaughter of horses during the First World War added a powerful impetus to the motorisation of road transport, and after the Armistice, this early interest was renewed with vigour, causing an enormous escalation in the sales of private cars as well as taxis, lorries and buses. Before the war, there had been only 1 car for every 330 of the population of America, 1 for every 600 persons in Great Britain and 1 for roughly every 1,000 Frenchmen and women. By 1919, however, car ownership had increased spectacularly to 1 vehicle for every 27 Americans, 180 Britons and 200 Frenchmen. During this postwar boom, the production of cars in France began to catch up rapidly with demand, making the French far more self-sufficient than their Anglo-Saxon neighbours. In fact, although it was already the third largest market in the world, Great Britain relied largely on imports from the USA and, indeed, France itself. Consequently, when the infant British motor industry – then comprising over 260 disparate, small firms, all woefully under-capitalised – failed to take the lead in Europe, it fell to French manufacturers to pioneer not just the technical configuration of the popular European automobile but also most of the techniques employed in its mass production and marketing.

By 1924, three flourishing volume-production car companies had been established in France – Peugeot, Renault and Citroën – of which the Societié Anonyme Automobiles Citroën ranked as the youngest, having been founded in 1919. But even though his famous double chevron badge did not appear on the radiator cowling of a motor car until a long time after Renault's or Peugeot's, André Citroën can rightly be numbered among those early pioneers who laid down the technical principles of the cars we drive today. Yet even at the outset, Citroën was never the spanner-wielding *Practical Mechanics* kind of car man with sump-oil beneath his fingernails and axle-grease in his hair, habitually dressed in dirt-stained overalls. Unlike Ford or Renault, he was never directly responsible for the design of the products that bore his name, much less even for the building and testing of the prototypes. Ford and Renault were essentially car-builders who became businessmen and industrialists through force of circumstance. Citroën was exactly the reverse!

A specialist in automotive manufacturing technology rather than an automobile engineer *per se*, his role in bringing the popular family car on to the European stage was that of a production expert and organiser. In short, he was a conductor rather than a composer. Even so, despite this lack of hands-on interest, either as a driver or mechanic, he was well qualified to understand the technicalities of car design and could argue abstruse theoretics on equal terms with his employees. This was not always the case among the famous names who founded other great automobile marques.

Right from the start of his career, solving the technical problems of large-scale industrial production was the engineering challenge that really interested him. Rather than becoming involved in the details of automobile design or the invention of new products or processes, his life's work was to be concerned with devising ever more brilliant ways of manufacturing and marketing the ideas spawned by the many other gifted engineers he employed and supported. In

Always the family man, André Citroën shows off his first car, the Type A, to his parents-in-law, M. and Mme Bingen. As usual, his wife is at the wheel. Some contemporary commentators claimed, unkindly, that she was in the driving seat throughout his career.

short, unlike most other early European motor car firms run by practical men or *garagistes,* and which developed out of the carriage-building, bicycle-making or agricultural engineering trades, the expertise of the Citroën company sprang not from a light-industrial or workshop background, but from the far more substantial skills of heavy engineering. This fact was to be of great importance when the time came for André Citroën to start making cars. Firstly, it gave him the resources to begin manufacturing on a grand scale, so that the output of Citroën vehicles quickly overtook that of his rivals, propelling him to first place in the league of French car manufacturers within a relatively short time. But secondly, it also gave Citroën's designers a very great measure of technological independence. Thus, when (much later) André Citroën decided to abandon the manufacture of conventionally-engineered motor cars in favour of a series of radically innovative new products, his company was able to realise these revolutionary ambitions from within its own technical resources, instead of being limited by a lack of skill and imagination on the part of outside suppliers, a factor which so often led to the failure of less self-sufficient would-be innovators in the automotive world.

Exactly when or how Citroën decided to enter the car business is unrecorded; all that is known for certain is why. Indeed, to provide a profitable new occupation for the workers and machinery of the Quai de Javel factory, he could just as well have turned to making bicycles, sewing-machines or even pots and pans. But in the light of his famous and characteristically extravagant saying of 1923, '*Dès l'instant où une idée est bonne, le prix n'a pas d'importance*' ('the moment an idea is right, its price becomes of no importance') there can be no doubt that, having decided to build a car bearing the double chevron badge, André Citroën proposed to spare no effort or expense to ensure that it was the best of its kind. But exactly what kind of a car would it be?

In truth, Citroën never made so much as a mark on paper to define his thinking on the detailed rights and wrongs of car construction, either as a design brief, an engineering blueprint or stylist's sketch. Without such documentary evidence, it is hard to say precisely what he had in mind at the outset or, indeed, exactly when the act of conception that led to the birth of the Double Chevron marque actually took place. However, it is known that, as early as 1915, Citroën invited two well-established car designers from Panhard – Messieurs Artault and Dufresne – to produce the prototype of a large and luxurious performance car, using a four-cylinder 18CV version of the Silent Knight engine, ready for production as soon as the war ended. Whether he intended to market this car as a Mors or under his own name is a matter for speculation, but in the event, Citroën abandoned the project and the design was sold to Gabriel Voisin, who made it the cornerstone of his own prestigious marque, founded in 1920. With relatively little modification year by year, Voisin produced this car until 1927, with great success. Purchased by such notables as Rudolf Valentino, Josephine Baker and H.G. Wells, the speedy and elegant Type C1 became the favourite of the fashionable fast set during the early twenties. Everybody who was anybody had to have one, especially after Dominique

The Silent Knight-engined sports tourer designed by Artault & Dufresne, originally commissioned by André Citroën, as subsequently produced by Voisin in 1922.

Lamberjack (Voisin's friend and chief concessionaire) drove one from Paris to Nice in 11 hours 30 minutes, knocking more than an hour off the previous best time for this classic run.

One of the more flamboyant of Citroën's fellow *habitués* at Maxim's restaurant, Gabriel Voisin (1880–1973), was a transport pioneer both in the air and on the ground. Working always from first principles, he was consistently ahead of his time in all that he did, at work and at play. Throughout his long and eventful life, he never failed to demonstrate exceptional originality and individuality of thought. The first man ever to build aircraft on a factory basis for sale to private customers, including the machine in which Henry Farman made the world's first closed-circuit 1 kilometre flight in 1908, he went on to produce no less than 10,000 aeroplanes for the French and British Air Forces during the First World War. But then, finding the demand for aircraft much reduced in peacetime, he turned his attention to the automobile – or rather to constructing highly-advanced and innovative cars that were as much like aircraft as possible. In 1923, he produced an aerodynamic, lightweight, all-aluminium racing version of the C1, featuring the world's first chassisless monocoque bodyshell, and entered it in that year's Grand Prix de l'ACF held at Tours, where it came fifth, despite having an engine only half as powerful as that of the winning Sunbeam. An architect by training, Voisin also collaborated with le Corbusier in developing a system of industrialised, prefabricated buildings, and later, in sponsoring a visionary plan for the redevelopment of Paris. Known as *le Plan Voisin*, this was drawn up by the

Announced by a fanfare of publicity in the spring of 1919, André Citroën's first car, the 10 hp Type A, was the first mass-produced European car. Unlike other French cars of its era the Type A came fully equipped with tyres, lamps and even a self-starter, ready for the road. Eventually it was made available in a wide variety of body styles, all based on one standard chassis, engine and transmission, in accord with Citroën's mass-production and mass-marketing formula.

revolutionary designer in 1925 and exhibited in his famous Pavilion d'Esprit Nouveau at the Paris Exhibition of Decorative Arts. But although this scheme anticipated the city's modern-day motor traffic demands with prescient accuracy, at the time it was rejected by the authorities as nothing more than futuristic madness!

Clearly, the events of the First World War had made a profound impact on Citroën's thinking, causing him to revise his plans altogether, for in July 1917 he requested another well-known designer, Jules Salomon, the creator of the popular le Zèbre light car, to produce quite a different type of vehicle – a car designed not for the amusement and pleasure of the most privileged members of society, but for the everyday needs of the ordinary man in the street.

As an entrepreneur whose remarkable commercial acumen was combined with a deep social awareness, Citroën had already realised that the world had changed forever. Inspired by the example of Henry Ford and the Model T, he had decided that the future of the automobile lay as a tool of work and business for the middle classes rather than as a plaything for the rich.

So it happened that, against the advice of many of Citroën's closest friends and advisers, in January 1919 the newspapers of France carried a series of advertisements announcing the impending arrival of a completely new kind of car – a mass-produced vehicle that came fully-equipped and ready for the road, at a single, all-inclusive price. Costing only 7,250 francs in its simplest form, this new car was not only cheaper to buy than anything else then being offered on the market, but it was also far less expensive to run. These advertisements – the first of their kind – caused a sensation, and within a fortnight over 16,000 enquiries were received, a flood that increased to a torrent when, in June, an example was put on display in a showroom on the Champs-Elysées.

Already, during the previous month, the earliest examples of this first true Citroën – the 1,327 cc 10 hp Type A – had begun to roll out of the totally reconstructed and re-organised facilities at the Quai de Javel. The first European car to be built using American mass-production techniques, the Type A Citroën came to its buyer fully finished and fitted out, unlike most other cars available at the time, which were normally supplied as a rolling chassis plus engine for completion by a specialist coachbuilder. There was nothing else to buy; the car came complete with bodywork, hood, wheels, tyres, electric lights, horn, tools and even an electric self-starter as standard equipment.

The Type A Citroën was also the first car in Europe to have its steering wheel mounted on the left, so setting the pattern adopted by other mass producers. Although the rule of the road established in France by Napoleon dictated that vehicles should keep to the right side of the road when passing, the earliest continental manufacturers placed the steering wheel on the right, next to the kerb, so that the driver or chauffeur could see the edge of the poorly made roads. This practice was maintained by luxury marques until after the Second World War. Citroën, on the other hand, always catered for the owner-driver, and so he positioned the driving seat of his cars so that the gearstick could be

The Type A in mass-production at the Quai de Javel factory in 1919. At that time, the assembly line was not yet fully mechanised and the cars were pushed along the raised ramps by hand. Even so, Citroën's construction methods were far in advance of any other European car manufacturer.

operated by the driver's right hand, and so that the person at the wheel had better visibility ahead when overtaking.

Available in a choice of eight different body styles and capable of 38 mpg and a top speed of 40 m.p.h., the Type A was an instant success. At first, thirty vehicles left the factory daily, but soon this output had risen to over fifty cars a day, so that by the end of 1919, 2,810 Citroëns were on the road. The first of these was said to be the example sold to a certain Monsieur Testemolle from Beaulieu in the Dordogne, on 7 July 1919. Later, M. Testemolle visited the Quai de Javel with his car, to be met by André Citroën in person. To the accompaniment of a fanfare of trumpets played by a large brass band, Citroën no. 000,001 was decorated with a commemorative chassis-plate, in a ceremonial reception. By the end of 1920, a further 12,244 cars had been built, although by this time the price had risen by almost 50 per cent, to 12,500 francs for the *Torpedo* or open-tourer version.

In 1921, however, the Type A was replaced by the Type B2 two- and four-seaters, equipped with a more powerful 1,452 cc four-cylinder engine, while the following year, the famous 5CV Type C series (also designed by Jules Salomon, assisted by Edmond Moyet) joined the Citroën range. An outstandingly robust and reliable light car, powered by a 7.5 hp 856 cc engine, this was available initially as either a closed- or open-topped two-seater cabriolet, or later, in C5 form, as the immortal Cloverleaf three-seater drop-head coupé. Perhaps the first cars in the world to be aimed at the woman driver, the 5CV Petite Citrons were normally painted bright lemon-yellow, in a visual pun of their maker's name, and their

The interior of the Quai de Javel in 1920, showing completed Type A chassis awaiting marriage with their wood-framed bodywork, which was produced separately in the coachwork department.

success undoubtedly inspired a number of other famous small-car designs such as the Opel Laubfrosch in Germany and the Austin Seven in England.

Following the installation of a 500 metre-long moving-chain assembly-line system in 1923, production at the Quai de Javel works hit 100 cars a day, the first time such an output figure had ever been achieved in Europe, and an astonishing rate of production for that era. Sustaining such levels of output called for more than organisational genius, of course, and so, to expand the market for his products and find sufficient would-be motorists to absorb this prodigious flow of cars, André Citroën brought another of his remarkable talents to bear – his flair for advertising and marketing. A master salesman and publicist, Citroën soon devised a number of farsighted and innovative ideas to widen the market and create marque loyalty, including the concept of distribution through a network of franchised dealerships. Soon, a tied garage or showroom displaying his double chevron badge, selling and servicing Citroën products exclusively, was open for business in virtually every town in France – 5,000 dealers had been appointed by 1925, compared to the 200 listed at the outset in 1919 – in the first example of this now universal method of distributing and selling cars.

These early Citroëns also broke entirely new ground in marketing and customer-care techniques. For the very first time outside America, purchasers were offered a driver's manual and a list of approved Citroën repairers, together

The finishing hall at the Quai de Javel in 1922. The 8CV Type A has now been replaced by the more powerful 9CV B2, but the method of construction remains the same. Note the wide variety of body styles, open and closed.

First exhibited at the 1921 Paris Salon and sold between 1922 and 1925, the highly popular 5HP Type C was a real car in miniature and soon put paid to the cycle car as a means of cheap motoring. First available as a two-seater, but then from 1923 onwards as the three-seater Trefle or Cloverleaf C3 model, it had many imitators including the Austin Seven. Over eighty thousand were sold, at a price that never rose much higher than 15,000 old francs – half the price of most other cars during the twenties. Despite a huge continuing demand, production stopped when Citroën realised that he could build bigger and better cars, in greater numbers, for the same cost.

with a tariff of standard service charges, so that they were assured that any item of work, carried out by any distributor in France, would be done to the same standard and charged at the same price. The concept of standardised factory-made replacement parts was also introduced, so that owners could exchange a worn or broken component for a brand new item without waiting for the original piece to be repaired or reconditioned by a *garagiste*, as was the case in the motor trade hitherto. And, naturally, this comprehensive after-sales service was completed by the publication of accurately-illustrated spare-parts catalogues, in which the construction of each model was explained and detailed, down to the last nut and bolt. For most manufacturers at that time, the industrial process ended when a product left the factory and was sold. But for Citroën, it had only just begun. 'As soon as one sale ends, another more important sale commences. It is the after-sales service offered to the customer when he has already parted with his money that will decide whether he returns to buy from us a second time,' he later declared. Such an outlook is not unusual in the motor trade today, but in the early twenties it marked a revolution in sales and service methods. Yet in prizing so highly the ideals of quality control and customer care, Citroën was merely following the same business ethic practised by many other

The three-seater conduite intérieure town car was one of several new versions of the B2 introduced in October 1922. This model soon caught on among members of the medical profession for making their visits to patients, and thus came to be known as the Doctor's Coupé.

great Jewish retailers of his time – men like Simon Marks of Marks and Spencers in Britain, for example. Moreover, to ensure that the high standards of reliability and durability he claimed for his products were actually met, Citroën set up chemistry and physics laboratories at his factory to carry out analysis of raw materials and manufactured components on a routine basis, a precaution unheard of elsewhere in Europe.

André Citroën was also the inventor of the sales technique known today as direct-mail marketing, now a complex, computerised activity, but then much more a matter of laborious manual record-keeping. Supplied with information about potential customers by the dealers, a special department at the Quai de Javel kept vast card-index files of the names, addresses and requirements of likely prospects. In due course, all received a series of mailings containing catalogues and brochures, accompanied by a covering letter thanking them for visiting the showrooms and suggesting the ideal Citroën model for their needs. The text of the letter was uniform and duplicated, but the hand-written, individually addressed salutation and valediction gave each recipient the impression that it had been written by André Citroën personally, for his or her eyes alone. Thousands of these mailings were despatched each week throughout France; the method proved so successful that it was responsible, so it was claimed, for over 15 per cent of Citroën's sales.

The unusual B2 'Caddy Sport' introduced in limited numbers in 1923 – just 300 were made. A lightened, souped-up version of the standard B2 tourer, it was Europe's first popular sports car. Aimed specifically at women drivers, it offered the joys of sporting motoring at rallies and concours d'élégance *for a fraction of the price of true performance cars from makers such as Bugatti and Delage. Owners included Mistinguette and Josephine Baker. Top speed was 56 mph!*

All kinds of novel advertising and publicity initiatives were employed to establish the Citroën marque and foster brand loyalty. During 1920, various endurance trials and economy runs were staged, the results of which enabled Citroën to claim that his 10 hp Type B2 Type A was the most economical car in the world. Next, a caravan of cars toured rural France like a travelling circus, to demonstrate the advantages of Citroën motoring in out-of-the-way places where no dealer existed. A sales-training school for concessionaires was established, and a company journal, the *Bulletin Citroën*, was introduced. Full-page advertising campaigns were mounted in the national and regional press, while thousands of posters were stuck up on walls and hoardings and most other large, flat, permanent surfaces visible from the road, and later, Citroën hire-purchase and insurance schemes were created. For the benefit of those who somehow managed to miss the ubiquitous sight of the double chevron symbol painted on the sides of hotels and houses, no less than 150,000 roadsigns bearing the Citroën badge were also erected across the length and breadth of France, as a gift to the nation from *le patron* of Javel. Then, on the morning of 4 October 1924, the date of the opening of the seventeenth Paris Motor Show, the capital city came to a standstill as its citizens stopped work and craned their necks to see an aeroplane writing the name 'Citroën' across the sky high above the Arc de Triomphe in huge letters of white smoke, the first time that this novel form of advertising had been seen in France. The inscription stretched 5 kilometres from end to end; even in the days when his business was comparatively small, Citroën was in the habit of thinking big!

It was the hallmark of André Citroën's genius as an industrialist that his interest in, and mastery of, large-scale volume-production methods did not stop short at the factory gates, but extended right down the line into distribution, sales and customer service. Despite the high degree of mechanisation of the production process at the Quai de Javel, the system never became dehumanised or lost sight of its purpose. In the modern phrase, Automobiles Citroën was 'customer-driven'. Through his flair for marketing and his deep, intuitive understanding of consumer motivation and psychology, Citroën created not just a marque but a brand, endowing his company and its products with a recognisable character and forging a strong human relationship with his customers. What was more, in creating the unique ethos of the double chevron brand, he established a property which soon became part of the popular culture of France, and thus, a familiar feature of the everyday lives of ordinary French men and women and their offspring. Even children were not forgotten as potential buyers of Citroën cars. 'I hope that the child who plays with his toy car won't just say "pass me my car" but "pass me my Citroën",' said *le patron* in 1925; and again, six years later: 'The first words that a baby should learn to pronounce are Mummy, Daddy and Citroën.'

To address this infant market and capture motorists at the earliest possible age, in 1923 he launched a range of miniature models of his cars, made by a specialist toy company. These sold just as well as the full-size cars. Beginning with around 15,000 purchases in 1923, by 1933 annual sales were exceeding

800,000 models! So successful was this pioneering Citroën toy venture, in fact, that the following year, another larger, much more expensive plaything was also produced – the Citroënette, a de luxe pedal- or electric-powered ⅕-scale model of the 5CV, which could be ridden in and driven just like the real thing. The car proved so popular that races were organised for children during the school holidays at resorts such as Deauville, where the famous beachside boardwalk provided a perfect racetrack. (The marketing of Citroën toys and models was discontinued after André Citroën's death. However, in 1938, during their State visit to France, King George VI and Queen Elizabeth were presented with two large-scale models of the Traction Avant, for Princess Elizabeth and Princess Margaret. One of these has survived, and can be seen today in the Royal Mews Collection at Buckingham Palace.)

Towards the end of March 1924, accompanied by his wife and various business associates and senior members of his staff, including Charles Rocherand, the first of his French biographers, André Citroën embarked at Cherbourg on the liner which was to carry him across the Atlantic on his second visit to the USA. On board also were several examples of the Citroën-Kegresse caterpillar-tracked car, together with their inventor Adolphe Kegresse, of whom we shall hear much more in Chapter Five. After arriving in New York on 4 April, Citroën spent several days sightseeing in Manhattan, combining business with pleasure by meeting numerous politicians, government officials, bankers and financiers, before travelling on to Detroit to renew his acquaintanceship with Henry Ford.

By now, the commercial triumph of the Model T had raised Henry Ford from the status of a humble farm mechanic to that of an industrial superstar or folk hero, America's first ever dollar billionaire, in the greatest personal success story the world had ever known. Although his 'Universal Car' had already been on the market for sixteen years, its sales were still increasing, since ever-rising production meant ever-falling prices, due to the economies of scale. During the previous year alone, over 2 million had been sold, some versions costing as little as $290, less than a third of the price charged in 1908, making a grand total of around 10 million to that date. Ultimately, over its nineteen-year lifespan, more than 15 million examples of the Model T were to be built, to the same basic formula. That year, with his profits once again topping $100 million (but still averaging only $50 per car), Ford was at the zenith of his career, firmly established as the largest car-maker in the world, and responsible for almost half the vehicles in America then built or being built. His 100 per cent shareholding in his company had recently been valued at $1 billion, making him by far the richest man in business history. Moreover, the original investors in the Ford Motor Company, bought out by the Ford family in 1919, had also done well out of the Model T. A $100 investment made in 1903 had realised $260,000 within sixteen years, having already yielded $95,000 in dividends over that period – the largest return on risk capital ever recorded. In addition, Henry Ford's own dividends, amounting to some $60 million, had been paid entirely free of income tax.

This enormous accretion of wealth had enabled Ford to build, at the point where the River Rouge flows into the River Detroit and onwards into Lake Erie, the largest industrial complex the world had ever seen. Opened in 1920, the vast

1,096 acre Rouge plant contained no less than 7,250,000 square feet of factory space and employed over 80,000 workers, in a gigantic demonstration of the self-sufficiency and independence that was both the keystone of Ford's personal philosophy and the essence of his business creed. At one end of this vertically-integrated mass-production process, a constant procession of boats and trains arrived at the Rouge site bringing coal and iron ore for the smelting furnaces which produced the all-important steel. And at the other end, they departed again, transporting the finished cars to the markets of the world at the rate of 5,000 a week.

This time, after making the customary tour of the Rouge and other Ford installations in the Detroit area, Citroën was invited to inspect some of the experimental work currently in progress in Ford's Engineering Laboratories. Henry Ford's success had been due in part to his interest in research and development, particularly in the field of metallurgy. He had been among the first automobile-makers to employ high-tensile vanadium steel for chassis and other parts, so giving the Model T its legendary lightness, strength and resilience. But this innovation was all too often carried out in a haphazard, capricious, empirical way that reflected Ford's beginnings as a farmboy mechanic, hobbyist and tinkerer.

Perhaps because his first foray in that field, the Model K of 1906, had proved unsuccessful, Ford held a prejudice against six-cylinder engines. So, as early as 1920, working on another hunch, he had begun to fiddle with a new and highly complex type of eight-cylinder motor. In this revolutionary power plant, the cylinders were arranged not in line but in a cruciform double-V configuration, with four pistons located above the central crankshaft and four below. Already, against the advice of the trained professional engineers on his staff, Ford had thrown vast resources into the task of perfecting this unorthodox piece of machinery, but without success. Apart from the problems of overcoming the inherent imbalance of this arrangement, when tested on the road, the dirt and water thrown up onto the underside group of cylinders caused ignition problems and misfiring. According to Charles Rocherand, who was present in the party, on seeing this X Engine and realising that it was theoretically unsound, André Citroën also shook his head in doubt. 'Very interesting, an admirable effort, but it will never work in practice,' he told his host. The Frenchman was not wrong in this observation, for this type of engine never entered production on a Ford or on any other make of automobile.

Citroën had brought with him something to show the Americans in return. Two full days of his visit were devoted to an extended demonstration of the Citroën-Kegresse half-track system, which Citroën hoped to sell to the US military authorities, with Ford acting as the licensee and manufacturer of the Citroën-Kegresse system in the USA, until such time as Citroën could open an American factory of his own. But although an example of the Model T Ford specially equipped with these caterpillar tracks was demonstrated in front of the American industrialist, nothing came of the project. For Citroën, this must have been a great disappointment. As a man of boundless optimism and imagination, he believed that this vast country of America, which had, as yet, few made-up roads, presented immense opportunities for his caterpillar cars. Able to travel equally well over sand, soil and snow as over tarmac, they were ideal for American conditions, civilian as well as military, he believed. Unfortunately, despite being shown the film of a convoy of Citroën-Kegresse vehicles making the first-ever crossing of the Sahara by motor car (see Chapter Five), Henry Ford was not convinced, doubtless due to the 'not-invented-here' syndrome; he had already experimented unsuccessfully with a half-track himself in 1918. Neither, for that matter, was the US Army convinced at that time, although many years later it adopted the caterpillar track principle to great effect. The M4 half-track vehicles used by the US Army in great numbers during the Second World War were direct descendents of the numerous Citroën-Kegresse lorries eventually purchased by the Americans.

Throughout his trip, André Citroën was hailed in the American press as the Henry Ford of France, but apart from an involvement in the motor car business and a shared belief in the principles of Taylorism, the two men had little in common. For André Citroën, surely one of the first Europeans to comprehend the huge significance and potential of America's industrial and economic might, this meeting with his hero Ford must have come as something of an anticlimax, being both commercially barren and socially frigid. But the outcome was hardly surprising: one man was progressive, liberal, sophisticated, pleasure-loving and Jewish; the other was conservative, provincial, puritanical, pessimistic in his view of fellow human beings, and anti-Semitic to boot.

As a man of the soil, born and bred in the spartan traditions of America's Midwest farming communities, Henry Ford had an instinctive distrust of city folk, be they the hordes of rootless native Black or White labourers that he employed in his factories or the smaller but no less threatening numbers of stateless Jewish immigrants – cosmopolitan intellectuals, businessmen and financiers – who were also arriving on American shores as refugees from Europe in ever-increasing numbers at that time. Abhorring the very changes in tradition that through his products he himself was introducing into America, and obsessed with the notion of imposing a new order on humanity through the principles of scientific management, he sought to control his employees' thoughts as well as their deeds. By supervising their leisure time with the same authoritarian methods that he exercised in managing their working hours, he even dictated the reading matter and musical entertainments permitted within his company.

Throughout the early twenties, the American auto tycoon had systematically conducted a crusade against what was, in his opinion, the all-corrupting influence of the Jews, a campaign so virulent and vitriolic that later, even Adolf Hitler acknowledged that it had provided him with inspiration and encouragement. Regularly, the *Dearborn Independent* (a local weekly newspaper owned by Henry Ford and actually printed on Ford Motor Company premises) published anti-Semitic articles blaming rapacious international Jewish bankers and destructive Jewish Bolshevik revolutionaries for all the imaginable evils of the world, from liberalism and unionism to Negro jazz music. A digest of these articles, some written by Ford himself, was published under the title *The International Jew*. Widely circulated in Europe, it was eventually translated into German and circulated within the Nazi Party. In addition, Ford disseminated copies of the notorious and highly defamatory booklet *The Protocols of the Elders of Zion*. Purporting to be extracts from a series of lectures given at the First Zionist Congress held at Basle in 1897, these protocols, outlining a secret Jewish plan for subjugating the Gentiles and establishing a Jewish World State, were later exposed as a forgery concocted by the Tsarist secret police in 1905, to discredit Russian Jews. Eventually, in 1927, faced with a boycott of his products by the American Jewish community, Ford was obliged to retract his views and stop his anti-Semitic propaganda. Even so, until the end of his life, he still held on to his belief that the Jews were unproductive hucksters, traders, speculators and gamblers who contributed nothing to human welfare and whose hold on the world's banking and investment system was nothing but iniquitous. 'Money is the root of all eval [sic] unless used for good purpus [sic],' he wrote in his notebook.

Yet this prejudice was always directed collectively and never individually. On a man-to-man basis, the eccentric, capricious Henry Ford appears to have got on well with every Jew he ever met, André Citroën included, for on their parting, Henry Ford presented his guest with a signed photograph. This was to occupy a place of honour on Citroën's desk at the Quai de Javel for the rest of his life.

Despite the failure of the two motor magnates to agree on engineering matters, Citroën did not leave America empty-handed. Before returning to Paris via New York (where, on 20 April, he was guest of honour at a banquet organised by some of Wall Street's leading lights, including John D. Rockefeller), he made a detour to Philadelphia. Here, he met a far more sympathetic and like-minded character, the industrialist Edward Gowan Budd, who was an innovator and pioneer after his own heart. Having begun in business as a maker of railway wagons, Budd had gone on to develop a revolutionary process for constructing all-metal car and railway carriage bodies by welding together large, pre-formed panels, stamped from sheet steel by giant hydraulic presses. Seeing for the first time just how quickly and simply these steel panels could be assembled into durable, weatherproof vehicle bodies, Citroën did not hesitate; immediately, he took up the European rights to this patented technique and agreed to purchase from Budd the tools and presses that he would need in order to introduce the process in his own factories.

Up till that moment, the building of bodies had presented serious problems to Citroën – difficulties, indeed, that were holding back the efficiency and profitability of operations at the Quai de Javel. Although the production of engines, transmissions and chassis was by now highly mechanised, the assembly of bodies was not. In common with all other European car-makers at that time, Citroën was still using the techniques of the horse and carriage era, constructing bodies manually by attaching pre-formed metal panels to hand-built wooden frames. The process was complicated, lengthy and laborious, so much so that the flow of completed bodies could never quite keep up with the output of completed chassis. And to make matters worse, once assembled, these wooden-framed bodies had to be painted by hand with several coats of slow-drying lacquer. By switching to Budd's all-steel method and using the new quick-drying nitro-cellulose spray-painting process developed by Du Pont de Nemours (another American company), he could overcome this blockage, increase output, reduce prices and boost demand still further. Better still, with the all-steel system, it was possible to build stronger, safer, fully-enclosed all-weather saloon and limousine-style bodies cheaply and efficiently, instead of the open drop-head tourers that up till then had been the mainstay of his range.

Immediately following his return to Paris, his deputy and chief of production G.-M. Haardt went back to Philadelphia with a team of engineers to prepare and organise this next great stage in the expansion of Citroën's industrial empire. The trip marked the beginning of regular fact-finding visits to the USA by Citroën engineers; thereafter, all were required to learn English, and lessons

Nothing better illustrates the significance of André Citroën's arrival on the French motoring scene than this photo taken on the Boulevard des Italiens in Paris in about 1922. The little owner-driven Citroën 5CV threading its way through the big Renault taxis and chauffeur-driven limousines marked a transport revolution – the end of the old order under which only the rich could afford to run a car. A Citroën B2 taxi can also be seen, at the kerb behind the Renault. Citroën's Paris taxi business commenced in 1921.

were instituted at the factory. By the autumn of 1924, 156 2,000 ton presses and over 800 other machine tools had been installed in a new factory located at Saint-Ouen on the northern outskirts of Paris, close to the foundry which had recently been opened at Clichy for the casting of engine blocks and other components. The investment costs of this improvement programme were enormous, committing the company to massive debts, but Citroën was sanguine about the risk. When Haardt asked him why he insisted on forging ahead at such a furious pace, expanding by revolution instead of by gradual evolution, he replied: 'One advances faster by taking giant steps instead of little shuffles.'

Consequently, on the Citroën stand at the Paris Motor Show that October, there duly appeared the very first example of the all-steel-bodied car to be built in Europe, the B10 Tout Acier model, constructed using the chassis and mechanical parts of the old B2. This was superseded the following year by a new and improved design, the 10 hp B12, which also featured drum brakes on all four wheels, another Citroën innovation. By the end of 1925, production of this model alone was regularly reaching – and sometimes exceeding – 500 cars a day. Of the 600,000 vehicles registered as running on the French roads that year, no less than 175,000 – almost 30 per cent – were Citroëns. As André Citroën had predicted at the outset, within six short years of commencing operations, the double chevron marque had overtaken its older established continental competitors – Renault, Peugeot and Fiat – to become the fourth largest car company in the world, topped only by the American giants, Ford, General Motors and Chrysler.

CHAPTER FOUR

The Talk of London and Paris

By 1925, Automobiles Citroën was well established as an international business with thriving interests not just throughout Western Europe but also in the Far East and South America. As early as 1920, Felix Schwab had begun to build an export department, making a world tour to recruit foreign dealers and promote the sales of Citroën vehicles abroad. Already, over 21,000 cars per year were being exported – almost a third of production – to places as far afield as China, Indo-China and Japan. During 1924, wholly-owned subsidiary companies were established in Belgium, Switzerland, the Netherlands, Italy, Denmark and Germany, following the pattern founded by André Citroën's first foreign *filiale* (subsidiary), Citroën Cars Ltd. Incorporated in Great Britain on 27 July 1923, initially this company numbered André Citroën, G.-M. Haardt, Felix Schwab and Daniel Metz as its directors.

The first Citroën cars to be sold in the UK arrived in 1920, imported by the London concessionaire Gaston Ltd. Here a row of chauffeur-driven Type A models supplied by Gastons is lined up outside Harrods in Knightsbridge that year ready to convey customers home from the Piano Sale. At that time, Harrods was actually a Citroën stockist!

The first Citroën cars to arrive in the British Isles had done so three years earlier, when, in 1920, the American-owned import agents Gaston Ltd obtained a concession to act as sole UK distributors, operating from showrooms in Great Portland Street and Piccadilly, London. The Type A very soon achieved a high reputation for robust construction, reliability, economy and low running costs among British motorists. 'I have yet to see one broken down,' said the leading motoring correspondent W.F. Bradley, reviewing an example in *The Autocar*.

This reputation was reinforced by the success of two Type B2 cars which Gaston's entered in the 1922 Scottish Reliability Trials. Finishing first and second out of a field of eleven starters, the pair covered a thousand miles of difficult highland motoring within six days, the leading car averaging 36.8 mpg for the distance to win the Scottish Cup, then Great Britain's top fuel economy award. When it joined the range that year, the little Type C proved more popular still, so that Gaston's sales for the three-year period were soon approaching 5,000 vehicles. These results were judged so encouraging in Paris that it was

At the Paris Salon of October 1924, André Citroën played another of his trump cards by announcing the arrival of all-steel bodies for his 10 hp B2 cars, thereafter known as B10s. Although stronger, safer and more weather-proof than the wood-framed coachwork used hitherto, these 'tout-acier' bodies were welded together from a large number of small stampings with the many joints concealed by lead soldering, and thus were somewhat less durable than the large unitary pressed-steel structures used on modern cars.

*Besides the all-steel saloon, Citroën
continued to offer a traditional 'torpedo'
or open tourer model in the B10 range, for
those who preferred fresh-air motoring.
This too was built by the tout-acier process.*

decided that a nationwide network of dealers and service agents should be set
up in the United Kingdom along the lines of that already created in France. As
the London-based Gaston company lacked the resources for such an expansion,
it was further agreed that this network should be controlled by the newly-
established *filiale*, Citroën Cars Ltd. Like the London sales office of André
Citroën's gearwheel business and the separate Citroën-Kegresse company
already established, this would be run by André Citroën's Dutch cousin Daniel
Metz, a British resident. Before long, over fifty garages had been recruited, the
first being Worthing Motors Ltd, which is still a Citroën dealer today.

To act as the hub of this network, in August 1923, Citroën Cars Ltd opened
new showrooms, workshops, stores and offices at Brook Green, Hammersmith,
in West London. Advertised as 'The Largest Motor Car Service Station in the
World', this modern, three-storey building with 100,000 square feet of floorspace
enabled Citroën to offer its customers, owners and dealers a comprehensive
range of services never before offered to British motorists in one location. Just
like a modern garage, the Citroën Building sold fuel and accessories as well as
cars, retailing replacement parts over the counter and providing a 'quick-fit'
exhaust and tyre change service. Full lubrication, maintenance and repair
facilities were also provided, as well as a paintshop and a carwash. The building
also functioned as a distribution depot, preparing cars delivered from France by

Initially, the 10 hp B10 came in a wide range of body styles to suit the greatest possible variety of customers and purposes. The saloon and tourer were built by the new all-steel method but the rest were coach-built in the traditional manner. But from the spring of 1925 onwards, carpentry was abandoned at the Quai de Javel and all but the all-steel saloon and tourer were discontinued.

The all-steel B12 conduite intérieure, available between October 1925 and 1926, was similar to the B10 saloon but had a stronger chassis and brakes on all four wheels. The idea of an inside position for the owner-driver was still a novelty. In most enclosed automobiles produced before the B10, the owner sat comfortably inside the vehicle in a separate compartment at the back while the chauffeur sat outside in the open air, exposed to the dust, wind and rain, an arrangement inherited from the days of the horse and carriage.

sea and rail via its own goods siding at the rear. Its large, flat roof, reached by an electric lift, provided space enough for cars to be test-run after servicing or repair, or for vehicles arriving from the factory to be parked ready for collection.

These changes brought immediate results. During the last three months of 1923, 1,509 cars were imported by Citroën Cars Ltd to add to the 1,500 already sold by Gaston's, making total sales of 3,009 – a figure which equates to almost 5 per cent of the 71,396 cars produced by British manufacturers that year, the first in which such statistics were recorded. But over the following two years, Citroën Cars' sales results were even more impressive. The ending of the wartime McKenna import duties in 1924 brought down the prices of French cars by as much as 20 per cent, which led to a huge increase in Citroën deliveries in the United Kingdom, with annual imports more than doubling from 3,080 in 1924 to 6,655 vehicles in 1925.

Not surprisingly, this *laissez-faire* policy on the part of the British government did not last for very long. In an attempt to stem the rising tide of imports (31,781 cars worth £5.9 million that year alone), early in 1925 it announced its intention to re-impose the McKenna duties the following year, in order to protect home producers. For André Citroën, the conclusion was inescapable;

like Henry Ford – and the tyre-manufacturing Michelin brothers also – he would have to establish his own production facilities in Britain. That way, not only would his cars avoid the re-erected barriers to trade in the United Kingdom, but by qualifying as British-made and therefore eligible for preferential tariff status, they would also gain a price advantage in the valuable markets of the British Commonwealth presently denied to the products of the French motor industry, including the right-hand-drive vehicles then being built at his own Paris factories. However, this new factory would have to be very much more than just an assembly point, putting together components made in France and shipped across the Channel. French-made components were also subject to the same punitive 33⅓ per cent McKenna duties as were applied to completed cars, so the factory would have to operate as self-sufficiently as was possible, buying in from British suppliers whatever parts it could not manufacture for itself, and importing only major items such as engines, transmissions and body pressings from France.

With this objective in mind, André Citroën instructed Daniel Metz to begin a search for factory premises in England. Metz did not have far to look. Just a few miles along the Great West Road lay the ideal place, located on a brand new

Also in 1926 Citroën opened his British assembly plant at Slough, the first of his factories outside France. In this picture of the Slough production line taken that year, the B12 model (known in the UK as the 12–24 hp) is being finished ready for delivery. Note the no-smoking sign: this policy, first introduced by André Citroën, still endures within all Citroën factories and office premises today.

industrial estate, already equipped with suitable buildings and facilities and ready for immediate occupation. Owned by the Slough Trading Company, co-founded by Sir Percival Perry, formerly Managing Director of Henry Ford's British assembly plant at Trafford Park, Manchester from 1909 to 1919, and Managing Director of the Ford Motor Company from 1928 to 1948, this factory stood just yards from the very site where (as we shall see in Chapter Five) a demonstration of the Citroën-Kegresse caterpillar car had taken place just three years earlier. Already equipped with the railway sidings that would be essential for handling freight wagons bringing supplies from Paris, the Slough factory satisfied all requirements, and Daniel Metz reported to *le patron* his recommendation to proceed. Characteristically, André Citroën did not hesitate, and on 31 July 1925 the lease was signed. By the end of the year, production of British-built Citroëns had begun.

On Thursday 18 February 1926, André Citroën opened his first foreign factory in person, thus beginning a tradition of Citroën residence at Slough which endures to this day. Production was destined to continue at the Slough works for exactly forty years. For the first few months, the 5 hp Cloverleaf alone was built at the Slough works, but then in September 1926, despite the fact that this very popular car was still selling well, production was discontinued in favour of the new, all-steel-bodied 9CV 12.24 hp B12 model.

By the autumn of 1926, the Slough factory was in full operation, turning out right-hand-drive cars at the rate of 500 a month. So, to celebrate this latest success, André Citroën arranged an excursion to London for his French associates and *confrères*, to show them his newly-created British organisation. At 3.30 p.m. on 26 October, a group of over one hundred leading Citroën concessionaires plus a sizeable number of France's top motoring journalists and correspondents met at the Gare du Nord in Paris and boarded the boat train to Boulogne, intent on three days of non-stop festivities. On arriving at the port, the revellers embarked on the ferryboat *Maid of Orleans*, to arrive on English soil later that evening, their spirits only slightly dampened by the rough crossing. At Folkestone, another special train awaited them, made up of several Pullman coaches hauled by a locomotive decorated with an immense double chevron emblem. Arriving at Victoria station, where accommodation had been reserved at the Victoria Hotel, the members of 'Monsieur Citroën's Party' (as the gathering was politely described in the British press) were greeted by André Citroën in person, accompanied by Daniel Metz and Felix Schwab, the co-directors of Citroën Cars Ltd.

The following day, the ceremonies began in earnest with a magnificent luncheon for seven hundred French and British guests, served in the ballroom of the Victoria Hotel, on tables adorned by decorations featuring the Double Chevron trademark intertwined with the *Tricolore* and the Union Flag. At the table of honour, surrounded by a throng of distinguished guests and celebrities, sat André Citroën himself, with Ettore Bugatti at his right hand. Later that afternoon, the party spilled out onto the streets of London, to witness the official opening of the grandiose new showrooms in Piccadilly, and then on to visit the London Motor Show, then running at Olympia, where, needless to say, the Citroën stand was among the most impressive on view.

The celebrations came to a climax on the third day of the trip, Thursday 28 October, when the entire party was conveyed to Slough in a procession of Citroën limousines, to enjoy a guided tour of the new British factory. Here, the operation of the production line and workings of the machinery and equipment were explained by André Citroën personally. That evening, the party returned to France. But before departing, the agents and pressmen sent André Citroën a congratulatory telegram, thanking the '*Grand Animateur*' of their three-day tour for his generous hospitality and praising him for his work in establishing Automobiles Citroën's pre-eminent position in Great Britain.

Twelve months later, the celebrations of Citroën's party were repeated when the journey was staged again – in the opposite direction. On 6 October 1927, a party of seventy British Citroën agents left Victoria station bound for Paris, where, on arrival at the Gare du Nord, they were met by André Citroën and his wife. After a sightseeing trip round the capital, M. Citroën led his party on a guided tour of the Quai de Javel factory and, later, joined them for a convivial evening at the *Folies Bergère*. The next day, host and guests met again on the Citroën stand at the Paris Salon motor show before making an excursion to Versailles. Naturally, the trip concluded with the traditional lavish banquet.

Citroën's new London premises at Devonshire House, Piccadilly (a huge office block constructed on the site of the former London mansion of the Dukes of Devonshire, almost opposite the Ritz Hotel), were surely the most elaborate and extravagant motor car showrooms ever created anywhere in the world. Opened in 1926, they were certainly far more magnificent even than the splendid showrooms which André Citroën was later to create on the Champs-Elysées and at the Place de l'Opéra in Paris. A monument to *le patron*'s characteristic largesse, the place was indeed *une folie de grandeur*. Although when the lease was signed the framework for the ten-storey building had already been erected, the entire centre section was promptly dismantled and replaced by a cage of massive steel girders to create a huge, open, three-storey vault, eight bays wide and clad entirely with marble. Unashamedly lavish and luxurious, the decor was modelled on Napoleon's tomb at les Invalides in Paris. Entering the 12,000 square foot showroom through one of the three central doorways on its 100 foot-long Piccadilly frontage, prospective customers found themselves on a balustraded balcony from which they could view as many as forty cars displayed on the marble-floored rotunda below, reached by a curving flight of carved marble stairs and illuminated by enormous, glittering chandeliers. The impression was that of a temple, dedicated to the worship of the automobile; hundreds of devotees came every day to pay their homage before the sign of the double chevron. But by no means everyone was impressed with the brave new motorised world being introduced onto the streets of London by Citroën and his rivals. Bemoaning the passing of the horse-drawn carriage and the hansom cab, Sir Max Beerbohm complained bitterly at the way that the capital was being

The exterior of Citroën's London showrooms at Devonshire House, Piccadilly, opened in 1927 and closed in 1935. Note that Green Park underground station had not then been built. Now somewhat less magnificent than in André Citroën's time, these premises are still used as motorcar showrooms today, but not by the Citroën company.

'vulgarised, democratised, commercialised, standardised and ruined beyond redemption' by the arrival of the car. What were Piccadilly and Park Lane without their private palaces such as Devonshire House and Grosvenor House? What real contribution to civilisation was being made by the hideous, high blocks of hotels, flats, offices and car showrooms that were springing up to take their place, Beerbohm plaintively enquired.

In Paris during the mid-twenties, however, it was hardly necessary to visit a car showroom to see signs of André Citroën; the unmistakable traces of his activities abounded everywhere. With typical Jewish chutzpah, he never missed an opportunity to display his name before the public to draw attention to his products, employing a blatant showmanship that was often mistaken by his critics as an exhibitionist craving for personal publicity. By day, a huge fleet of over five thousand taxi cabs run by Citroën's own taxi company (founded in 1924) circulated about the capital, painted black and lemon-yellow and bearing his double chevron badge on their doors. Passing pedestrians hummed or whistled a catchy song extolling the virtues of his cars, with the words '*Citron, citron, Citroën, Double Chevron, voitures champion*'. This tune, the winner of a song contest that he had recently organised, had been recorded by the Citroën Orchestra and was issued on discs bearing the Citroën label. By night, between

The B14G of 1927 was the first car in the world to be equipped with servo-operated brakes. Output was at the rate of 400 units a day. By now Citroën's Paris factories employed over 35,000 workers, while his French commercial network totalled over 5,000 agents.

1925 and 1934, his name was flashed in letters of light 100 feet high, by 250,000 electric lightbulbs wired to the Eiffel Tower by 600 kilometres of cable and visible for sixty miles in all directions.

This *coup de publicité* – which surely ranks as the ultimate bright advertising idea – was actually the inspiration of an Italian, Fernand Jacopozzi, who specialised in organising fairground lightshows and illuminations. On hearing Jacopozzi's proposals, at first Citroën modestly demurred at the idea, perhaps abashed at the thought of the huge electricity bills that he would face. But when he learned that Henry Ford had also been approached, he changed his mind. Apparently, the American had not only indicated that he was willing to sign a contract for exclusive rights to the illuminations, but that he was also prepared to buy the entire Eiffel Tower outright and to ship it back to the USA! Thus, at a gala ceremony held on 4 July 1925, accompanied by his wife and three of his four children (his fourth child, a daughter, Solange, had been born the year before but did not survive infancy: she died of pneumonia in November 1924, aged twenty-two months), André Citroën – now aged forty-seven and at the height of his fame – switched on this amazing signal of his achievements. As he did so, he would surely have remembered his first visit to the tower, as a schoolboy, thirty-eight years earlier.

The ceremony coincided with the opening of the highly influential international Exposition des Arts Decoratifs et Industriels, which occupied a site

First seen at the Paris Salon motor show in October 1927, the B14G was an improved version of the 1,539cc B14 model, which had been introduced in 1925 to replace the 1,453cc B12. The Citroën tradition of annual improvements, year by year, was by now firmly established and expected.

At the Paris Exposition des Arts Decoratifs in 1925, the fashionable painter Sonia Delaunay
exhibited this Citroën B12 cabriolet. Decorated with a multi-coloured chequerboard motif, the car was
accompanied by models wearing clothes made from a fabric bearing an identical art-deco design.

on the Esplanade des Invalides beneath the shadow of the Eiffel Tower and also
at the Grand Palais across the Pont Alexandre III on the right bank of the Seine.
A sensational *tour de force* of organisation on the part of the French government,
the huge exhibition gave its name to, and provided the motive force for, the Art
Deco movement which swept Europe and America during the following decade.
Although it was intended to promote traditional craftsmanship in the decorative
arts, it was largely from the symbols of the new Machine Age that the majority of
exhibitors drew their inspiration: the wings of aircraft, the bows of liners and the
gears and steering wheels of motor cars were universal motifs. In fact, the theme
of the exhibits on view in the Pavillon de l'Esprit Nouveau, organised by the
revolutionary architect and intellectual le Corbusier, argued against the use of
decoration, embellishment or beautification of any kind. Another exhibitor was
the Simultanist painter, decorator and designer Sonia Delaunay, who showed an
'Orphist' car, boldly painted in a chequerboard pattern of bright colours, in
which there rode models wearing matching garments, similarly checked.
Needless to say, the car that she chose to decorate was a Citroën B12 Cabriolet.

Citroën's gigantic advertising sign on the Eiffel Tower provided a beacon to
guide the American airman Charles Lindbergh when, on the evening of 20 May
1927, piloting the *Spirit of St Louis*, he made his approach to le Bourget airport
after completing the world's first solo, non-stop, 5,809 kilometre-long transatlantic
flight. This widely-reported event gave Citroën the opportunity to demonstrate his

In May 1927, a huge party took place at the Quai de Javel to welcome the American aviator Charles Lindberg, who had just made the first solo air crossing of the the Atlantic, in his plane The Spirit of St Louis. *In this photograph, Lindberg is the tall man on Citroën's left, with M.T. Herrick, the American Ambassador, on his right.*

enterprise and flair for publicity once again, by inviting the American aviator to attend a grand reception and buffet at the Quai de Javel the following Saturday, 27 May, accompanied by the highly popular US Ambassador to France, Myron T. Herrick, with whom Citroën had been on friendly terms since the war. Addressing a crowd of 10,000 employees from a hastily-erected platform, Citroën welcomed Lindberg in the name of the mechanical engineers and automobile workers of France, who saluted their colleagues across the Atlantic for constructing 'the marvellous engine that made this epic flight possible'. Lindberg's plane should rightly be called the *Spirit of Detroit*, Citroën suggested, adding that it was through the efforts and achievements of the citizens of this town that almost every American worker now possessed a car. The global impact of this masterstroke of public relations was enormous. Newspaper readers around the world were given the impression that Lindberg had endured the dangers and discomforts of his 32 hour 33 minute flight merely to enjoy the privilege of meeting André Citroën and of making a sightseeing tour of his factory.

Earlier that month (May 1927) André Citroën had entertained another very important person at the Quai de Javel – the Prince of Wales, who, following in his uncle's footsteps, had become a fervent francophile and a frequent visitor to Paris. A leader of fashion, particularly in matters of dress, the Prince was wearing the baggy, checked tweed plus-fours and double-knotted tie that became his trademark. It is recorded in the legends of the Citroën company that, as *le patron* guided the natty young Prince through the assembly shop, pointing out this or that feature of technical interest, a loud, irreverent voice rang out with the remark, '*Dis donc! Si son phalzar fait des petits, j'en retiens un!*' ('Gor blimey! If his trousers ever have kids, I'll have a pair!')

The year of the great Art Deco exhibition – 1925 – had seen the arrival in Paris of another celebrity who played a key role in the André Citroën story; the dusky American dancer and singer Josephine Baker, the star of the sensational *Revue Nègre* which had opened to wild applause at the Théâtre des Champs-Elysées, marking the coming of the Jazz Age to France. For years to come, she was the most talked-about woman in Paris – an Ebony Venus whose erotic dancing and sinuous, naked beauty gave jaded *demi-mondaines* a fresh interpretation of sexuality. Actually half-Spanish-Jewish by birth and a mulatto rather than a Negress, Josephine Baker's act was, by all accounts, amazing to behold. Described by one reviewer as 'a barbaric dance . . . a triumph of lewdness and a return to prehistoric morality', and by another as 'a powerful challenge to civilisation in the name of primitive instinct', it consisted mainly of a series of frenetic gyrations and contortions through which she cavorted with total abandonment, dressed only in a belt of bananas, and with 'her gilded body with breasts thrust forward like a figure head, moving in spasms of desire', to the rhythms of Ragtime and the Charleston. The famous New Orleans clarinettist Sidney Bechet played in her band, and became the first of many famous American Negro jazz musicians to make his home in Paris.

In common with most of the audience of sophisticates who flocked to see her performance (Georges Simenon was another fan), André Citroën was captivated

Between 1924 and 1934, the Eiffel Tower was illuminated with the word Citroen, spelled out in giant, radiant letters by 250,000 electric lightbulbs visible for sixty miles in all directions.

and returned again and again. Before long, the Black Pearl was to be seen driving about Paris in a boat-tailed B14 Sport cabriolet which he had presented to her. She returned the compliment by singing that she had only two loves in her life, her country and Citroën. Whether she was referring to the man or simply to the motor car is an interesting ambiguity that has never been resolved.

In truth, it is unlikely that the relationship was anything other than platonic. Like many young men brought up in the absence of their fathers by their mothers, Citroën's great love of women was not that of the compulsive womaniser but of a genuine worshipper of femininity. Whereas Gabriel Voisin spent his money on beautiful females, preferring the pleasures of the private dining room to those of the casino, Citroën found his excitement at the green baize table rather than on the *chaise-longue*, bestowing his emotions on his family and his factory rather than on a string of actresses. He was particularly affectionate towards his children, and enjoyed nothing more than the regular family holidays taken in the mountains or by the seaside. For their visits to Deauville, Citroën presented them with a half-size replica car, complete in every

By now, Citroën's reputation as a bon vivant and gambler had spread far beyond his native land and was attracting press comment around the world, as headlined in this report published in the gossip columns of the British newspaper, the Sketch, *published in September 1924.*

THE FRENCH MOTOR-CAR MANUFACTURER WHOSE PLAY HAS BEEN THE SENSATION OF DEAUVILLE THIS YEAR : M. ANDRÉ CITROËN.

M. André Citroën, the French motor-car manufacturer, has been gambling in an imperial style at Deauville this year, and is said to have broken all records for the Casino by winning £50,000 in six hours, and playing up his amazing luck till he had made £162,000. He then, however, dropped some of this big "pile"; but he left Deauville with £112,500—quite a comfortable little profit, even for a millionaire.—[*Photograph by Keystone View Co.*]

respect and fitted with a proper engine, modified so as not to exceed a top speed of 20 mph By special permission of the Deauville police, the three Citroën children were allowed to drive this car about the town themselves, unaccompanied by an adult, as well as to enter the many Concours d'Elégance held in this centre of fashion. One year, they did so with Maurice Chevalier riding as their passenger.

Like Josephine Baker, André Citroën was never out of the news throughout the twenties. It was almost as if he was an entertainer rather than an industrialist. But even if he had been the manufacturer of some obscure device which sold well without the need for advertising, it would have been impossible for him to achieve complete secrecy and anonymity in his personal life, such was the worldwide interest in his gambling exploits. For example, on 3 September 1924 the popular London scandal-sheet the *Daily Sketch* carried a lurid gossip-column report under the headline 'French car maker strikes lucky at Deauville', which described how Monsieur André Citroën had been seen gambling at the seaside resort again that year, in the style of an emperor. According to the *Sketch*, Citroën had beaten all previous records at the casino by winning £50,000 in six hours at the tables, only to gamble all his chips on one final spin of the roulette wheel, which brought him the astounding windfall of £162,000. In today's money, that win would be worth around £3 million. He was not always so lucky, however. On another notable occasion, he was reported to have dropped no less than $500,000 in a ten-hour sitting at Deauville Casino.

Win or lose, Citroën was renowned for his largesse, more than once presenting a car to the croupier concerned as a token of his appreciation! Often, he gave cars away as tips to hotel servants. Indeed, his impulsive generosity was legendary and not confined to his servants or employees. Once, when eating incognito at a bistro, he heard a diner at an adjacent table defending the merits of his cars. Without saying anything, he got up and pressed into the amateur salesman's hand a signed note, or *bon de commande*, entitling the lucky fellow to call at the factory and collect a brand new car. Another time, when playing baccarat at Deauville, he grew impatient with the large crowd of spectators which, as usual, had gathered around the tables to watch him play. Pausing for a moment, he handed a 10,000 franc chip over his shoulder to the woman behind him with the remark: 'Be so kind as to take this and stop breathing down the back of my neck.' And as a gift to the people of Paris, made entirely without strings attached, he arranged for the Place de la Concorde and the Arc de Triomphe to be permanently illuminated, paying the resulting electricity bill for many years although no advertising sign or sales message was involved in the display.

Without the evidence of a profit and loss account, it is impossible to say to what extent André Citroën's gambling habits affected the financial health of his firm and contributed to its eventual bankruptcy. Citroën believed that the publicity his exploits brought him came cheap at the price, and when tackled on the subject by Haardt, he is said to have remarked: 'Believe me, Georges, I do not mix business with pleasure. Although, for me, gaming is one of the best things in life, life itself is not a game.' Certainly, huge though they may seem today, the sums spent on gambling would have been petty cash compared to the fortune staked on the company itself. The profits retained in the business were substantial, and there can be no suggestion that his firm was bled white through under-investment due to his gambling losses. Clearly, Citroën was far less irresponsible and feckless than many other wealthy Parisian employers in those madcap times, '*les Années Folles*'. At the height of its success, Automobiles Citroën had annual revenues of over a billion francs, making its founder one of the richest men in the world. But unlike Henry Ford, who paid himself $30 million a year while his workers earned only $5 a day, Citroën lived on a modest scale, at least for a motor magnate. There was no château in the Loire, no yacht or villa on the Côte d'Azur, no string of racehorses at Chantilly and no collection of priceless paintings or *objets d'art* at his holiday villa at Deauville or his home in Paris. This was still no more than a rented apartment, occupying two floors at 31 rue Octave-Feuillet in Passy and furnished with reproduction furniture in the elaborate eighteenth-century '*Style Rothschild*' manner admired by many other *haut-bourgeois* Jewish businessmen. Apart from his factories, Citroën never owned any property or real estate. Such material encumbrances did not interest him. Nor, for that matter, did expensive luxury cars; his chauffeur-driven Hispano-Suiza was kept largely for ceremonial duties, or for the use of his wife. Indeed, it seems that Madame Citroën (1892–1955) was far more interested in motor cars than he was, or at least in driving them. As a leading member of the Automobile Club Féminin de Paris, she had been one of the first women to gain a driving permit in France.

Undoubtedly, it was thanks to her influence that Automobiles Citroën made a point of introducing products designed for, and marketed directly at, the newly-emancipated female market, such as the 5CV. Apparently, Madame Citroën was also the driving force in André Citroën's social life; as an elegant, fashionable woman (invariably dressed in outfits designed by her friend Coco Chanel), she delighted in the role of society hostess, especially when entertaining the very many important persons, including royalty, that her husband was required to amuse in the course of his business life.

But apart from gambling, the relaxation that pleased André Citroën most was music. Nothing affected him more than to hear a good tune well played, be it an operatic aria, a popular chanson, a Negro jazz blues or a military march played by the brass band that he had founded at the Quai de Javel, the Fanfare Citroën. As a surprise entertainment for his family, one evening early in February 1927, he arranged an impromptu private concert at their Passy apartment. At this soirée, the highlight was a guest appearance by an infant prodigy currently visiting Paris, whose virtuoso performance of Lalo's *Symphonie Espagnole* with the Orchestre Lamoureux conducted by the famous maestro Paul Paray was the talk of the town. The young violinist who delighted the Citroën children on that memorable occasion was none other than Yehudi Menuhin, then making his debut in the French capital at the outset of his professional career, aged only ten.

One year later, on New Year's Eve 1928, Citroën arranged another musical soirée at his home for the amusement of his family and friends. But this time he invited a rather different (but no less famous) musician to perform – Jack Hylton, the celebrated English dance band leader, who had just arrived in Paris from London at the beginning of a European tour. Such was the international prestige of the French motor magnate that Jack Hylton and his musicians had agreed to play without a fee, merely for the privilege of entertaining Citroën and his guests. The only stipulation was that Citroën should be responsible for conveying the band to an engagement in Hamburg the following day. Thus it had been arranged with a Dutch airline for them all to be flown to Germany immediately after the party, at his expense. But on the morning of 31 December, the weather turned against Citroën's plans, and all flights from le Bourget airport were cancelled indefinitely, due to poor visibility. It looked as if it would now be impossible for the band to play for Citroën that night and still have time to arrive in Germany by the scheduled Paris–Hamburg train service, in order to honour their contracted appearance there the following night. But Citroën did not intend to be beaten by the fog – if there was no time for the band to make the journey by the normal express, then a special train would have to be laid on, regardless of expense. Problem-solving was Citroën's speciality, and this little difficulty presented a particular challenge. Fortunately, an old friend from his days at the Ecole Polytechnique had since become a Director of the French Northern Railway Company, and thus, with one simple phone call, the *petit contretemps* was soon overcome. That night, Citroën danced the Charleston to the sounds of the great Jack Hylton and his Orchestra, surrounded as usual by *tout le beau-monde*, including such notables as Hugh 'Bendor' Grosvenor, the expatriate 2nd Duke of Westminster (reputedly England's wealthiest man), who was accompanied by his current paramour, Coco Chanel. And by way of compensation for his lack of sleep, Hylton was rewarded by the gift of a splendid Citroën six-cylinder sports saloon.

In short, whereas the strait-laced Henry Ford disapproved of the popularist consumer culture that he himself had helped to create, urging his workers to amuse themselves innocently by singing folk songs and holding square-dances, André Citroën embraced the spirit of the Jazz Age with enthusiasm. While certain Jewish antique and art dealers were busily engaged in exporting the rarefied treasures of European high culture to the USA for the gratification of American millionaires, Citroën led in importing the raw, unrefined vitality of American popular culture into Europe, for the pleasure of the common man, so much so that he actually symbolised the ethos of that era. By being simultaneously both a progressive, innovative industrialist and social reformer and a capricious, spendthrift socialite, he personified the stark contrast between gravity and frivolity that was so typical of the 'Roaring Twenties'.

PART 2: THE EXPLORER

CHAPTER FIVE

Caterpillars that Crossed the Sahara

In contrast to his cousins in the British royal family, the ill-fated Nicholas II, Tsar of all the Russias, was an early motoring enthusiast who welcomed the arrival of the horseless carriage without reservation. His grandfather, Tsar Alexander II, was probably the first man ever to buy a motor car; in 1864 or thereabouts, he purchased Jean-Joseph Etienne Lenoir's three-wheeled carriage which the previous year had become the first internal combustion-engined vehicle to run on the streets of Paris, powered by an engine which ran on coal-gas.

By the turn of the century, Tsar Nicholas II had begun to amass a large and impressive motor transport fleet, which eventually included a Rolls-Royce Silver Ghost, several Delaunay-Bellevilles and a Packard powered by an enormous 6.9 litre V12 engine, the first of its kind. To manage this collection, in 1905 he appointed as his personal *garagiste* a certain Adolphe Kegresse, a Frenchman of Central European extraction, born in 1879 at Héricault in the Haute-Saône district of eastern France.

Unfortunately, due to the harsh winter climate and the lack of good roads in Russia, the Tsar's vehicles could only be used for half the year at best. Accordingly, he instructed Monsieur Kegresse (whose official title was Technical Director of the Imperial Motor Transport Corps) to devise a method of propulsion that would allow him to drive his cars between St Petersburg and Moscow, across the snow. The resulting invention was eventually to prove as useful an asset to André Citroën's fast-growing empire as it would have been to the Tsar's, had the Revolution not intervened to spoil His Imperial Highness's plans.

Adolphe Kegresse was an intelligent, resourceful and inventive engineer. Instead of attempting to employ the heavy, hinged metal plates used in the tracks of a tank or crawler tractor, he developed an ingenious, detachable, lightweight caterpillar-track device to replace the rear wheels of a car. This functioned like a moving railway track, constantly unrolling under the vehicle. Consisting of flexible, endless rubber bands running on sprung bogies pivoting from the rear axle, these caterpillar tracks provided the necessary grip and support to carry a loaded vehicle across soft snow or sand as well as rocky, cratered surfaces, so that Kegresse's caterpillar cars were equally at home in

boggy moorland country as on desert or mountainous terrain. In his own words,
they could 'travel at all speeds either over deep snow and ice or roads covered
with lightly packed snow, or on dry and stony roads – and then leave the road
and proceed to travel across country without stopping or slowing down'. In
short, he had made the vehicle suit the ground, instead of attempting to make
the ground suit the vehicle as had so far always been the case in both road and
railway transportation. By 1913, the Système Kegresse had been perfected,
patents had been filed in France as well as in Russia, and the concept of the half-
track motor vehicle was a working reality.

Four years later, at the outbreak of the Russian Revolution, M. Kegresse found
himself without a job and eventually returned to France via Finland. Arriving in
Paris in 1920, he soon made contact with André Citroën through the help of M.
Jacques Schwob de Héricault, a partner in the Société des Engrenages Citroën,
whose family owned a large textile manufacturing business in Kegresse's home
town. Quite possibly, the two had known each other since their school-days.

With the agricultural tractor still in its infancy and the modern four-wheel-drive
utility vehicle not yet invented, André Citroën was quick to realise the potential of
this ingenious system and immediately acquired sole rights to Kegresse's
invention, forming a special company – the Société Citroën-Kegresse-Hinstin – to
provide the inventor with the necessary funds and facilities to manufacture and
exploit the concept of autochenilles, or self-propelled caterpillar-tracked vehicles,
on a large scale, using the chassis and four-cylinder engine of his standard-
production 1,452 cc 10 hp B2 touring car as a basis for the venture.

Ultimately, a wide range of these Citroën-Kegresse half-track vehicles was
produced, initially with the original friction-drive system, although later, larger,
more powerful types were equipped with a positive sprocket-drive arrangement
in which the forward of the two pulleys was driven and the sprung bogies of the
track unit were attached to the chassis frame from a central pivot-point.

Classed as light tractors and marketed as a replacement for the carthorse, these
autochenilles – assembled at a special factory at Courbevoie, and then later at
Levallois, both on the outskirts of Paris – proved to be an immediate commercial
success. Capable of climbing a 1 in 3 gradient and of travelling at 30 mph on the
flat, they soon found employment in a wide variety of civilian and military roles,
and throughout the twenties and thirties they were used extensively throughout
Europe in farming and forestry work, pulling ploughs and hauling wagons and
barges, as well as towing field guns in service with the armies of France, Belgium,
Poland and Great Britain. In fact, surviving examples were prized by the Germans
in the Second World War, who repaired and reconditioned all that they could
find, before pressing them into service on the Russian Front.

Undoubtedly, this rapid acceptance of Kegresse's revolutionary idea was due
in no small measure to the famous series of demonstrations and endurance
expeditions, or 'raids', which the master publicist André Citroën staged to show
off the caterpillar car's remarkable cross-country abilities. The first of these took
place in February 1921, at a snow trial held at Mont Revard in the Alps; but
then, in September that year, under the supervision of the French military

The cross-country abilities of the first production examples of the Citroën-Kegresse caterpillar car, based on the B2 chassis, were convincingly demonstrated at snow trials held on Mont Revard near Chambery in the French Alps, in February 1921.

As another typical Citroën publicity stunt, in September 1924 three caterpillar cars travelled from Paris to Arcachon via Bordeaux, one of them towing a massive 'Maison Roulante'. Weighing three and a half tons, this caravan was probably the world's first Portakabin!

authorities, three autochenilles travelled from Paris to Arcachon on the Atlantic coast of France, one of them towing a large caravan, or *maison roulante*, the size of a small two-storey house and weighing 3½ tons. Here, at the huge Pilat sand dune, the highest in Europe, various tests and experiments were carried out, culminating in an assault on the summit, 344 feet above sea level. This the caterpillar cars ascended without problems, despite the 1 in 6 gradient, proving that for moving over sand and snow alike, the Système Citroën-Kegresse had an almost unlimited scope.

During the first week of July 1922, a further important demonstration was held in England for the benefit of influential British journalists and important potential military and civilian customers. This was staged at a vast former military transport depot located at Slough, 20 miles west of London, known locally as 'The Dump', where scrapped army lorries had once been collected for reconditioning, after the First World War. The open land of this disused salvage yard provided a suitably difficult obstacle course over which the Kegresse could show its paces. Watched by a large gathering of spectators, including André Citroën himself, in heavy rain, two vehicles climbed up and down the slippery banks of a gravel pit where, in places, the gradient exceeded 45°. Next, one of the vehicles was attached by a tow rope to a pair of railway wagons filled with

The Citroën-Kegresse half-track system as fitted to a Model T Ford. This vehicle accompanied André Citroën on his visit to America in March 1924, where it was shown to Henry Ford. Alas, the American motor-magnate was unimpressed.

people, a load which it started from rest and towed with ease, running alongside the railway line over a ploughed field. Later, both Kegresses set off on a journey by road from London to Cambridge and back, a 108 mile round trip which was covered at an average speed of 21 m.p.h., with no difficulties whatsoever being experienced en route. In its report dated 15 July 1922, *Light Car and Cyclecar* magazine published pictures of the Kegresse ascending a 1 in 12 slope at Slough and commented that this demonstration had provided a convincing evidence of the Kegresse's extraordinary hill-climbing abilities and its unique dual road and cross-country powers.

To capitalise on this acclaim, a British subsidiary, Citroën-Kegresse Ltd, was quickly established in London. Registered on 21 August 1922, this company numbered André Citroën, Daniel Metz, Marcel Lourde and the British military vehicle expert Major-General Sir Ernest Swinton as its founding directors. Over the following ten years, around 200 Citroën-Kegresse vehicles were sold on the British civilian market, plus eight examples delivered to the British Army in 1924–6 for use as battery staff cars by the Royal Artillery. All of them were supplied from Paris, the great majority in left-hand-drive form, crated up in knock-down kits to be assembled at the Citroën depot at Hammersmith or, later, at the Citroën Cars Ltd factory at Slough, which opened in 1926, built on the very site where the Kegresse demonstration had taken place four years earlier.

In recruiting General Swinton to his colours, André Citroën had enlisted a loyal and stalwart ally. Over the next thirty years, the General – known to military

Adolphe Kegresse driving the only known example of a right-hand-drive Citroën-Kegresse Type B2 caterpillar car, at the Talbot proving ground near Acton, West London, in April 1924.

historians as the father of the tank and the first commander of the Tank Corps – was to prove invaluable as an *éminence grise* behind the scenes in the Anglo-Saxon world, liaising with the British and Commonwealth military and civil authorities from his quarters at All Souls College, Oxford, where he later held the position of Chichele Professor of Military History. Thanks to his time in the army, his service in the War Cabinet Secretariat and his association with Prime Minister Lloyd George, Swinton had high-level connections throughout Whitehall and Westminster, and his work behind the scenes was to prove indispensable in paving the way for the coming Citroën-Kegresse expeditions in Africa and India, by securing permission for their routes to cross British territory.

From his experiences as a transport and logistics specialist in the First World War, André Citroën understood the cross-country limitations of conventional-wheeled motor vehicles. So when Adolphe Kegresse first demonstrated the caterpillar-track principle before him over a pile of builder's sand at Saint-Denis one Sunday morning in October 1920, he grasped the implications of this development immediately. Firstly, the fact that the problem of locomotion over sand, snow and mud had been solved appealed to him as an engineer, industrialist and motor manufacturer, and he was keen to exploit the technique to his own commercial advantage without delay. But secondly, he also welcomed the invention from a more dispassionate point of view, aware of its wider long-term strategic significance to the French economy as a whole. Now, with a vehicle that needed no roads, it would be possible to open up new military and trading routes in the colonial territories of Africa and the Orient, where paved

André Citroën scored a huge publicity coup in England when he contrived to have Queen Mary and the Princess Mary photographed riding in a 'caterpillar car' during military manoeuvres at Aldershot in May 1923. The resulting reports and pictures filled the British newspapers the following day, but the Citroën-Kegresse vehicle was never purchased in large numbers by the British Army.

roads and railways were still lacking. It only remained to prove that fact before the eyes of the world at large – by staging the first ever crossing of the Sahara desert by motor vehicle.

As an engineer, Citroën realised that the effect of the Kegresse system was to reduce the amount of horsepower needed to overcome the obstacles of off-road motoring, so that, fitted with caterpillar tracks, smaller, lighter cars with less thirsty engines could accomplish what heavier, more powerful, conventional-wheeled vehicles had so far been unable to achieve in trackless terrain. Thus equipped, even his little 10 hp B2 town car had the power, stamina and range to cross the desert, and for the moment at least, could be regarded as the only practical, economical and reliable means of motorised transport in the wilderness of the Sahara.

Ever since the French had begun their colonisation of North Africa in the 1880s (actually incorporating Algeria into metropolitan France in 1881), the problem of establishing communications and maintaining military and political control over the vast trackless territory of the Sahara region had greatly concerned the government in Paris. But when in 1912 the territory of Niger was also annexed, the establishment of a land route from the Mediterranean down through the desert to French Equatorial Africa and then onwards across the interior to the east coast and Madagascar became a strategic priority rather than merely the pipedream of would-be adventurers, keen to rival the achievements of Livingstone and Stanley in exploring the uncharted regions of the Dark Continent. The arrival of transport aircraft promised an answer by ending the age-old reliance on the camel train; but even so, the problem of logistics had still to be solved. Staging posts with landing strips, repair facilities, fuel and water dumps and radio stations had still to be constructed and supplied, and thus opening up a route traversable by motor vehicles was seen to be an essential and unavoidable step forward in the civilisation of French Africa. This fact was amply underscored when, in February 1920, attempting to fly between Algiers and Timbuktu, an aircraft carrying the regional military commander, General Lapperine, was blown off course by a sandstorm and crash-landed in the desert. A column of conventional-wheeled motor vehicles immediately set out on a rescue attempt, but due to the appalling difficulties of the terrain, all met with accident or breakdown, and sadly, the General, wounded in the crash, perished of thirst before help could arrive. His terrible ordeal lasted for fifteen days, in temperatures of 123°F.

Indeed, General Lapperine had been the first man to attempt to organise a crossing of the Sahara by motor vehicle. As early as 1916, an expedition led by a certain Commandant Bettembourg had attempted to make an exploratory journey along the old camel route between the oases of Wargla and In Salah. This mission covered a mere tenth of the total 2,000 mile distance between, to the north, the railhead at Touggourt in Algeria and, to the south, the ultimate objective of Timbuktu, the mysterious City of Salt that lies on the River Niger in French Sudan, now known as Mali. Only one vehicle got through undamaged, taking twenty days to cover 470 miles, most of that time being spent digging it out of the sand. Consequently, the rate of progress made by Bettembourg's convoy of conventional, four-wheeled vehicles was no faster than that of the camels they were intended to replace. By 1920, three successive expeditions under Lapperine's direction had still proved incapable of conquering the obstacles and challenges put in the way of motorised transport by the world's greatest desert. Covering 3½ million square miles (sixteen times the area of France), the Sahara is not just an endless sea of shifting sand entirely devoid of flora and fauna; it also contains several mountain ranges with peaks as high and as extensive as those of the Alps. And although the mean temperature of the Sahara is not actually as high as its reputation suggests, it exhibits daily a punishingly wide extreme of heat and cold which puts excessive stress on man and machine alike, alternately boiling a car's radiator dry by day and freezing it solid by night.

Not surprisingly, these events and their implications created much public interest in France, and not least among the men who were about to form the Société Citroën-Kegresse-Hinstin. According to André Citroën himself:

the first idea of a trans-Saharan raid was born during the war, which proved how necessary were the resources of our Equatorial African territories to the metropolis, not only in men but in supplies of all sorts, from the oil-products of Senegal to the rubber of Guinea and the Congo. It showed that this wealth could not achieve its real value until the *bloc africain* was realised by the establishment of rapid, safe and permanent communications between our various possessions in the Black Continent.

Announced by André Citroën in the autumn of 1922, the Raid Sahara was the first crossing of the desert by motor vehicle. The 4,000 mile expedition from Algiers to Timbuktu and back was reported throughout the world.

Despite his penchant for gambling, Citroën believed that, in all industrial enterprises, success was a question of applying scientific analysis to every problem and of adopting a vigorous organisational logic which anticipated every tiny detail, leaving nothing to chance. And despite the aura of romance and adventure surrounding the mission, the proposed crossing of the Sahara by his Citroën autochenilles was exactly that – an industrial venture to be carried out using the very same carefully calculated industrial and logistical techniques which had served him so well in his previous endeavours. Before the expedition could begin, three tasks had first to be accomplished – to prepare and test the machines, to trace out and organise the itinerary and to recruit and train the personnel. Thus, in the winter of 1921/2, several caterpillar cars were despatched to the Touggourt region of southern Algeria to begin reconnoitring a route for the expedition.

In charge of this trial run was Louis Audouin-Dubreuil, a former cavalry officer-turned-airman and explorer, who was already regarded as an expert on desert operations. Aged thirty-five, he was a veteran of General Lappérine's various exploits, and had since built up an extensive knowledge of the area. In fact, he had become infatuated with the Sahara, forming an unrequited love affair with the wilderness that was to continue unabated throughout his life. Thirty years on, when in his late sixties, Audouin-Dubreuil was still to be found risking his life to explore its barren charms, this time making solo journeys in a

2CV. Short, rotund and robust, his jovial personality made an amusing foil to the lanky and somewhat sang-froid character who was to lead the trans-Sahara expedition itself – Georges-Marie Haardt.

As has often been observed, few French industrialists have ever deserved the soubriquet '*patron*' more than André Citroën. A paternalist in the best sense of the word, he was regarded as a father-figure by his associates and employees, who gathered round him to form a veritable family of disciples. Throughout his career, Citroën never lost the uncanny ability always to find the right men for the job, and then, having enlisted their skills and talents, to fire their enthusiasm and foster their long-term loyalty. None of his activities show this gift more clearly than the case of the Croisière expeditions, which although carried out in his name, to the enhancement of his personal reputation, for obvious reasons, were never under his direct day-to-day control.

In choosing Haardt as leader, Citroën picked a man with the very highest qualifications, from the senior echelons of his firm. Now the Director-General of Citroën's gear-making and car-building factories, Haardt had already been among Citroën's closest, most trusted colleagues for over fifteen years, their association having begun while working together at the Mors company. According to General Swinton, who knew him well, Haardt was 'physically a fine specimen, of unusual height, with great personal charm. He had a passion for all things English, spoke the language extremely well and was always dressed immaculately, by a London tailor.' As a founding director of Citroën Cars Ltd, Haardt made many visits to the United Kingdom, and not just on business. According to a persistent rumour then circulating in France, for many years he had conducted a secret romantic liaison with a lady belonging to the highest rank of British Society.

If ever such proof were needed, Haardt was a living contradiction of the dubious proposition that the man of action is inevitably a philistine. Fastidious in his manners and epicurean in his tastes, Haardt had an artistic side to his temperament which made him something of an aesthete and a dandy. His apartment in the rue de Rivoli in Paris, overlooking the Tuileries gardens, contained an extraordinary collection of paintings, bronzes, antiques and Art Nouveau glassware, of which he was undoubtedly a genuine connoisseur. In one corner was a display of rare African butterflies, in another several priceless Ming dynasty Chinese vases, while the walls were entirely covered by scores of valuable prints and pictures produced by celebrated contemporary artists – many of them Haardt's personal friends – and also by several no less impressive canvases painted by Haardt himself. And by the time his travels in Africa were over, this collection of antiquities and *objets d'art* would be hugely enhanced.

Nothing if not a professional, André Citroën was aware that this first motorised trans-Saharan crossing could be no pleasure trip or charabanc outing, staged by reckless amateur adventurers. Failure was unthinkable, for the dangers of the desert were such that even a minor mishap or mistake would result in disastrous consequences. Much more than merely the lives of his friends and employees was at risk – the prestige of the double chevron marque would also be at stake. The 'raid' was to be the first journey of exploration ever to be conducted directly under the unforgiving eyes of the world's press, with regular news bulletins appearing in the newspapers as soon as radio and telegraph reports were received in Paris from the desert. Moreover, the entire journey was to be recorded on film for showing in cinema newsreels in Europe and America later on. Hence the meticulous preparations, tests and rehearsals carried out both in Africa and in France, which led to many important modifications being carried out to the design, construction and equipment of the vehicles, including the fitting of auxiliary radiators.

But by the autumn of 1922, just two years after his first meeting with Adolphe Kegresse, all was ready for the attempt, and a fleet of fifteen autochenilles had been assembled in Africa ready for the departure. Five were to carry the expedition all the way across the Sahara to Timbuktu and back, while the other ten were to act as supply vehicles, going only part of the way. One group of supply cars started out ahead from Touggourt to deliver supplies to In Salah, while the other drove straight to Timbuktu from the coast at Dakar to deposit a store of fuel and spares ready for the expedition's arrival at Timbuktu.

The plan was to make the 2,000 mile outward journey in eight stages, spread over a total of twenty-two days, covering an average of 100 miles during every day spent on the move. Thus, at daybreak on 17 December 1922, ten brave men in five little caterpillar cars rolled out of Touggourt, the railhead south-east of Algiers, at the start of a journey that was to mark a turning point in the history of Africa. Painted white to resist the heat of the sun, each bore a strange, brightly-coloured heraldic emblem taken from ancient Egyptian mythology. At the head of the convoy was the Golden Scarab, the command vehicle carrying Haardt and driven by the mechanic Maurice Billy. Next followed the Silver Crescent, bearing Audouin-Dubreuil, with Maurice Penaud at the wheel. Then came the Flying Tortoise, driven by Roger Prudhomme and carrying the expedition's filming equipment and its official geographer and cinematographer Paul Castelman. After that followed the Apis Bull, driven by René Raboud and carrying the expedition's guide and interpreter, Adjutant Chapuis, an officer in the French colonial forces. Bringing up the rear came the Crawling Caterpillar, driven by the driver-mechanic Fernand Billy, accompanied by Flight-Lieutenant Georges Estienne. Fittingly, Georges Estienne was the son of the French tank and armoured car pioneer General Estienne, a Gallic equivalent of General Swinton. Also included in the party was a mascot: Haardt's little white-coated Sealyham terrier, Flossie (who duly became the role model for the world's most famous fictional canine adventuress – Milou, in Hergé's celebrated *Tintin* strip cartoons). In her owner's own words: 'Before becoming a globe-trotter Flossie was well-known at the Citroën works at the Quai de Javel for her good manners and cheerful character.'

All five vehicles contained 2 tons of stores, a reservoir holding 8 gallons of drinking water and a fuel tank brimming with 50 gallons of petrol. Each was equipped with a collapsible tent attached to its bodywork, which could quickly be lowered for shelter at night. All carried rifles and a plentiful supply of

Although travelling at a mere 20 mph, the little 10 hp B2 Citroën caterpillar cars could cover three thousand miles of desert in the time (one week) that it took a camel train to cross a mere one hundred miles of sand. Acknowledging the dangers of their mission, the vehicles carried rifles and machine-guns, plus plentiful supplies of ammunition. For protection at night they were formed up in a circle, like a Wild West wagon train.

ammunition for the protection of its crew. And as a stark reminder of the dangers of the mission, three were armed with heavy machine guns, mounted in a visible position, as a deterrent to the notorious *rezzous*, or bands of roving robbers, which, despite official military protection, the expedition fully expected to encounter en route. Each day, the convoy resumed its journey at 5 a.m., well before dawn, and after pausing briefly for lunch at midday, continued relentlessly onwards until 10 p.m., well past sunset, driving on by the light of its headlamps. At night, the caterpillar cars were drawn up in a circle round a campfire with their machine guns pointing outwards, like the vehicles of a wild west wagon train.

Four days later, the little column reached the fort of In Salah at the end of the first leg of its journey, having covered 600 miles at an average speed of 20 m.p.h., ten times the pace of a camel train. After two days' rest at this last outpost of civilisation, the expedition pressed on again into trackless territory, across the plains of Tidikelt, up through the lunar landscape of the mountainous Hoggar region, with peaks as high as 9,000 feet, and then across the Tanezrouft, the legendary 'desert of unquenchable thirst'. This was the Sahara of popular imagination, a vast, uncharted sea of shifting sand, entirely featureless except for its endless rows of rippling dunes, some rising steeply up to impressive heights, like the crests of massive waves. Here, with no well or oasis for 300 miles in any direction, the slightest navigational error would have spelled doom for the expedition; with no path to follow, Haardt's men steered by sextant and compass, as if travelling by boat. Crossing this sea of sand, surprised by sudden, terrifying storms, countless caravans had already been lost without trace, buried beneath its treacherous surface. In his diary, Haardt recorded that his path was strewn with the skeletons of innumerable camels which had perished through exhaustion, their sun-bleached skulls and vertebrae providing the only signposts to the route ahead.

On New Year's Eve 1923, the party arrived at Tin Zaouten in the French Sudan, 1,250 miles from their starting point at Touggourt. Champagne was served at the campfire that night, but there was no time to pause for lengthier celebrations. New Year's Day was spent on the move as usual, and by 4 January the expedition had reached the fort of Bourem on the banks of the Niger. Here, after almost 2,000 miles of insufferable heat and seemingly interminable desert, the sight of the broad waters of the river sparkling in the moonlight must have been an unforgettable spectacle. Now passing through the fertile country of French West Africa, with the vastness of Algeria behind them, Haardt and his men turned west to follow the Niger across the scrubby savannah lands of the French Sudan, their passage observed from the brush by herds of antelope and gazelle, and from the cloudless sky by circling vultures. Two days later, they arrived at the gates of the ancient city of Timbuktu, to be welcomed by an immense throng of a multitude of races, creeds and colours. According to Haardt, the applause was tumultuous; thousands of its inhabitants rushed out and gathered around the vehicles to express their congratulations in at least twenty different languages. To this polyglot din was added the ululations of camels and horses and the noise made by native bandsmen attempting to play the '*Marseillaise*' on curious, primitive musical instruments.

The following morning – on 7 January 1923, twenty days after setting out from Touggourt – the column of Citroën-Kegresse cars entered the gates of Timbuktu in triumph. For hundreds of years, until its conquest by the French in 1893, this ancient and mysterious mud-brick city had been forbidden territory to Europeans, on pain of death. But now, at a short ceremony held in the city's great central square, the customary meeting place of traders and travellers since the dawn of recorded history, but recently renamed the Place Joffre by its new masters, Haardt and his party were formally received by the French Colonial Governor. Presenting the first mail to be delivered from the mother country across the Sahara, and inaugurating what was planned to be a regular postal service, speaking on behalf of the Minister of State for Posts and Telegraphs, Haardt remarked: 'As a result of our efforts we hope to see a revival of the old caravan routes which long ago linked Algeria and Tunisia with the Niger, even in the times of Charlemagne.'

Next, the leaders of the expedition reported by wireless telegram to their patron at the Quai de Javel that their mission had been safely and successfully accomplished, exactly on schedule. By return came the following jubilant message, phrased in the stilted official language of the era:

At this moment of your reaching the Pearl of the Niger, having accomplished by your superhuman efforts the work of Titans towards the cause of humanity and the triumph of French industry, may I greet your arrival and express from the bottom of my heart the joy that I feel as a result of your achievement.

But the self-congratulatory tone could be forgiven. Truly, as André Citroën had predicted, 'Le chameau est mort – la Citroën le remplace.' After two thousand years in the service of mankind, the camel was dead, replaced by the Citroën motor vehicle.

Following three weeks' rest and recuperation at Timbuktu, spent filming and photographing in the city, hunting game in the vicinity and overhauling their caterpillar cars ready for the return journey, on 26 January Haardt's team set off again, to retrace its steps over the same laborious route back to Touggourt, where – so it was now planned – they would rendezvous with André Citroën himself. But, initially, the leaders went on ahead alone, floating down the broad, majestic, slow-moving Niger on barges, to meet the caterpillar cars and the other personnel at Bourem, where supply vehicles also waited to refuel and revictual them. On the river, they hunted duck, crocodiles and hippopotamuses, and on its banks, gazelles and warthogs. Entertained by the tribesmen of the villages that he passed, the aesthete Haardt admired the statuesque, bronze-skinned Negresses who danced before him to the savage beat of the tom-tom, observing that they were 'devoid even of the artistic convention of a fig-leaf', and that their naked breasts 'rivalled the best productions of classical art'.

Together once more, on 10 February 1923, the convoy of caterpillar cars and its crews set off northwards, homeward bound for Algeria and France. Making its usual steady pace of 20 m.p.h., and covering more than 120 miles each day, by 16 February it was back deep in the heart of the Tanezrouft, where, at this time of the year, the daily range of temperature was at its most extreme. By day, the scorching heat was enough to melt the grease in the rollers of the caterpillar tracks, so that frequent stops had to be made to lubricate the cars. By night, the men shivered in their tents, wrapped in blankets and wearing scarves and greatcoats, unable to find so much as a twig to make a fire. On 18 February, the peaks of the Hoggar came into view again, and at midday on 19 February, the fort of Tamanrasset. Here, 5,000 feet above sea level, a refreshingly cool breeze blew down from the mountains to provide a welcome respite from the furnace heat of the desert below, so Haardt halted for a day to pay homage at the grave of General Laperine and to dine with an assembly of friendly Tuareg chieftains.

Two days later, approaching Tadjmout, the column was stopped by two Chaamba camelmen, who reported the news that further caterpillar cars of a different type had been sighted at the oasis the previous evening. Moreover, the passenger in one of them was a white woman! Haardt had no doubt that this was André Citroën's party, on its way to meet him, and that the lady in question was Madame Citroën, 'a fearless traveller who had no hesitation in accompanying her husband so far into the desert'.

*On 24 February 1923, accompanied by his wife, André Citroën himself drove a caterpillar car to
meet the homecoming expedition and rendezvous with his friend G-M. Haardt near the oasis of
Tadjmout. This is one of the very few pictures ever taken showing Citroën at the wheel of a motor car.*

At 11 a.m. on 24 February, near the well of Tadjmout, the two old friends were
reunited in a scene of jubilation vividly described by Haardt himself:

> Suddenly, two caterpillar cars of the sporting torpedo-bodied type bounded
> out of the palm-groves surrounding the oasis. We recognised in one of them
> Monsieur and Madame Citroën and their mechanic Guegan, and in the other,
> Adolphe Kegresse and his assistant Ferraci. The cars stopped several yards
> from us and we rushed forward and embraced. General emotion ensued,
> which we cannot describe. All we can say is that we lived through one of the
> most joyous hours of our existence. . . . M. Citroën had thought of everything.
> He had even brought us the mail from France. The mechanics were not
> forgotten and M. Citroën warmly praised our devoted assistants.

Le patron had not forgotten to bring the champagne either, and an impromptu
party was soon in swing beside the vehicles. Haardt records that a pleasant hour
was spent sitting on the ground, exchanging congratulatory toasts and swapping
travellers' tales, with both the sparkling wine and the elated conversation being

A triumphal homecoming for the heroes. M. and Mme Citroën greet Haardt and Audouin-Dubreuil on their return to Paris, 17 March 1923. On André Citroën's left is Colonel Estienne, the French tank pioneer.

raptly absorbed by the originator and guiding light of the mission. Unlike the celebrated meeting between Livingstone and Stanley, the encounter between these two intrepid African explorers was captured on film. The camera records that both Monsieur and Madame Citroën were suitably dressed for the occasion, wearing the highly-polished boots, riding breeches, khaki drill tunics and pith helmets then considered *de rigueur* for desert wear. Somehow, Madame Citroën's Parisienne chicness momentarily brought the style of a *concours d'élégance* in the Bois de Boulogne to the palm-fringed oasis of Tadjmout. The whole scene had about it the elaborately stage-managed atmosphere of a perfectly-designed and accessorised film set, which indeed it was.

On 26 February, the entire cavalcade made a triumphal entry into the fort of In Salah, the walls of which had been decorated with *Tricolore* flags. Surrounded by cavalry and camelry adorned with the finest ceremonial costumes and regalia, the seven caterpillar cars advanced through the gates in parade order, to be greeted by the military commander-in-chief of the region, acting on behalf of the Governor-General of Algeria. Also present in the welcoming party at André Citroën's invitation was General Estienne, who had also made a special trip from France to be reunited with his son. All the Arab chieftains of the district were also assembled for the feasting and festivities, which went on long into the night.

'Le chameau est mort – la Citroën le remplace!' After two thousand years in the service of mankind, the camel is dead, replaced as a means of desert travel and commerce by the Citroën automobile!

As darkness fell, the shrill sound of Saharan music could still be heard mingling with the enthusiastic shouts of the crowd.

Summoned by a telegraphic call of duty from the Quai de Javel, the following day Monsieur and Madame Citroën left at speed for Paris, while Haardt with his men and machines pressed on to Ougla, where, arriving on 5 March, once again they were given a tremendous welcome. Over five hundred camelmen were assembled to see them arrive. Finally, on 7 March 1923, the column reached its departure point at Touggourt, twelve weeks after starting out, having covered over 4,300 miles of desert terrain in forty days of travel. The vast distances of the Saharan wilderness had been conquered; the little Citroën caterpillar cars had shown that, in the time that it took a camel to cross a hundred miles of sand, an automobile could cross no less than three thousand. Among the many Anglo-Saxon newspapers that kept a watching brief on the Citroën Sahara mission from beginning to end was *The Times*. In a leading article published on 11 January 1923, 'The Thunderer' declared: 'That men can endure such a journey seems wonderful; that machines have conquered it, a miracle.'

CHAPTER SIX

An African Adventure

After the excitements of his African excursion, André Citroën returned to everyday routine. Even so, as he sat in his office at the Quai de Javel, surrounded once more by the ceaseless activities of his beloved factory, assailed by the drumbeat of the presses and the cymbal-like sound of sheet-metal parts being beaten into shape – a deafening noise that was normally nothing but music to his ears – his mind was elsewhere, lost in memories of the eerie silence of the empty desert. His travels through those vast open spaces, camping by night at remote, palm-fringed oases and drinking champagne below the North African moon, had fired his imagination and he was keen to exploit the commercial possibilities of trans-Saharan travel.

The result was an astounding scheme that demonstrated all the hallmarks of Citroën's fatal combination of originality, adventurousness and over-confidence – an Arabian fantasy almost as far-fetched as the story of *One Thousand and One Nights*. His idea was to set up a regular transport service from Colomb-Bechar to Timbuktu – by caterpillar car, of course. On payment of the not inconsiderable sum of 40,000 francs for a return ticket, well-heeled travellers could experience the same Saharan adventure that he and his wife had enjoyed, except that, instead of camping out, the passengers would stay in a chain of Grand Luxe Fort-Hotels that he intended to create at the oases along the route. These would be equipped with every civilised convenience including running hot and cold water, and would be lavishly furnished and decorated in the Arabian style. As the highlight of their tour, guests would spend one night of the twenty-four-day round trip under canvas, when an exotic and elaborate dinner would be served in an immense tent. After the meal, as the guests reclined on carpets, a cabaret would be performed by native musicians, dancers, jugglers and snake charmers. Fifty years ahead of his time, André Citroën had invented the Club Méditerranée Safari Holiday!

Overcome with enthusiasm for his grandiose scheme, Citroën issued orders for the inauguration of the Compagnie Trans-Africaine Citroën, and began to organise the venture with his usual meticulous attention to detail. Immediately, staff were engaged and a programme of hotel construction embarked upon in North Africa. A publicity and advertising campaign was mounted throughout Europe, and brochures were printed by Citroën's own printing presses at the Quai de Javel. Simultaneously, a fleet of seventy vehicles was prepared. The little 10 hp Citroën caterpillar cars were considered too humble for the task of transporting the wealthy passengers that André Citroën hoped to attract, and so much larger and more comfortable 15 hp Mors cars equipped with Kegresse tracks were employed.

Within eighteen months, all was ready for the inaugural trip, scheduled to depart for Timbuktu on 6 January 1925. The distinguished guests invited to join Monsieur and Madame Citroën on this maiden voyage across the desert were no less important persons than His Majesty Albert I, the King of the Belgians, Maréchal Pétain, Chief of Staff of the French Army, and Monsieur Steeg, the Governor-General of Algeria, accompanied by their respective spouses. But the great occasion was not to be. At the very last moment, on 2 January, the entire event was suddenly cancelled on André Citroën's personal instructions. The explanation given was that reports from southern Morocco indicated a resumption of warlike activity among the dissident tribesmen there. The military authorities had given notice that they could no longer guarantee the safety of the party and declined all responsibility in the event of a hostile incident. In consequence, the French government had withdrawn its permission. Evidently, it went against the army's interests to encourage tourism in the Sahara, even by such notables as their own Commander-in-Chief! Faced with both a humiliating failure and the loss of a small fortune, André Citroën abandoned the whole undertaking forthwith, liquidating the company and disposing of its vehicles. (Later he learned from travellers who had been in the region at the time, that there had been no disturbances of any kind: someone had invented the scare to spoil his plans.) Suspecting treachery in official quarters and the intervention of his rival Louis Renault behind the scenes, he refused to discuss the affair again for the rest of his life. Indeed, when within a few months the Renault firm announced its intention to open a similar service using conventional-wheeled vehicles, it met with no official obstacles of the kind that had thwarted Citroën.

This débâcle was the first reverse that Citroën had suffered in his meteoric rise to fame and fortune. Moreover, it was evidence that, behind the scenes, in certain influential circles, a reactionary tide of resentment and hostility was building up at the over-reaching adventures of the parvenu 'little Jew of Javel', as he was unkindly described by an increasing number of conservative opponents, including Louis Renault. Citroën's enterprising, unconventional approach, which broke unwritten rules and breached the barriers of precedent, had begun to offend opinion among traditionalists, who considered his methods vulgar or, at best, not quite *comme il faut*.

But with his usual resilience and optimism, Citroën soon shrugged off the setback, turning his back on his enemies to concentrate on more promising avenues of exploration. Confidence restored, he soon conceived a venture even more sensational and spectacular than the trans-Sahara mission – a full-scale, 12,500 mile coast-to-coast crossing of the Black Continent of Africa by caterpillar cars. This, the famous Citroën Central African Expedition, popularly known as the '*Croisière Noire*', would be very much more than a '*Raid Sportif*' or proving-run-cum-rally like the previous affair, however. Staffed and equipped as a genuine scientific expedition, it would embrace the fields of geology, meteorology, zoology, ethnology and anthropology, as well as geography and cartography; and because its progress was to be recorded in detail at every stage by a travelling photographer, cinematographer and artist, it would also have a serious cultural and political purpose.

Certainly, the favourable reception that the proposal met with in high places suggested that there was no real reason for Citroën to suppose that the entire French establishment was against him, *en bloc*. The President of the Republic, M. Gaston Doumergue, gave the project his blessing, on behalf of the Colonial Ministry, seeing it as a way of establishing a strategic land route from French North Africa to the nation's inaccessible possessions on the east coast of the continent, in Djibouti and Madagascar. Other important institutions such as the Société de Géographie Française and the Museum of National History endorsed and sponsored the expedition.

Undertaken within the space of ten months, between October 1924 and July 1925, this expedition was a hazardous, trail-blazing journey from Algiers to Mombasa (and then on by sea to Madagascar) by way of the Sahara, Niger and the Sudan, traversing desert, bush, savannah, swamps, rivers and tropical forests along an unmapped, roadless route never before conquered by motor vehicles.

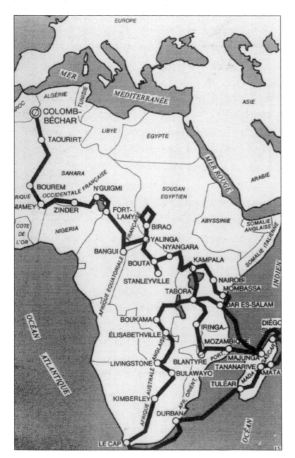

The route of the Citroën Trans-African expedition 1924/25. After leaving Kampala, the convoy of caterpillar cars split into four parties, each taking a separate route south before joining up again at Cape Town.

Encamped near Am-Defok in French Equatorial Africa, early in February 1925, Haardt, Bettembourg and Audouin-Dubreuil plan the next stage of their trek across the African continent.

Yet once again, all the caterpillar cars came through the ordeal unscathed. En route, the expedition shot about 90,000 feet of film and took 8,000 photographs, produced over 300 botanical drawings and fifteen books of sketches and collected samples of over 300 mammals, 800 birds and 1,500 insects, many of which were unknown to science at that time.

As before, the expedition was led by Georges-Marie Haardt (who had now relinquished his position as managing director of Citroën's factories to concentrate on the challenge), with Louis Audouin-Dubreuil acting as second-in-command and Commandant Bettembourg (leader of the French Army's abortive 1916 trans-Sahara mission) as adjutant. Other key members of the sixteen-strong team included the engineer Charles Brull, director of research at Citroën's laboratories, Dr Eugene Bergonie, a doctor of medicine-cum-zoologist, the distinguished artist Alexandre Jacovleff, and Leon Poirier, a cinema pioneer who had just completed a science fiction film based on the legend of Atlantis.

Eight Type B2 Citroën-Kegresse vehicles took part in the expedition itself, but many more were employed in the five auxiliary logistical expeditions which met up with the main force en route, to supply it with food, water, petrol, spare parts and other essentials. Just as in the Sahara crossing, the autochenilles carried heraldic emblems denoting their function – a symbolic dove marked the combined cookhouse and sickbay vehicle, for example – but this time, they also pulled trailers loaded with tents and supplies.

Turning its back on civilisation, the mission set out to conquer the Dark Continent on 28 October 1924, leaving from the French Foreign Legion fort at Colomb-Bechar in north-western Algeria. Moving from oasis to oasis, to begin with Haardt and his team made excellent progress across the Sahara, reaching Bourem on the Niger on 19 November, before continuing on to Niamey, further down the river. News raced ahead of the vehicles as native runners carried reports of the approaching convoy to their rulers. On arrival in Niamey on 24 November, the party were greeted by 3,000 excited horsemen and camel-riders who had gathered there from miles around to witness the coming of the intrepid Frenchmen and their strange mechanical monsters, marvelling at the way that they crept along like giant insects, devouring all obstacles in their paths with an insatiable appetite for progress, scarcely less voracious than that which motivated André Citroën himself.

From there, the autochenilles headed due east, running parallel to Nigeria's northern border and, initially, covering the ground at a fair pace. By 1 December, they had reached Tessaoua, where they visited Sultan Barmou, who presided over a harem of one hundred women. Five days later, they were at Zinder, an age-old trading centre and slave market, standing at the crossroads of the ancient trade routes of Central Africa. But then, en route for Lake Chad, came the first of the many long, hard battles with the wilderness that were to tax both men and machines to the limit. In the absence of so much as a beaten track, a path had to be hacked out by hand with machetes through near-solid walls of grass, standing as tall as a man, and in which great herds of elephants browsed. Haardt's vehicle suffered a breakdown when it got stuck in an enormous rut near Bande. Consequently, the calm, reed-fringed waters of the lake were not sighted until dawn on 18 December. Next, the expedition turned southwards again, onwards through the savannah towards Fort Lamy, the capital of what was then French Equatorial Africa. Here, on 24 December, the entire local European community turned out to join the explorers in celebrating Christmas and rejoicing in their already remarkable achievement.

Haardt and his men rested at Fort Lamy until 3 January 1925, welcoming in the New Year, writing reports, shooting both cinema films and wild game, and preparing the indomitable little Citroëns for the next leg of the marathon, by far the most difficult and dangerous that they had yet encountered. The route now took them further southwards through a wild and remote region of dense bush and huge trees, sparsely populated by hostile bands of bizarre, plate-lipped people and ferocious, tattooed 'panthermen', whose religion involved making human sacrifices, or so it was feared by less primitive tribes.

On 11 January, they bivouacked near Bangui, on the border of the Sudan and the Belgian Congo, before penetrating further southwards into the equatorial jungle. The first 400 miles of this part of the journey were relatively easy to negotiate, because a track had already been cleared for them by a huge army of natives recruited by the Belgians. But thereafter, the going was agonisingly slow, and it was not until 12 March that they reached Stanleyville, following in the footsteps of the British explorer-journalist Henry Morton Stanley, who had established the Congo Free State for the Belgians fifty years earlier, and whose magic powers, according to the natives, were strong enough to blow rocks apart. Like Stanley, Haardt had also to engineer almost supernatural feats to create a path forward for his vehicles through the dense, steaming foliage. Many broad rivers had to be crossed, but the few rickety bridges that existed were unable to take the weight of anything as heavy as a car. The only answer was to lash logs to dug-out canoes to construct makeshift rafts, and then winch these platforms and their loads across the raging torrents, inch by inch. Meanwhile, danger of another sort was ever-present, as hostile tribesmen armed with bows and poison-tipped arrows lurked in the surrounding jungle. Once more, news of the expedition's progress – or lack of it – was telegraphed from village to village by jungle drums. The atmosphere was tense and sometimes even overwrought; once, the artist Jacovleff was sent into ecstasy by the sight of the immense, rainbow-coloured butterflies that flitted gracefully from one exotic plant to the next. On another occasion, when sketching the portrait of the chief of a more friendly tribe of natives, he was embarrassed to be offered the chief's daughter as a gift. With his usual charm and diplomacy, Haardt tactfully declined the offer on his colleague's behalf, explaining away the expedition's lack of female companions as a penance imposed by his own headman, André Citroën.

Having covered 5,600 miles of virgin territory in a little under five months, the group rested for eleven days at Stanleyville before proceeding by a northerly detour to Kampala, at the head of Lake Victoria, in the British colonial territory of Uganda. From the outset, it had been planned that here the convoy would split into four two-vehicle groups, each making its own way to the Indian Ocean coast by a different route, before reuniting in Madagascar. Audouin-Dubreuil and his companions headed for Mombasa via Nairobi, skirting Mount Kilimanjaro and climbing to over 9,500 feet above sea level at one point. The second group, led by Commandant Bettembourg, set course east for Dar-es-Salaam, crossing Lake Victoria by boat and the Wami River by a pontoon bridge 60 yards long, which they constructed themselves. After paying homage at the spot in Zambia where Livingstone died in 1873, they reached the coast on 15 May 1925. The third group, led by Charles Brull, travelled all the way south by made-up roads through Rhodesia to Cape Town, before sailing to Madagascar from Durban in early August. In Bulawayo, they encountered the Prince of Wales – later to become King Edward VIII and, subsequently, after his abdication, the Duke of Windsor – who was in the middle of a four-month, 10,000 mile-long, official tour of Southern Africa. Declaring that he had been following news of the progress of the expedition and was interested in meeting the man whose pioneering spirit energised the mission, the Prince requested a tête-à-tête with André Citroën in Paris at the earliest opportunity. He had already met Henry Ford, at Fairlane in October 1924.

The fourth group under Haardt's direction had the hardest time of all, making for Beira in Mozambique through Nyasaland and Northern and Southern Rhodesia (now known as Malawi, Zambia and Zimbabwe) by a route that the British colonial authorities then considered impossible. On the most hazardous

Their route took them across rivers swollen to raging torrents by the coming of the rainy season . . .

through hostile jungle and swamps inhabited by hippopotami, as here on the River Maroway . . .

over rickety, makeshift bridges, improvised from logs, near Buta in the Congo . . .

and through savannah land thick with elephant grass so high that navigation could only be made by compass, as in British East Africa.

stage, between Kampala and Blantyre, it often took an hour to cover half a mile as, lashed by torrential rain, they hacked their way with axes and spades through gloomy forests, steering by compass. Some days ended with the explorers being no more than 5 miles nearer their destination. After that nightmare, the final 435 mile run through open country from Blantyre to Beira should have been child's play, yet it was anything but that. First, the battered Citroëns had to battle their way across the mud of the Dabo, a huge, soggy plain, thickly carpeted by tall grass, where the sun beat down like a golden sledgehammer on the heads of the exhausted men, hauling their autochenilles out of the morass with ropes. Then came trial by fire! Fanned by a stiff westerly breeze, it raced towards the explorers faster than they could drive their cumbersome caterpillar cars over such treacherous terrain. Just as it seemed that there would be no escape from the conflagration, the wind changed course and Haardt and his men were able to find a way through the burning grass, fleeing with their rubber caterpillar tracks ablaze, their canvas tents smouldering and the flames scorching the clothes on their backs. Having reached Beira, the party embarked on the French liner *General Galliéni* and sailed for Madagascar on 20 June, reaching the island five days later, eight months after starting out from Colomb-Bechar.

On returning to Paris by sea that autumn, Haardt and his team were given a jubilant welcome. Hailed as conquering heroes, they were fêted in a series of gala receptions and celebratory banquets organised by André Citroën and attended by the French president and prime minister, plus innumerable senior military and governmental figures, together with the principal personalities of the double chevron company and France's leading journalists and commentators.

Throughout its travels, the progress of the Citroën Central African Mission had been charted almost daily by reports in the international press, and both at home and abroad, an enormous public interest in its achievements had been aroused. To satisfy this curiosity in the mysteries of the Dark Continent – a fascination in the life of the 'noble savage' and all things primitive was in vogue among sophisticated people at that time – a lavish exhibition of the expedition's vehicles and trophies was mounted at the Louvre. Later, Haardt's own personal caterpillar car – the Scarabée d'Or (Golden Beetle) – was put on permanent display at the Army Museum at les Invalides. And when Leon Poiret's film of the expedition was completed the following year, needless to say, it was screened in triumph at ceremonial premières in all the major capitals of Europe.

The London première eventually took place at the Plaza Theatre on 16 January 1928, at a gala performance in aid of the Royal National Lifeboat Institution, as had been the case in November 1923, when Queen Mary attended a gala performance of the trans-Saharan expedition film, given at the Victoria Palace Theatre. This time, the Prince of Wales was guest of honour. The Prince not only attended the performance, but gave a dinner party before it, his guests being the Duke and Duchess of York (later King George VI and Queen Elizabeth), Monsieur and Madame Citroën, Messieurs Haardt, Audouin-Dubreuil and numerous members of the Royal Household. The performance was preceded by a *tableau vivant* depicting the meeting of Livingstone and

Stanley, and during the film an orchestra played music based on native melodies recorded by the expedition during its trans-African journey. After the film show, the Prince of Wales accompanied André Citroën on stage, and as President of the RNLI, thanked the French motor magnate for his generosity in raising funds. Later, Citroën was elected an Honorary Life Governor of the RNLI. (Clearly, both Citroën and his products enjoyed unusual prestige and popularity among the British aristocracy and governing classes throughout the twenties. It is interesting to note that at one point towards the end of the decade, Citroën Cars Ltd published a series of posters and advertisements featuring a remarkable testimonial written by none other than the distinguished Conservative politician and lawyer F.E. Smith, the 1st Earl of Birkenhead, a close political ally and associate of Winston Churchill.)

In short, the whole Croisière Noire episode amounted to a remarkable demonstration of André Citroën's powerful promotional machine. Reputedly, the expedition had cost him over £100,000 (more like £10 million in today's money), but so valuable was the publicity and prestige it generated that the venture was considered highly profitable, far more so than participation in grand prix races and motor sport events, in which *le patron* had little personal interest. Such matters he was content to leave to men like Bugatti and Voisin.

Meanwhile, at the Quai de Javel, the lathes and presses continued to turn, churning out cars at an ever-increasing rate to meet a seemingly inexhaustable demand. In the economic boom of the late twenties, France experienced what amounted to a second revolution, in which the *ancien régime* was overturned in favour of a new aristocracy of creativity and enterprise. Talent took precedence over title, new money reigned supreme over inherited wealth, and as the nation embarked on its long love-hate relationship with the USA, traditional French values were usurped by a modish egalitarianism. Paris became the focal point or capital city of this new transatlantic culture. Somehow, its unique atmosphere acted as a catalyst in the process of creation, by attracting and absorbing American elements, animal, vegetable and mineral, and then recycling this rich material into literature, painting and music which were then re-exported back to the USA as great art. Without a doubt, the enthusiastic adoption by Whites of Black American folk music would never have taken place at that time had Negro musicians and dancers not been welcomed in Paris and made respectable, as the creators of jazz, by French socialites and intellectuals.

By 1925, more than 5,000 wealthy Americans a week were arriving in Paris, disgorged by the boat-trains that were fed in turn by the *Ile-de-France*, the *Mauretania* and other huge transatlantic luxury liners which docked regularly at Cherbourg. Eager for the European experience, these refugees from Prohibition truly lived '*wie Gott im Frankreich*' ('like God in France', in the old German-Jewish phrase) thanks to an exchange rate that gave them 25 francs to the dollar. On $20 a week, they could live in comfort, on $40, in enormous style; the average Frenchman then earned the equivalent of only $9 a week. Grand Luxe hotels like the Ritz and the Crillon became virtual colonies of Uncle Sam, while the great Parisian couturiers and *parfumiers* – Lanvin, Patoux, Coty, Cartier,

Chanel and Schiaparelli – all did a roaring trade. Life in Paris was one long party, as young American heirs and heiresses imitated the prodigal excesses of society hostesses like Peggy Guggenheim, Nancy Cunard and Elsa Maxwell, to create a cosmopolitan plutocracy in which native French champagne-progressives and *bien-pensants* like André Citroën participated with enthusiasm, much to the chagrin of traditionalists and conservatives.

Creative talent thrived in this frenetic atmosphere where, as long as transgressions were committed in the name of art, the only unpardonable sin was to be boring. Just as it had in the Belle Epoque, the City of Light once again played host to a cast of internationally famous artists: in the cinema, René Clair and Jean Renoir; in painting, Picasso, Braque, Matisse, Chagall, Dali and Duchamp; in music, Milhaud, Ravel and Poulenc; in literature, Apollinaire, Proust, Gide, Cocteau, Mauriac, Valéry and Simenon.

And to this roll-call of fame were added the names of Anglo-Saxon expatriates such as Ernest Hemingway, Scott Fitzgerald, Ezra Pound, Man Ray, Aaron Copland, Alexander Calder and James Joyce, who frequented Gertrude Stein's salon in the rue de Fleurus or hung out in the cafés of Montparnasse: La Coupole, La Rotonde and Le Dôme, often sponging off their richer compatriots. 'There was so much money about that, even if you had none yourself, you could always live as though you had an inexhaustible supply,' Scott Fitzgerald is supposed to have recalled in later years. Cole Porter and George Gershwin were also there *en passant*, and Gershwin's rhapsody *An American in Paris*, with its clever evocation of traffic sounds, is said to have captured in music the frenetic easy-come, easy-go atmosphere of the Parisian social scene.

But it was really in the spheres of industry and commerce that the effects of this *nouveau riche* revolution were most strongly felt. Output of manufactured goods soared, and unemployment was virtually abolished. With the help of three million immigrant workers, within ten years industrial productivity was increased by 38 per cent over 1918 levels, and as more and more peasants left the self-sufficiency of the land to find better material opportunities in the factories, a new consumer society was created. This overall prosperity and optimism was reflected in higher living standards, reduced working hours and the universal adoption of Britain's '*le weekend*', as had been enjoyed by André Citroën's employees for the past ten years.

Thanks largely to the seriously undervalued franc, no other European country prospered more greatly in the twenties than France, and no French company did better than Automobiles Citroën. By 1928, there were 976,000 automobiles on the roads there – 1 for every 41 inhabitants – and no less than 350,000 of these cars were Citroëns. The company's Paris factories had now achieved a production capacity of 800 vehicles a day, double that of its two main French rivals. It employed 35,000 production workers in France alone and had fourteen zone distributors in France and North Africa, plus ten subsidiary sales companies in other countries around the world. Its overseas sales represented 45 per cent of all French motor industry exports, without counting the contribution made by its foreign factories at Slough, Brussels, Cologne and

Milan. That year, its home production totalled 72,356 vehicles; the following year, it was to reach a staggering 102,891 vehicles, more than the output of its two main rivals Renault and Peugeot combined, and over one-third of the output of the entire British motor industry for that year. A whole generation was to pass before such levels of production were seen again in the European motor industry and the output of the Citroën firm topped 100,000 units per annum again, in 1951.

Encouraged by this success, at the 1928 Paris Motor Show, Citroën introduced two new models, the AC4 and the AC6, each available in up to sixteen standard body styles, plus seven utility versions of the AC4 and four of the AC6. The pair created a sensation. Together, they marked the seventh change in the line begun less than ten years earlier, and both were a move upmarket, offering greater technical refinement and a higher degree of performance and comfort than their predecessors. Thus, in bringing out the AC4 and AC6, Citroën abandoned the opportunity to create a simple, inexpensive and economical people's car that would fill the gap created by the demise of the Type C models, to consolidate his position as an international supplier of robust, reliable, well-engineered cars and utility vehicles, conventionally designed in the Ford and Chrysler manner. The four-cylinder AC4 was derived directly from the earlier B14, but featured an all-new, high-revving 1,628 cc engine designed by Arthur-Leon Michelat, the former chief engineer of Delage, while the 2,442 cc AC6 – Citroën's first six-cylinder-engined car – was entirely new in every respect.

At the 1928 Paris Motor Show, Citroën introduced his first six-cylinder model, in the American style. This is the C6E 'Grand Tourisme' version, built in 1929.

Completely American in style and concept, the long, spacious and stylish AC6 lay somewhere between a popular mass-produced model and a coach-built luxury car, and consequently it offered the middle-class customer extraordinary value for money. But, naturally, it never caught on among rich and fashionable motorists, accustomed to more exclusive motor cars.

Enormous sums of money were invested in the tooling and production of these two new cars; hundreds of costly, sophisticated machine tools were imported from the USA. Almost as much again was spent on marketing them. At the high point, Automobiles Citroën regularly spent 2 per cent of its revenues on advertising and promotion, far more than any other motor manufacturer in the world. And yet, for all its flamboyance and panache, Citroën's publicity was rational, factual and informative. Despite the fact that he called his advertising department the 'propaganda service', it produced none of the fanciful nonsense seen in most American car advertisements of that era, which claimed for machines the speed and agility of birds or animals and offered few concrete, objective facts about performance, in terms of engineering content or the economics of ownership. Like Voisin, Citroën opposed (and tried to remedy) 'the hopeless incompetence with which people in the machine age use machines, and the absurd criteria by which they assess their merits', like children looking for an excuse to buy a new toy. He had nothing but contempt for charlatans who attempted to bamboozle or short-change the public. And, despite his reputation as a publicist and showman, he was one of the few car-makers of his age who did not address his customers as infants and who was not prepared to sell them mere playthings.

To launch the AC4 and AC6 models, a massive advertising campaign was staged throughout France and, once a month, Citroën took the back page of all the largest-selling newspapers in the country (total circulation: 15 million copies) to publicise his products. Posters, brochures and catalogues were produced in profusion, photographed and designed by Citroën's own studios and printed on Citroën's own presses at the Quai de Javel. These were the work of Pierre Louys, a supremely gifted photographer and graphic designer who had joined Citroën's staff in 1920, at the age of twenty-seven, having trained at the Ecole des Beaux-Arts in Paris. It was Louys who first came up with the idea of photographing cars in attractive outdoor locations, surrounded by beautiful girls, to associate Citroën's products with natural beauty and feminine elegance. For years he toured France to find the right settings for his *chef*'s latest cars, in Brittany, Provence, the Auvergne and the Loire, and as a result of his untiring efforts, the Citroën marque came to be associated with the ambiance of la belle France in the minds of the motoring public.

Evidently, André Citroën exerted a magnetic pull over men of talent like Louys, attracting them into his orbit and propelling them on to great achievement by his encouragement and patronage. According to Charles Rocherand, who was employed at the Quai de Javel in the twenties, and who subsequently wrote the first biography of Citroën, published in 1938, his boss always refused to take no for an answer, or to follow the easy, well-trodden route:

He managed to create among his fellow directors and personnel an attitude of mind which he called the beehive mentality. The dynamism that emanated from the patron found its way down to all levels and encouraged remarkable efforts and developments. He would set out with a blissful certainty of achieving his objectives and therefore he succeeded in a whole series of areas where others had failed. . . . His energy and ability made him one of the great leaders.

Other ex-employees or associates praised his warmth, generosity and humanity. Unlike certain other motor magnates of his era, he never adopted an authoritarian approach to his inferiors: 'What other people could only obtain by issuing orders, he knew how to obtain with a smile or with a cheerful handshake,' wrote the leading French motoring writer Pierre Dumont. Every day, he made a tour of his factory, greeting all those that he met by name, asking after the health of their wives and families. To Citroën, the social welfare of his staff was always of paramount importance; in 1927, he became the first employer in France to pay his salaried employees a Christmas bonus of an extra month's pay, a provision that is nowadays not just customary throughout most countries in the EU but statutory, though not, alas, in the UK.

The success of the AC4/AC6 range was immediate, and within two years of its introduction, over 140,000 examples had been sold. Thus, by the end of the decade, just ten years after starting up his motor manufacturing business, André Citroën had achieved his objectives and established his marque as a major force in the automotive world. With its annual production rate now topping 100,000, and with almost half a million Citroën vehicles having been made and sold, his company had by now overtaken all its rivals to become the largest motor manufacturer in Europe.

Yet something was missing. On the road, his American-style products were beginning to seem decidely dated and old-fashioned compared with the exciting new ideas coming from the more adventurous minor manufacturers. Standing high off the ground, they looked boxy and clumsy in contrast with the long, lean, low look then in fashion among the leading designers and coachbuilders of *voitures de luxe*. Something altogether more stylish, sophisticated and technically advanced was called for, André Citroën decided.

Hitherto, his success had been founded on an astute exploitation of the principles of mass production, so as to reduce prices to the minimum while at the same time maximising sales by an outstanding flexibility in manufacturing and assembly methods – a system which also allowed for a very wide variety of different body-style options to be offered. The time had now come to add another factor to his formula, by introducing highly-advanced engineering ideas and a greater originality of design. This would permit an even more ruthless exploitation of the laws of economics, by making it possible to carry out very long production runs of each new model. What he needed was a car so far ahead of its time that it wouldn't matter to his customers if it had been in production for two years or for twenty.

CHAPTER SEVEN

An Eastern Odyssey

No sooner had Georges-Marie Haardt returned to Paris in triumph after completing his trans-African mission than he and André Citroën began to plan a sequel, an epic of adventure and discovery that would eclipse even the Croisière Noire in its audacity. The Citroën company had now reached the absolute zenith of its fortunes, employing over 32,000 persons at its Paris factories, which covered a total 850,000 square metres of floorspace and housed over 12,500 machine tools of the latest type. To the two friends and partners, the omens seemed so encouraging that there appeared to be no limit to what could be achieved or afforded in the future. They therefore resolved that the third Citroën expedition should be nothing short of the ultimate test of men and machines – an assault on the last great challenge of land travel, a coast-to-coast journey across the Asian continent from west to east, so far unconquered by the motor car. If successfully accomplished, the adventure would live forever in the history books, a permanent testimony to the power of the automobile in demolishing geographical, cultural and political barriers around the world.

So it was that five years later, in March 1931, Haardt and Audouin-Dubreuil, together with numerous other veterans of the Croisière Noire, set out from France on a bold new mission of geographic and scientific exploration, the Citroën Central Asian Expedition, popularly known as the 'Croisière Jaune' ('Yellow Cruise'). Their aim was to make the first ever motorised crossing of Central Asia, covering the 8,000 miles from the Mediterranean to the China Sea within nine months; and by a route so difficult and dangerous that their achievement would come to join that of Hannibal and his elephants in the eternally enduring legends of travel. Sponsored and supported by the French and British governments, the National Geographical Society of America and the Pathé Nathan newsreel company (which planned to make a film about the adventure), the expedition had taken over three years to organise and prepare; simply reconnoitring the route, obtaining all the necessary official travel documents and establishing supply bases for the provision of fuel and spare parts had been a mammoth task in itself.

The original plan had been to drive straight across the European and Asian land masses from west to east, avoiding the mountains of the Great Divide by skirting round the Caspian Sea, and then travelling along the 40th parallel through Russian Turkestan to Sinkiang before retracing Marco Polo's route along the ancient Silk Road caravan trail to China. But this idea had eventually been abandoned due to the uncertain political situation in the USSR and the worsening state of diplomatic relations between the Soviet and French governments. Instead, an even more hazardous route was chosen, detouring south via Afghanistan and crossing one of the most daunting natural barriers in the world, the mountains of the Pamir and Hindu Kush ranges, travelling through the Afghan corridor and over the Wakhir Pass, reaching an altitude of over 16,000 feet, higher than any motor vehicle had ever gone before.

In this new plan, the Citroën trans-Asia mission was to be split into a two-pronged attack, with one column of smaller, lighter caterpillar cars, the Pamir Group led by Haardt and Audouin-Dubreuil, setting off eastwards from Beirut, bound for Peking, while another force, the China Group led by Victor Point and using the original heavier vehicles, advanced westwards from Tsien-Tsin, having travelled to its starting point by way of Moscow on the Trans-Siberian Railway. The two groups would then rendezvous at the ancient Silk Road trading town of Kashgar – for centuries past the traditional meeting place of travellers from the East and the West – before returning together to the Chinese capital along another route through Mongolia and across the Gobi Desert. Already, a third force led by a certain Vladimir Petropavloski had been despatched to set up a chain of supply bases to refuel and revictual the two main convoys, a 6,000 mile round trek across China that was an expedition in its own right.

Initially, the project was viewed with suspicion by the Chinese, who thought that it might be a military mission in disguise. But after much diplomatic wrangling, the permission of the Nationalist government in Nanking, led by Marshal Chiang Kai-Shek was finally obtained, on the condition that a party of Chinese scientists and observers joined the China Group, and that the mission

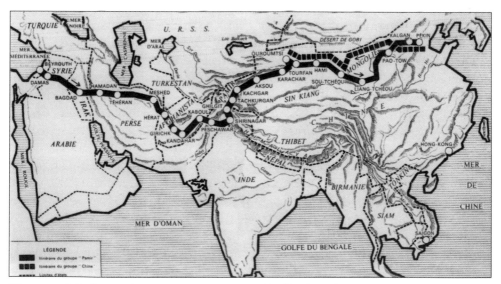

The route of the Citroën Central Asian Expedition 1931/32. In fact, the Croisière Jaune was planned as a two-pronged mission, one party travelling west to east from Beirut to Peking, the other travelling in the opposite direction. Their intention was to rendezvous at Kashgar before returning together to Peking, by a different route. But unfortunately, events did not go according to plan!

was renamed the Great Sino-French Expedition of the Nineteenth Year. Any activity which might affect the sovereignty or national defence of China, such as surveying or archaeological excavation, was forbidden, and both filming with cine cameras and the use of radio communications were to be closely supervised.

Unfortunately, in February 1931, just six weeks before the forty-strong expedition was due to depart from France, word came from Afghanistan that a revolution had broken out in the north, and that the route over the Wakhir Pass was now impassable. But with over 50 tons of fuel and supplies worth millions of francs already in position in a supply chain stretching right across Central Asia, the cancellation or postponement of the enterprise was far too costly to contemplate. After so much time and money had been invested in the preparations, defeat was out of the question. The only alternative was to find another route through to Chinese Turkestan, by way of British India, and to attempt to motor across one of the virtually inaccessible passes of the central Himalayas.

On learning of the setback, Haardt immediately made a trip to London to seek assistance from the British authorities and to enlist the help of General Sir Ernest Swinton, who had done so much to pave the way for the Croisière Noire in its journey through East and South Africa. From his days in the army and the War Cabinet Secretariat and his service with Prime Minister Lloyd George, Swinton knew everyone worth knowing. As he put it himself in his autobiography:

My value to [André Citroën] lay in the innumerable contacts my varied life had enabled me to make. I never remember being unable to arrange a meeting with anyone that he [or Haardt] wished to see, from the Prince of Wales downwards. I had access to almost every British Government department. Two successive British Ambassadors in Paris were my personal friends and I knew many of the Governors in the British territories that Citroën wished to traverse, in addition to the [then] outgoing and incoming Viceroys of India [Lord Irwin and Lord Willingdon].

General Swinton was therefore well qualified to assist his friend Haardt with introductions at the Foreign Office, the War Office, the India Office and the Air Ministry, all of which were eager to help in every way. Formalities were waived, and Haardt was quickly given permission to use the Gilgit route through the mountains, a track that was normally open only to British military and diplomatic personnel.

General Swinton was also instrumental in securing the services of Colonel Sir Vivian Gabriel, an old India hand who had organised the Durbar for King George V in 1912, and who, according to Swinton, had an unrivalled knowledge of India and its peoples. Sir Vivian volunteered to travel out to India on the next boat to reconnoitre the Gilgit Pass on the spot, and to report to Haardt in three months' time, when the Pamir Group reached Srinagar in the foothills of the Himalayas.

Meanwhile, the expedition began to prepare for its departure from Paris, as if very little of importance had happened to alter its plans, other than a change of route. With Haardt would travel his lieutenant and second-in-command Louis Audouin-Dubreuil, together with André Goerger and Henri Pecqueur, who acted as General Secretary and Paymaster to the mission, the painter Alexandre Jacovleff, the writer and historian Georges Lefevre (who had been commissioned to produce a book about the journey), the distinguished archaeologist Joseph Hackin (curator of the Guimet Museum of Oriental antiquities in Paris) and the American writer and photographer Maynard Owen Williams (who, as its Chief Correspondent, accompanied the mission as the official delegate of the National Geographic Society of Washington) plus a further fifteen men to do the work of drivers, mechanics, radio operators, cinema cameramen and sound recordists. A total of seven light-weight four-cylinder caterpillar cars (six Type P17 and one Type P14), all towing trailers, were required to carry the Pamir Group and its equipment. Each had a specialist function, such as command car, cinema car, radio car and cookhouse vehicle, and as in the Croisière Noire, all bore a symbol acting as both a means of identification and as a talisman to ward off bad luck. The radio car with its generator and powerful short-wave transmitter would enable them to maintain contact with their fellows in the second group, and also with their headquarters in Paris, through various relay stations and listening posts, including two French warships anchored at Shanghai and Hong Kong.

Travelling towards them in the opposite direction would be the China Group, a team of eighteen men led by Lieutenant-Commander Victor Point, riding in seven six-cylinder Type P21 caterpillar cars of the heavy-duty military pattern originally intended for use by the expedition, plus two Type C6F conventional lorries. Like those of the Pamir Group, the autochenilles of the China Group

The caterpillar cars used by the China Group were of the larger 2,442 cc six-cylinder C6F Type. Normally employed in France as military transport, all towed trailers. One was equipped as a radio communications vehicle, to send regular signals to André Citroën who waited for news at the expedition's headquarters in Paris.

were specially adapted and equipped as radio, cinema, workshop and mess cars, and were manned by ten driver-mechanics accompanied by the engineer Charles Brull (Director of the Citroën laboratories), the cinematographer Georges Specht, the archaeologist Jean Carl, the naturalist André Reymond, the doctor Robert Delastre and the radio specialist Roger Kervizic. But it was also planned that, en route, two other Europeans resident in China would join the party. The first of these extraordinary characters was the multilingual White Russian civil engineer Vladimir Petropavlosky, usually known as 'Petro' (who later took up British citizenship, joined the British Army and became a sort of James Bond figure in the shadowy world of espionage). The other was no less a personage than the French geologist, palaeontologist, philosopher, mystic and freethinker, Père Pierre Teilhard de Chardin (1881–1955). A Jesuit priest, he had lived and worked as a missionary in China for many years and was partly responsible for the discovery of *Homo Sinanthropus*, the prehistoric Peking Man. Long after the Citroën mission, his theological unorthodoxy led him to develop the concept of the noosphere, the unconscious union of thought among human beings, a doctrine that was regarded as heretical by the Catholic Church. During his lifetime, his superiors placed an embargo on his philosophical work, and so his famous book *The Phenomenon of Man*, a seminal work setting out his transcendental studies, remained unpublished until after his death.

A 1,628 cc four-cylinder-engined Type P17 Citroën-Kegresse caterpillar car bivouaced near Beirut, at the start of the Citroën Trans-Asian expedition in March 1931. Note the Stars and Stripes flown alongside the Tricolore, *in recognition of the participation of the National Geographic Society of the USA.*

Eventually, all were ready at their departure points, and early on the morning of 14 April 1931, Haardt's party started up their caterpillar cars to set out from Beirut for Kabul, travelling via Damascus, Baghdad, Tehran, Herat and Kandahar, across terrain that was reminiscent of their earlier journeys. After leaving Kabul on 14 June, the expedition made a south-easterly detour across the Afghan high plateau before descending through the Jalalabad basin, where, for the first time, the explorers felt on their cheeks the hot breath of a wind blowing up from the Indian plains like the blast from an open furnace door. When the thermometer rose to 50°C, the petrol vaporised in the tanks and the cars began to lose power. And the nights seemed even hotter than the days, for then the rocks gave out their stored-up heat like mighty radiators.

Early one morning towards the end of June, the rough track through the Khyber Pass suddenly gave way to a proper, macadamised highway, and Haardt and his men found themselves at the North-West Frontier post of Landi Khana, the gateway to British India. Here an immaculately turned-out Gurkha guard officered by an Englishman formed up and presented arms in welcome. Over drinks at the guard post, the party were invited to luncheon in the officers' mess at the nearby Landi Kotal Fort, where the garrison commander, Brigadier-General Sandeman, was awaiting their arrival, along with Colonel Gabriel. The expedition's diarist Georges Lefevre recorded that at the sunbaked entrance to the Fort – a place which evidently had seen much heavy fighting – they were met by Colonel Gabriel accompanied by General Sandeman and his staff, together with a guard of honour formed by the two regiments of the garrison, Rattray's Sikhs and the Gordon Highlanders, the latter parading in full Highland dress together with its Pipes and Drums. 'Their music had not the wild frenzy of that of the Afghans, but was a more restrained manifestation of the same warlike tribal spirit,' the bemused Frenchman observed.

After lunch, but not before many farewell toasts had been drunk, the expedition set off again eastwards on the road to Peshawar. Here Haardt took advantage of the hospitality of the officers of the Khyber Rifles and the Royal Air Force, which placed its workshops and engineering resources at his disposal, making possible certain technical adjustments and repairs to the vehicles. Then, after passing through the Punjab to Rawalpindi, the caterpillar cars began the slow, laborious climb up through the foothills of the Himalayas, to Srinagar, the capital of the state of Kashmir, where they were welcomed by the British Resident, his Highness the Maharajah Sir Hari Singh. Srinagar, the 'Venice of India', lies on the shores of a lake more than 5,000 feet above sea level, and was renowned as a pleasure resort for British officers and officials in India, who found in its cool mountain climate and its famous houseboats and floating hotels a refuge from the heat and dust of the plains. The Maharajah of Kashmir had invited the members of the expedition to be his guests during their stay in his capital, and Haardt and his men enjoyed a brief few days of relaxation in one of these luxuriously appointed houseboats, waited upon by a staff of fifty Sikh servants, impressive in their scarlet turbans and upright, martial bearing. One afternoon, they were entertained at an official garden party held in the world-

famed Shalimar Garden, the impressive setting of the ancient palace of the
Mogul emperors. Even so, they had little time to enjoy the polo, golf, tennis,
shooting and fishing for which the resort was acclaimed. For in spite of its social
and sporting attractions, Srinagar was but the starting point of the truly arduous
and serious part of their mission. The difficulties and dangers of a journey
across the Himalayas lay ahead, and a constant reminder of their impending
exertions rested in the stockpile of food, fuel and equipment, including steel
hawsers and oxygen cylinders, sent out from Paris via Bombay and Lahore, and
which was now stacked beside their camp.

Poring over the maps provided by the British, Haardt began to realise just how
difficult a task he had set himself. His aim was to carry on up the trail over the
13,775 ft-high Burzil Pass to Gilgit, and there to connect with his original
planned route to Kashgar through the Kharakoram range, on the track that
debouched from the Wakhir Pass, a journey he estimated would take him at least
forty-five days to complete. Although local opinion maintained that it would be
quite impossible to take a vehicle beyond Gilgit, Haardt believed that it could be
done, and that he would still be able to arrive in Kashgar on schedule, to make
the planned reunion with Victor Point's China Group on or around 20 July. The
Pamir Group's caterpillar cars had been specially designed so that they could be

*Travelling from west to east on the first leg of its journey, the Pamir Group convoy crossed the plains
of Iraq and Persia, heading for Tehran. On arrival there at the end of April 1931, Haardt and his
men were given a ceremonial welcome by the Shah.*

progressively lightened by stripping them down bit by bit to their basic engine and chassis; if the worse came to the worst, they could even be dismantled entirely and carried over difficult ground by pack-mules. But it wasn't so much a problem of the terrain as a problem of logistics, Colonel Gabriel pointed out. A forty-five-day march at these altitudes called for a minimum weight of 1,000 lb of baggage for each European – food, warm clothing, sleeping bags, tents and other camping equipment – to say nothing of the fuel and spares required for the vehicles. It therefore followed that to support Haardt's party, consisting as it did of twenty-three Europeans, French and British, it would need over 400 men or 200 pack-horses to carry the huge weight of supplies involved – 10 tons or more, not counting the scientific equipment and cameras and the fuel and spares for the cars. If all seven of the vehicles were to attempt the trip, the number of porters and animals would have to be doubled, an impossible congregation to supply and sustain in these conditions. In any event, government regulations stipulated that the number of Europeans permitted to cross the mountains in any one party was limited to five.

The only possible solution was to divide the expedition into three smaller groups, each travelling to Gilgit separately, and with their successive departures staggered at intervals of eight days, so that the second party could use the porters and ponies sent back by the first, and so forth. This meant that the last party would not arrive at Kashgar until twenty-four days after the first. Moreover, only two vehicles and their drivers would be able to continue; the rest would have to return to France immediately. Baggage was to be limited to just 600 lb per person, which must have been a hardship for the fastidious, immaculately-dressed Haardt, who normally insisted on a clean change of collar and shirt every day, no matter where he was travelling. To add to his worries, on 29 June a disturbing radio message was received, reporting that Point's mission had encountered fighting between Chinese forces and Muslim rebels in Sinkiang, and that their arrival at Kashgar would be delayed.

On 12 July, Haardt's party – the second – set off on the slow climb up into the mountains and over the Burzil Pass with the remaining two vehicles, the Golden Scarab and the Silver Crescent. Three-and-a-half months had elapsed since they had set out from Beirut, during which time they had covered some 3,500 miles, But the next 500 miles would take them almost as long again to traverse. On one occasion, it took ten hours to cover a bare 4 miles. Recent heavy rain had turned the rivers into raging torrents, destroying bridges and washing away the track, while landslides had reduced the surface on the treacherous 45° slopes to a scree as loose as shingle on a beach. In places, the trail passed along ledges only 4 feet wide – 7 inches narrower than the track of the vehicles – with sheer cliffs rising above on one side and yawning drops into chasms on the other. In the Burzil Pass itself, although it was summer, 20 feet of snow had fallen, so that the party had to inch their way along at less than 1 m.p.h., continually probing the surface ahead for ice caverns beneath the crust, into which the cars might suddenly plunge. At most river crossings, it was judged necessary for the porters to lug the 2 ton cars across the rickety wooden bridges with hawsers. Since it was

Arriving literally on the top of the world, the expedition's second vehicle, the Silver Crescent, reached the summit of the Burzil Pass at the end of July. Ironically, this achievement marked the crest of André Citroën's fortunes. From now on, the path would be downhill.

far too dangerous for the driver to remain at the wheel, each vehicle had to be steered from behind with ropes arranged like reins. On one occasion, the track gave way entirely beneath the Golden Scarab, leaving it suspended on a precipice overhanging the River Astor. It took five hours of improvised engineering with jacks, crowbars and winches to haul it back onto solid ground.

But by dint of sheer perseverance and perspiration, on 21 July Haardt's party finally reached the village of Astor, perched high on a pinnacle overlooking the junction of two mighty gorges, a place so remote and ringed by towering peaks that no wheeled vehicle – not even a cart – had ever been seen there before. Here, the natives fled at the sight of the caterpillar cars crawling slowly along the track, frightened lest the mountain spirits should be offended at the sound of their engines rending the silence of the sacred peaks. Pressing on towards Gilgit, and now on the steep downhill slopes, Haardt was still optimistic that the cars could get through under their own power, even though, at these altitudes, their engines only developed half their normal output. Far more worrying was the fact that it was now three weeks since any news had been received from Victor Point. But further along the valley, they came to a place where the entire mountainside had collapsed, undermined by the rain, leaving a surface of loose rubble and shale so unstable that the merest footstep would send a shower of

In attempting to cross the Burzil Pass, the expedition followed a mule track where no wheeled vehicle had ever travelled before. Near Astor the rocky track gave way beneath the leading vehicle, leaving it suspended precariously over a gorge. It took five hours of back-breaking work to rebuild the path beneath the Golden Scarab before Haardt and his men could continue.

Now reduced to just two vehicles, the convoy was slowed down near Gilgit by unexpected early snowfalls. At this altitude – over 4,500 metres, higher than any car had ever reached before – the lack of oxygen affected both men and machines. At one point it took the caterpillar cars eighteen hours to creep a mere 8 km across the snow and scree.

stones sliding down into the ravine a thousand feet below. Before this obstacle could be crossed, a new path would have to be built. Even with the two cars now stripped down to the barest minimum, the going was so perilous that it soon became necessary to dismantle them entirely. At dawn on 25 July, a start was made to divide them into 60 lb loads which could be carried by the ponies and mules; by the afternoon, the ground was covered with engines, gearboxes, wheels, tracks and brake-drums, arranged in rows, as if in the Citroën factory. By 27 July, the landslide had been passed and the cars reassembled and restarted. By 2 August, they were once again rolling along down the broad valley of the Indus, making progress at an encouraging rate, in conditions which, after the previous struggles, seemed almost too good to be true. Two days later the convoy arrived at Gilgit, where the whole population awaited its arrival. It had taken almost 1,200 hours of continuous work to cross the mountains; the astonishing endurance and tenacity of the expedition had so impressed the natives of the region that hundreds gathered simply to watch the wheels and tracks of the caterpillar cars revolve.

Unfortunately, Haardt's satisfaction and relief at achieving his objective was to be short-lived. At the Gilgit telegraph station there awaited a telegram from Audouin-Dubreuil, despatched from Peshwari on 25 July. Following eight days behind him, the third party – which carried the Pamir Group's single wireless set – had at last received the long-awaited radio signal from their fellows in the China Group, now in the independent Chinese province of Sinkiang, which had been relayed via Hong Kong. The news was not good. Victor Point and his team had also run into trouble and were seriously delayed. Worse than that, their path had actually been diverted. Far from nearing Kashgar to wait for the Pamir Group, as planned, they were now detained at Urumchi, 800 miles to the north. What had happened?

Why were they stranded there, so far off course, and in the wrong direction? There was no way of telling. The only thing that could be said with any certainty was that the proposed reunion of the two motor columns was now completely impossible. Clearly, it was pointless to waste time and energy continuing the journey over the Hunza Gorges and the Karakorum Mountains with the cars; they would run out of fuel long before reaching Urumchi. Instead, it was imperative to press onwards by the fastest means and route, to find out what misfortune had befallen the China Group, even if that meant abandoning the original purpose of the mission. So, to make the rendezvous with Point – who obviously needed urgent assistance – there was only one sensible course of action: Haardt and Audouin-Dubreuil, together with the scientists, photographer and cinema crew, would have to continue on horseback, leaving the vehicles and their drivers behind. Of the two cars which had come so far, the Silver Crescent was presented to the government of India and left at Gilgit (where it remains today) in commemoration of the first motor car journey undertaken in the region. The other autochenille – Haardt's own Golden Scarab – was dismantled and taken back to Paris. Formerly in the Citroën Collection, it can now be seen at the le Mans automobile museum.

In July 1931 the members of the China Group (heading from east to west) were held prisoners at Urumchi by the warlord Marshal King. The tracks of the caterpillar cars were removed to prevent their captors from driving the vehicles away and leaving the Frenchmen stranded without transport.

But if Haardt was disappointed by the breakdown in communications between the two parties and the consequent abandonment of the autochenilles, his anxiety was nothing in comparison to the worry that André Citroën experienced while waiting for news in Paris that summer. When planning the expedition he had anticipated that, thanks to the miraculous new medium of radio, he would have no problems whatsoever in maintaining daily contact with both groups on the other side of the world, passing instructions and exchanging information through the airwaves as easily as though across a conference table at the Quai de Javel. For him, radio was not so much a useful tool of management and control as an instrument of democracy, allowing an instantaneous dialogue linking the citizens of every nation and not merely just their rulers. By transcending the geographical and political barriers that had prevented the fast and free exchange of ideas in the past, it would surely lead to a new age of international understanding and cooperation, he believed. Citroën had been the first motor manufacturer in the world to offer his customers the entertainment of car radios – the Radioën was introduced in 1928 – and had even considered starting up a commercial radio station of his own, a sort of prototype Radio Luxembourg. That this wonder of modern science had failed and that he and his colleagues had been thrown back into a reliance on telegrams must have been intolerably frustrating to the French technocrat, particularly as he was shortly due to embark on a visit to the USA, a journey which would place him even further out of touch with events in Central Asia. He had already despatched three cars by rail across Russia as a gift for the local warlord, Marshal King, to smooth the path of the expedition through the province of Sinkiang. Now, short of pursuing the matter through diplomatic channels, there was nothing more he could do to influence events or intervene on behalf of his colleagues stranded at Urumchi, well beyond the farthest reaches of his own commercial empire and, indeed, beyond the borders of the civilised world.

Marooned in Sinkiang, Victor Point and his party had been experiencing difficulties equally as great as those encountered by Haardt, but of a different kind. Whereas the Pamir Group had been forced to overcome almost insuperable natural barriers, the obstacles placed in the path of the China Group were almost all man-made. Indeed, since leaving Tientsin on 6 April 1931, the expedition had suffered from repeated setbacks. Even before they reached Peking, their cars began to break down due to a technical problem with the adjustment of the track-band pulleys. Their entire stock of spares was soon used up, and on reaching the Chinese capital they were obliged to cable André Citroën in Paris to send a supply of replacements by rail. On 24 April, Point's party reached the Great Wall of China at Kalgan, where it was to await the arrival of the new track bands and also the delegation of eight Chinese scientists which was to accompany the mission. Although the tracks were soon delivered, the wait was to be a long one, and it was not until 24 May that the Chinese arrived and the caterpillar cars were able to continue on their way to Mongolia. 'In China it does not pay to be in a hurry, and travellers who are in haste never arrive,' Father Teilhard de Chardin prophetically observed, with all the sang-froid of the true philosopher.

By 27 May, they had reached the fringes of the Gobi Desert, travelling across roadless terrain at a rate of over 70 miles per day, almost ten times faster than the camel trains they passed. Loaded up with over 1,800 gallons of petrol for the 1,250 mile crossing, the expedition experienced the continual risk of fires ignited by the incessant electrical storms overhead. On 2 June, they were halted by a violent sandstorm, and again on 6 June, when their petrol cans began exploding in the intense heat, destroying their reserves. Now they had just enough to travel 120 miles, yet the next supply dump, established earlier by Petro, was at Suchow, twice that distance away. While the others halted, Point and Petro were forced to go ahead to collect more fuel. Fortunately, the supply dump – buried underground – had not been interfered with, and on 15 June all nine vehicles entered Suchow. Like the Sahara, the Gobi had been conquered by Citroën cars.

It was to take them five days to cover the 250 miles between Suchow and the Sinkiang frontier, where, at the Min-Shui Pass, the Mongolian plateau gave way to rolling plains. On their way, they encountered ominous warnings of trouble to the West. Sure enough, when, on 28 June, they arrived at the outskirts of the oasis of Hami, they found the houses in flames and the villages abandoned. A revolt had broken out in Sinkiang, and evidence of fighting between Chinese troops and Muslim insurgents was all around them, including the distant sound of gunfire. According to Lefevre, over the next few days the horrified Europeans witnessed scenes of cruelty and carnage which, by their appalling barbarity, showed that Central Asia had scarcely changed since the days of Genghis Khan. To add to the unpleasantness, they also experienced constant friction with their passengers, the Chinese scientists, who refused to acknowledge Point's authority.

Fortunately, Hami itself was still in government hands. But on entering the city, Point was informed by the officer commanding the Chinese garrison that orders had been received from the Governor-General of Sinkiang, Marshal King Shu-Jen, that instead of being allowed to continue towards Aksu and Kashgar, as had been promised, they were to proceed under escort to Urumchi. In effect, the Marshal had revoked the permit of safe conduct through his province granted before the start of the mission. The reason given was that the expedition had been seen photographing scenes of fighting 'detrimental to the national dignity of China', but, in truth, Marshal King was upset because the gift of three motor cars offered at the outset by André Citroën had failed to arrive. The China Group, still including the Chinese scientists and observers, duly left Hami for Urumchi on 1 July, crossing through the infamous Turfan depression, a stifling hell-hole 85 feet below sea level, where the heat reached an intolerable 50°C.

Urumchi was reached on 19 July, but instead of entering the town and surrendering, Point gave orders that the mission should set up camp outside the walls and, to prevent the seizure of its vehicles, to immobilise them by removing the caterpillar tracks. Here, with its passports and official recognition cancelled by the Nanking government as well as by the regime in Sinkiang, the China Group was to remain under virtual arrest for forty-three days, forbidden to use its radio to communicate with the outside world. Throughout this period of captivity, the only consolation for Point and his comrades was that they had at last escaped from the suffocating presence of the Chinese delegation, which had returned eastwards.

Realising that without outside intervention they could well remain stranded at Urumchi for the rest of their lives, like a number of other unfortunate Europeans caught up in the civil war, Point and his men put their minds to devising a clever ruse to get word of their plight to Haardt, who was then in the middle of the Himalayas and unaware that he and his group had already been barred from entering Sinkiang. Pretending to stage a party to celebrate the centenary of the founding of the Third French Republic, on 24 July they raised their radio aerial, disguised as a flagpole flying the *Tricolore*, and transmitted a clandestine message in Morse code. When their guards demanded to know why they had started an engine at night, they explained that they needed a motor generator to play their gramophone (this, of course, was actually the wind-up type). So while the Frenchmen appeared to be listening to a record of the '*Marseillaise*' blaring out across the camp, unknown to Marshal King and their captors, their radio was actually sending out the vital signal that was picked up by listening posts around the world, including the French sloop *Regulus* at Hong

Kong. This, of course, was the brief and somewhat cryptic message ultimately received by Haardt at Gilgit ten days later, on 4 August.

But serious as were the troubles of the expedition, those of Marshal King and the Chinese authorities were graver still. By now, the rebellion around Hami had swelled to such a level that the very continuance of Chinese supremacy in Sinkiang was threatened. The news from the fighting zone was one long tale of disaster – a government army of 8,000 soldiers had been slaughtered by the rebels. Without reinforcements to head them off, soon the Muslims would be at Urumchi and in total control of the region. Yet, with telegraph lines cut, communication with the Chinese capital was impossible. Now the boot was on the other foot, and Marshal King needed help from the French. On 20 August, he summoned Point to his headquarters. 'Though your passports have been cancelled by Nanking, I shall authorise your chief M. Haardt to enter Sinkiang – but on one condition only. You must send your wireless expert to assist us in establishing radio communications with the capital,' the Marshal declared. Thus it was agreed that a week or so later – on 6 September – four caterpillar cars and their crews would be released from detention and allowed to set out for Aksou, in order to meet Haardt and the remnants of the Pamir Group coming up from Kashgar.

Such was the efficiency of the international telegraph system in the early thirties (a facility which Victor Point was now once again empowered to use), his leader received news of this development the very same day via the British Consul-General in Kashgar, who had received a wire from André Citroën in Paris who, in his turn, had heard from Urumchi via Peking. At the time, Haardt was passing through Misgar, a tiny village lying between the Karakorum Mountains and the Hindu Kush, en route to Kashgar and only two days' march from the Sinkiang border. The new situation, as Haardt understood it, was that his entry visa into Marshal King's territory, cancelled over a month before, had been renewed, and that he and his companions were now authorised to continue their march to Aksou and Urumchi, providing that the three Citroën cars and other equipment despatched from Tientsin for the Chinese Marshal on 3 April, and which had evidently fallen into the hands of the Muslim rebels, would be replaced immediately by a new consignment of vehicles sent directly from France via Moscow. In fact, this request was already being complied with by André Citroën. This was just as well, for an early autumn snowfall in the Burzil Pass had already ruled out a return through India. When the third relay, including Audouin-Dubreuil, caught up with him, and the remnants of the Pamir Group were reassembled, they would all be free to proceed – not, alas, with the caterpillar cars (which they had already been forced to abandon) but with horses, mules and camels instead. The road to China lay open before them.

And so it happened that the reunion of the two groups finally took place in the village of Islam-Bai, 12 miles outside Aksu, on 8 October. Then, when Haardt and Point together reached the camp at Urumchi, on 27 October, the whole expedition was gathered together under the same roof for the first time since leaving Paris seven months before. The expedition was now three months behind schedule in its journey, and the bitter weather of the Central Asian winter was only weeks away. Yet the task still remained to escape from the trap of Urumchi, by gaining permission from Marshal King to begin their return to Peking, a journey that would take at least six weeks.

In summing up the situation in his diary, Georges Lefevre wrote that, for half the united expedition, the journey so far had been a fabulous adventure, an odyssey over the roof of the world, providing, in a whole procession of enchanting scenes, a glimpse of heaven. But for the other, it had been a vision of hell, a nightmare march through suffocating heat and dust, punctuated only by encounters with tyrannical warlords and bloodthirsty brigands, in a landscape littered with dead, decaying animals and headless human corpses. Even so, within the camp there was now a general sense of optimism that the problems were over, and that at last it would be possible to get on with the mission and undertake some serious scientific and archaeological work. But it was not to be. Despite several meetings with the inscrutable ruler of Sinkiang, including an official banquet, the promised travel permits failed to materialise; Marshal King was far too busy with important affairs of State to attend to such trifling matters, it appeared. Haardt was now seriously worried at the thought of crossing the frozen heart of Asia in the depths of winter, and ordered preparations to insulate the vehicles with felt and the crews with sheepskins, both having started the trip equipped for semi-tropical conditions only.

The deadlock in negotiations was not broken until 20 November 1931, when the replacement cars arrived from Paris. A week later, a communal passport was issued by Marshal King, and at last the expedition was at liberty to depart. Almost five months had been wasted in the frustrations and ennui of Urumchi, during which time French diplomats had intervened constantly in the capitals of Europe, the USSR and Asia to overcome the caprices of a Chinese provincial governor and secure the release of the expedition, without success. Ironically, six months later, its gaoler and tormentor Marshal King also left his capital in a hurry, when a fresh invasion of Muslim rebels sparked off a general revolt among the populace of Sinkiang, and Urumchi was sacked.

Early on the morning of 12 February 1932, on the 315th day since Haardt departed from Beirut, his column of caterpillar cars arrived, at last, on the outskirts of the Chinese capital and passed under a massive archway – the Western Gate of the Forbidden City of Peking. As they drew up outside the Winter Palace, to be met by almost all of the Europeans living in Peking, the personnel of the Pamir Group calculated that they had covered precisely 7,219 miles in their crossing of Central Asia. As Victor Point had foreseen, the return journey across the Mongolian Plateau and the Gobi Desert had been an ordeal by ice. The cold was so extreme that hot soup turned solid within minutes when ladled into metal bowls. Similarly, even boiling water froze immediately when poured into the radiators, and it had proved impossible to turn off the engines, in case they were immediately transformed into useless blocks of solid steel and

On 12 February 1932 Haardt and his men arrived in Peking at the end of their 12,000 km trek.
But for the leader, the epic journey was soon to end in tragedy.

ice. When the cars broke down, as they frequently did, the mechanics had been forced to handle metal parts in 33° of frost, or to free frozen brake drums with blowtorches. At one point, it had taken them eight hours to cover 12 miles. At another, the car bearing Dr Maynard Owen William's collection of photographic plates had plunged through the ice of a frozen canal, but mercifully, no damage had been done to his work. Then finally, almost within sight of its destination, the mission had been forced to fight off a gang of marauding bandits, intent on stealing its equipment and provisions. All in all, during its eleven months of travel, the Citroën Central Asian Expedition had amassed over 5,000 photographs and 200,000 feet of film, plus many valuable drawings, ethnological documents, mineralogical specimens, objects of art and archaeology and a collection of unusual flora and fauna; despite all the setbacks it had encountered, its reputation as a serious scientific mission was assured.

After so long spent beyond the borders of civilisation, the luxuries of the great hotels of Peking must have come as a welcome change of habitat for the Frenchmen. But Haardt's stay there was to last only fifteen days. For by now, after three such missions, the explorers had become nomadic travellers, possessed by a restless urge to move ever onwards and unable to settle down. It was therefore decided that, as the next stage of its journey, the expedition's caterpillar cars would proceed from Shanghai by sea to Haiphong, calling in at Hong Kong en route. In Indo-China, they would explore a route between Hanoi and Saigon. There was even talk of continuing further through Siam, Burma, India and Southern Persia, and to rejoin the Baghdad road which would take them back to their original starting point at Beirut.

However, on 3 March, while in Shanghai (which was then in a state of turmoil, with fighting having broken out between the Chinese and the Japanese), Georges-Marie Haardt complained of feeling unwell. The expedition's medical man, Dr Dalastre, diagnosed a slight chill, an opinion confirmed by an English specialist resident in the city. Haardt had suffered from bronchial trouble since childhood, and the severely cold weather he had been through recently had clearly affected his chest, yet the illness was nothing that a few days rest would not put right. But after landing in Hong Kong on 12 March, in very cold and foggy conditions, Haardt was obliged to take to his hotel bed and summon the Governor's medical adviser, Professor Gerrard, who diagnosed a severe case of influenza and prescribed a rest of at least three weeks. On Tuesday 15 March pneumonia developed in the lower lobe of the left lung, and Haardt's temperature rose to 40°C. During the night, he experienced difficulty in breathing, and oxygen was administered. Towards 3 a.m. on 16 March, although his temperature went down, his breathing became slower and more feeble, and by 3.40 a.m. it was all over.

Was this dreadful blow an act of the gods – the revenge of the mountain spirits, as the superstitious people of the high Himalayas had forewarned? To André Citroën, it must have seemed as much. Learning of the terrible news by telegram in Paris later that day, he was stricken with despair at the loss of his closest friend and counsellor. Immediately, he despatched a reply: 'The man is dead but his work lives on. Bring back to France the body of your leader. I share your grief.'

And so the speech of congratulations which M. Paquier, the Governor-General of French Indo-China, had prepared for the welcome at Hanoi on 17 March was hastily rewritten into one of condolence. The day which was to have been a time of celebrations and rejoicing became an occasion of mourning and regret. Conceived in a mood of optimism and idealism that was typical of Citroën, the Croisière Jaune undertaking had turned out to be simultaneously a triumph and a tragedy. It had been a failure, in that nothing had gone according to schedule and that it had proved impossible for even a single caterpillar car to cross the Asian continent from coast to coast as planned. Yet, equally, it had been a resounding success. Thanks to the indomitable courage of Haardt and his men, an initial defeat had been reversed, and a salutary victory of human virtue over adversity had been achieved. The Citroën Central Asian Mission had set out with high hopes, in the expectancy that it would encounter nothing but benign weather and benevolent human behaviour. But the very opposite occurred, and it was subjected to the harshness and treachery of both man and nature in equal measure. Nevertheless, due principally to the perseverance and tenacity of its leaders, it had never once despaired of reaching its objective and of attaining its principal aims, albeit by an unforeseen course and at an unexpectedly heavy cost.

On 4 April 1932, a year to the day since the mission departed from Beirut, the members of the Citroën Central Asian Expedition and their vehicles lined the quay at Saigon to see Haardt's coffin placed aboard the steamer *Felix-Roussel*, bound for France. One month later, on 29 April, the boat anchored in the Marseilles Roads. A small man, dressed entirely in black and wearing a bowler hat, slowly clambered up the companion ladder and went below. André Citroën, who so recently, and in the very same place, had said farewell to Haardt for the last time, was now the first to salute the return to France of the mortal remains of the friend that he had lost – the trusted colleague who had fought beside him for fifteen years and whose life had been expended so tragically in his service.

Finally, on 30 November 1932, a distinguished gathering assembled in the great lecture hall of the Sorbonne in Paris to formally welcome home the surviving members of the Citroën Central Asian Expedition. The current President of the Republic, Monsieur Albert Lebrun, and two ex-presidents, Messieurs Millerand and Doumergue, were joined by high-ranking military and civilian notables, including Maréchal Pétain, the Generals Gamelin, Weygand and Gouraud, Vice-Admiral Durand-Viel, the Chief of Staff of the French Navy, and Monseigneur de Guebriant, head of the Diplomatic Service (and, of course, Major-General Sir Ernest Swinton of Citroën-Kegresse Ltd), to hear the President of the French Geographical Society award André Citroën the society's Gold Medal. In his speech of acceptance, Citroën rendered homage to the memory of his deeply-mourned friend, Georges-Marie Haardt, praising his inexhaustible patience and attention to detail and thanking all who had contributed – each in his own sphere – to an achievement without parallel in the history of geographical exploration. (The English version of the film of the Croisière Jaune, directed by André Sauvage and produced by Leon Poiret, was premiered at a Gala Performance in aid of the Royal National Lifeboat Institution, held at the Plaza Cinema, London, on Tuesday 13 November 1934, in the presence of HRH The Prince of Wales.)

According to the French author Sylvain Reiner, some three years later another box from China addressed to André Citroën arrived at the port of Marseilles – a large crate containing numerous *objets d'art* and Oriental rugs which G.-M. Haardt had purchased before his death, as additions to his own extensive collection and as presents for his friend and patron. The shipment of these treasures had been long delayed by the vicissitudes of war and the lethargy of the Chinese customs authorities; in fact, before they could be imported into France, a hefty sum in outstanding customs duties remained to be paid. So great had been the change in the fortunes of the Citroën firm and family over the intervening months that the money could not be found.

CHAPTER EIGHT

The Lord of the Ice

Besides the famous Croisière Jaune trans-Asian mission (and somewhat overshadowed by it), two other little-known but none the less interesting and important expeditions employing Citroën-Kegresse vehicles took place in the thirties. The first, staged in 1934, was an attempt to cross the Rocky Mountains in Canada, privately organised and funded by Charles Eugène Bedaux (1887–1944), a multi-millionaire American business management expert who had made his fortune as a leading exponent of F.W. Taylor's time and motion study methods. Bedaux had already acquired extensive experience of operating these Citroën caterpillar cars in Morocco and Kenya as well as Canada, and now aimed to open up a road route to link Edmonton in Alberta with the territories of Yukon and Alaska. By promising the French motor magnate a rich return in publicity, he persuaded André Citroën to provide his expedition with five specially-equipped vehicles similar to those used on the Central Asian expedition, based on the Type C4G car and powered by the same 1,767 cc four-cylinder engine.

A vehicle of the Croisière Blanche expedition negotiates a 40% gradient in the Canadian Rockies during the autumn of 1934.

The column set out north-westwards from Edmonton in early July 1934 and soon reached Fort St John without problems. But then, as it entered virgin territory in the Rockies, freak weather conditions turned the venture into a disaster; incessant heavy rain for days on end caused the tracks through ravines to become raging torrents, and the normally firm terrain was churned into a quagmire of mud. First, one vehicle was lost while attempting to cross a river on a makeshift log raft; next, two more were submerged when a rocky path gave way and they tumbled into a ravine. Now there were just two left to transport twenty-eight men and all the expedition's material and supplies. Once above the 55th parallel, things turned from bad to worse, and the accompanying horses and ponies also began to suffer through the fatal combination of severe damp and frost, which affected their hooves. Further progress through this densely-forested, unmapped wilderness in such appalling conditions was impossible, and the mission – thereafter known to Citroënistes as the 'Croisière Blanche' – was abandoned with the onset of winter at the end of September. One autochenille was later recovered from beneath the snows and donated to a museum in Saskatoon, where it can still be seen today.

A shadowy – perhaps even shady – figure, Charles Bedaux later became world-famous for his other adventures. A French-born naturalised American, Bedaux had emigrated to the USA in 1908, where he made his fortune as a business efficiency consultant. Returning to live in France, he purchased the Château de Cande near Angers, which he renovated at vast expense to use as a base for his European activities. As these included extensive business interests in Germany, he quickly formed high-level contacts with its Nazi leaders, and had dealings with Hitler from the moment the dictator came to power in 1933. When King Edward VIII abdicated from the throne to marry the American divorcée Wallis Simpson, Bedaux offered the use of his château to the ex-king, and it was here that the marriage of the Duke and Duchess of Windsor (as the couple were subsequently known) took place in June 1937. Later, Bedaux became friendly with the Windsors, and it was he who arranged the unfortunate visit to Germany made by the Duke and Duchess in 1937. Bedaux's widely-dispersed interests gave him the ideal cover to undertake both industrial and political espionage, but whether or not he was actually a Nazi agent has never been proved. During the Occupation of France, he certainly acted as an intermediary between Vichy and Berlin. Consequently, at the end of the war he was arrested by the Americans on suspicion of treason and taken to Miami. He committed suicide in prison there while awaiting trial.

At the same time that this expedition was taking place in Canada, a second fleet of Citroën autochenilles was engaged on a mission of exploration and discovery in even more extreme conditions on the other side of the globe, in Antarctica. In September 1933, André Citroën received an urgent telegram from the American industrialist Vincent Bendix of the Bendix Corporation, one of Citroën's associates and suppliers. The message made an unusual request – or, more precisely, an intriguing business proposition. A privately organised and financed scientific and geographical expedition was on the point of leaving the USA bound for Antarctica, Bendix reported. Led by Rear-Admiral Richard

Evelyn Byrd (1888–1957), already renowned as the leading polar explorer of that era, this expedition was to be equipped with every possible modern convenience and device. But it still lacked proper motor transport, as there was simply no suitable design to be found anywhere in the USA. Could Citroën help in providing a vehicle for carrying men and supplies over snow and ice, Vincent Bendix asked – a vehicle similar to the caterpillar-tracked car that the French motor magnate used himself on his Alpine holidays? A photograph had recently appeared in the American press, showing André Citroën riding through the snow at Saint-Moritz in such a car, accompanied by his friend Charlie Chaplin.

If the mission was successful, Citroën would not only have the honour of being the constructor of the very first motor vehicle to reach the South Pole, Bendix promised. It was understood that Admiral Byrd intended to name any new mountains that the expedition discovered in honour of its sponsors, who included Bendix, Henry Ford, John D. Rockefeller and several other American millionaire industrialists and philanthropists. If Citroën would be good enough to join in the project, the Frenchman could be sure that his name would also go down in history, recorded forever as a topographical feature on the maps of the Antarctic continent.

André Citroën needed no further persuasion. His unique Citroën-Kegresse half-tracked automobiles had already been the first motor vehicles to cross the sands of the Sahara Desert, the jungles of Central Africa and the snows of the Himalayan mountains. Now there was a chance that they would also be the first to conquer the hostile climate of the Antarctic. Previous attempts to use automobiles in this harsh environment had failed, and the motor cars and tractors taken there earlier by Shackleton and Scott had all proved useless. Even the Ford Snowmobile employed by Byrd on his first Antarctic expedition in 1929 had broken down after running a mere 75 miles.

Once again, Citroën succumbed to the promise of cheap publicity. Without hesitation, he agreed to provide Byrd with a pair of 2 ton lorries powered by the same engine as Citroën's current six-cylinder saloon car, modified with Kegresse rubber-band caterpillar tracks at the rear and steerable skis at the front. On 14 September he telegraphed his response to Messrs Bendix and Byrd in the USA: 'I am delighted to put at your disposal my autochenilles equipped identically to those which have already proved capable of traversing deep snow in Switzerland stop if you also require a full inventory of spare parts and the services of a specialist driver and mechanic, I will be glad to provide these also, free of charge.'

An answer from Admiral Byrd was received the following day: 'Warmest thanks for your invaluable collaboration and contribution in offering the use of your snow tractors stop I am honoured at the thought of carrying the prestige of the Citroën name to the Antarctic, but we will not require the assistance of your staff stop we already have a number of excellent mechanics among our party.'

With characteristic energy and drive, Citroën immediately put the skills and resources of the Citroën company into top gear to fulfil the request. Just a couple of months later, on 18 November 1933, two specially-built vehicles

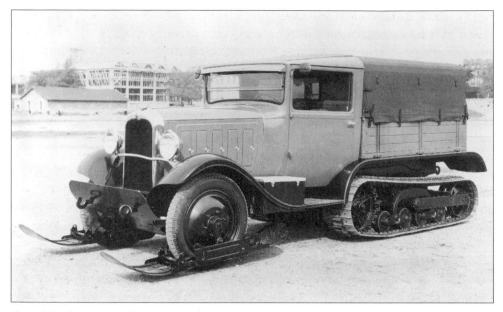

One of the three Type P15N six-cylinder Citroën-Kegresse lorries presented by André Citroën to Admiral Byrd, before its despatch from Paris to the Antarctic in November 1933.

painted in red with a yellow stripe (the Citroën factory colours) were duly despatched from Paris, for collection by the expedition in Wellington, New Zealand. In fact, the freighting arrangements via Brest, Newhaven and London Docks were handled by Citroën Cars Ltd at Slough. With the autochenilles went a goodwill message signed by André Citroën personally: 'To Rear-Admiral Richard E. Byrd, with my very best wishes for the success of your great enterprise, which you are conducting in the interests of science and for the benefit of all humanity'.

But no sooner had the vehicles departed when, on 22 October, Citroën received yet another telegram from Admiral Byrd: 'We have decided to attempt a complete crossing of the Antarctic continent using your caterpillar cars stop if successful, this will be an unprecedented achievement in the annals of geographical exploration stop can you please send a third tractor to New Zealand, in time to catch our steamer which departs for the Antarctic on January 5th stop with cordial greetings and our sincere thanks for all that you have done for us – signed R.E. Byrd.' André Citroën could hardly refuse. And so, in another remarkable demonstration of the organisational abilities for which he was justly famous, a third caterpillar car was on its way to New Zealand within the space of a mere six days.

But despite the superhuman efforts made on his behalf by Automobiles Citroën, nothing more was heard from Byrd at the Quai de Javel until August 1934, when another telegram was received from America, announcing that a radio message had been picked up from the Admiral's base at Little America, on the Ross Ice Shelf. This communication reported that the Citroën vehicles had already made history by being the first to travel 275 miles inland into the interior of the Antarctic continent, enduring temperatures ranging between 20° and 70°C below zero, without the slightest mechanical damage or engine malfunction.

If the waiting Frenchman hoped that this news marked the successful completion of the first stage in the trans-Antarctic trip, he was to be disappointed. Byrd's plans had changed once again, and the planned assault on the South Pole had been abandoned. In March 1934, he had ordered a party to set up an advance weather station, well below the 80th parallel, some 123 miles south-east of the Little America base. Here, he proposed to become the first man to endure a winter in the Polar interior – a five-month solitary stay which would include forty days and nights of continous darkness. From this tiny hut buried in the ice he would carry out meteorological observations and transmit a daily weather report back to base.

Thus, the work of the Citroën half-tracks, as reported to Paris, had been to lay a chain of supply dumps en route to another base or depot located at the foot of Mount McKinley, nearly 230 miles east of Little America. These were to be used to supply the traditional dog-sled teams and the fleet of three aircraft and an autogyro that Byrd had also brought with him on the mission for use when he mounted an alternative foray in the spring. This was to be an exploration of an

After being freighted via England and New Zealand, the lorries were unloaded on their arrival at Admiral Byrd's base on the Ross Ice Shelf in early 1934.

Two of the Citroën vehicles set out across the Ross Ice Shelf to supply Admiral Byrd's advance camp at Mount McKinley, thus becoming the first motor vehicles to reach the interior of the Antarctic continent.

unmapped coastal region near the Bay of Whales, which the American later christened Marie Byrd Land.

Although at the age of just forty-five Byrd was the youngest ever admiral in the US Navy, he was much more an aviator than a seaman by experience and inclination, and preferred to travel by air wherever possible. Born into a famous Southern family, he had graduated from the United States Naval Academy at Annapolis in 1912. But then, during the First World War, he had learned to fly, and thus had embarked on a lifelong love affair with the aeroplane, making his career in the navy as a pioneer of marine flight. In 1926, he became the first man to fly over the North Pole, and the following year he made the third non-stop transatlantic flight. In fact, Byrd had already led one mission to Antarctica in 1928–30 (ultimately, he made five), in the course of which he had established his Little America base and completed the double by becoming the first man to fly over the South Pole also.

Meanwhile, by July 1934 it was becoming obvious from the spasmodic, partly incoherent radio signals received from Byrd by his base camp at Little America that something was seriously wrong at the weather station. In fact, the combined effect of carbon monoxide fumes leaking from an oil stove with a faulty flue and exhaust gases escaping from a petrol generator was slowly poisoning the Admiral to death. Even if he had been aware of the intoxicating gases, the explorer would not have been able to remedy the situation by turning off either source, since the temperature outside the hut was hovering around minus 71°C.

There was only one solution. As it was still far too cold to use a dog-sled, on 4

August a three-man party set out through the freezing darkness in one of the Citroën half-tracks to rescue their leader, who by now was in a deep state of stupor, close to death. In the appalling conditions of the Antarctic midwinter, progress was almost impracticable. In the extreme winds and continuous blizzards which made the blackness of the endless night seem even more impenetrable, it was impossible to see the marker flags, so navigation had to be by dead reckoning. For this, the navigator was forced to lie with his compass on a metal-free sled towed behind the Citroën, signalling necessary changes in course to the driver by means of electrical switches linked to a panel of lights on the caterpillar tractor's dashboard. At the same time, the distance travelled was carefully measured by another man lying on the sled.

After crawling virtually non-stop at an average speed of 2 mph for almost a week, the rescue party reached the weather station at midnight on 11 August. They were just in time. Indeed, they found Byrd so emaciated and debilitated that they were unable to return immediately, and had to wait at the weather station for a further two months. It was not until 14 October that the Admiral was strong enough to make the trip back to Little America, by aircraft of course, just as he had arrived.

The following year, 1935, Byrd abandoned all thoughts of a motorised trans-continental land crossing and returned to the USA, to be hailed in the press as 'Lord of the Ice' or 'The Admiral of the Ends of the Earth', and welcomed as a national hero. Regrettably, however, the Citroën vehicles were left behind, and were never returned to Paris for inspection and display as agreed. Moreover, although the rugged robustness and dependability of these autochenilles undoubtedly saved the explorer's life, the promised films, publicity and personal endorsements also failed to materialise. But by then, André Citroën was past caring.

One aspect of the American expedition did go according to plan, however. During his explorations by air in the Antarctic, Byrd discovered several hitherto unknown mountains which he promptly named after his principal benefactors: Edsel Ford, John D. Rockefeller, William Ralston of the Purina Dog-Chow company, and William Horlick, the malted-milk drink king. The name of another generous supporter was unfortunately forgotten, and thus there is no Mount Double Chevron (twin-peaked or otherwise) towering above the polar snows today, to act as a memorial to André Citroën's pioneering spirit.

PART 3: THE ENTREPRENEUR

CHAPTER NINE

Boom Turns to Bust

In Paris, the party lingered on longer than elsewhere. The economic collapse brought on by the Wall Street Crash in October 1929, and which turned boom into bust almost overnight in the USA and Great Britain, arrived in France in slow motion, somewhat out of phase with the rest of the world, so that its full effects were not felt there for at least another two or three years. Indeed, at first it seemed to the French that the Great Depression would pass them by altogether; for months the only sign that the good times had ended was that the rich Americans had stopped arriving on their shores in droves. Soon, they would be replaced by another horde of refugees escaping from another form of prohibition – the Jews fleeing Nazi persecution in Germany.

However, when in September 1931 the British abandoned the gold standard and devalued the pound, the French were left high and dry, with the prices of their manufactured goods – and motor cars in particular – no longer as competitive as they had been throughout the twenties. By 1933, exports had fallen by over 40 per cent, and unemployment had begun to rise steeply, though never to the levels seen in the Anglo-Saxon countries. At its worst, in 1935, unemployment in France did not exceed more than half a million, or roughly 5 per cent of its working population, compared with the total of 2½ million jobless in Great Britain (22 per cent) and 12 million in the USA (23 per cent) recorded at the height of the Depression in these two countries during 1932. One reason was that, when they were no longer needed in the factories, around a million immigrant workers from Algeria, Italy and Poland were rounded up and sent back home; the peasants, of course, returned from the cities to the land of their own volition. Another was that in France, the whole process of industrialisation was much less advanced than in the UK and the USA. The majority of French workers (60 per cent) were still employed by small, privately-owned firms employing less than sixty people. By tightening their belts, these employers were able to retain their staff on reduced wages instead of sacking them outright and closing down their businesses for the duration as did many American bosses, such as Henry Ford.

Consequently, there were no hunger marches on the streets of Paris; social crisis was avoided, and the political unrest experienced much earlier elsewhere did not come to a head in France until 1934, when rioting organised by extremist right-wing groups took place outside the National Assembly. Ultimately, order was restored and the Republic was saved, but by then, France was no longer the carefree and prosperous nation that it had been at the turn of the decade. For the French – and André Citroën in particular – *les années folles* had become *les années difficiles*. Ironically, it was those few new large-scale enterprises such as his, whose successes had been the wonder of the twenties, that were the first to suffer from the new economic realities of the slump.

But in the light of the situation existing during late 1930, there was no reason for André Citroën to revoke his optimism or to revise his ambitious plans. So far as he was concerned, the fall in sales experienced that year was a temporary setback, explained by purely external, foreign factors; although the output of his British subsidiary had fallen by two-thirds within the past three years, his firm was still holding its own in the French market, and nothing fundamental had occurred to alter his analysis of future prospects in Europe. Viewed through his rose-tinted spectacles, which were focused to give a cosmopolitan, transatlantic perspective to events, the outlook continued to be one of boundless opportunities. American precedents showed that providing prices could be kept down by a continual increase in production, the potential demand was virtually insatiable. As long as people could be persuaded to upgrade or replace their cars on a regular basis, the market could never be completely saturated. In Europe, Citroën believed, this process of motorisation was sure to happen in the very same way – and after that, there would be Africa, India and Asia to satisfy! It was simply a matter of catching up with the American experience, using American practice, which at that time was about ten years in advance of the rest of the Western world.

And this process was already happening fast. Back in 1923, the American automobile industry had been thirty-eight times greater than the French in production terms. By 1928, it was only twenty times greater, and by 1932, a mere eight times greater. In just eight years, the number of new vehicles manufactured in France each year had quadrupled, from 60,900 units in 1922 to 225,600 in 1930, giving Automobiles Citroën a half share in the output of the second largest car-producing country in the world and a sixth share in the total output of all European motor manufacturers combined. Subsequently, of course, the production of cars by the French motor industry was to be overtaken by that of the British, but this did not occur until the second half of the decade. According to official statistics, in 1931 there were 1,689,400 vehicles on the roads of France (around a quarter of them lorries), and in 1932, 1,712,900, a substantial proportion of the European grand total motor vehicle population of 5,678,300 vehicles recorded that year.

In short, despite a reduction in its overseas sales, during 1930 the Double Chevron company continued to retain its hold on the home market, accounting for roughly 47 per cent of the total production achieved by the big three manufacturers – Citroën, Renault and Peugeot – combined. The latest generation of Citroën cars and commercial vehicles (the four-cylinder AC4 and six-cylinder AC6 series which had been launched at the 1928 Paris Motor Show) were still proving popular, thanks to a novel technical innovation added to their

Introduced for the 1929 model year, the robust and sturdy AC4 saloon marked yet another extremely successful step forward for Citroën. Featuring a new 1,628 cc engine, it came in a wide variety of passenger and light commercial body styles. A total of over 134,000 examples of all types were sold within two years.

specification in 1930 and marketed with an aggressive panache, in true Citroën fashion. Announced with posters and advertisements designed by Pierre Louys, featuring the motif of a swan floating placidly over the turbulent surface of a stormy sea, this was *le Moteur Flottant* ('Floating Power'), a vibration-damping engine mounting system using rubber blocks to insulate the motor from the chassis and body, a device licensed from Chrysler in America, but which had been originated in France by the engineer Pierre Lemaire. A grand total of 360,000 of these C series vehicles were made by the time that production ceased in 1932.

Two years previously, in tandem with the launch of the C4 and C6, Automobiles Citroën had entered the commercial vehicle market with a range of lorries developed from the chassis and mechanical elements of these two cars. The firm had produced light vans and pickup trucks since the beginning, of course, but these new medium- and heavy-duty vehicles marked a very successful new departure into virgin territory. By 1934, Citroën had captured 40 per cent of the market for utility vehicles in France. In typical Citroën style, these four- and six-cylinder-engined lorries were offered in a wide variety of forms and payloads from 500 kg to 2,000 kg, including an all-steel-bodied twenty-two-seater bus based on the 2 ton version. This vehicle led to another of André Citroën's pioneering commercial ventures, the Société Anonyme des Transports Citroën,

Citroën's second six-cylinder model, the C6F of 1931, in six-light saloon form. No less than twelve different styles of bodywork were available in conjunction with the same 2,442 cc engine, running gear and chassis.

a bus company inaugurated in November 1931 to operate a network of services in the Paris and Lyon regions. Before long, its activities had been expanded throughout rural France, to convey countrydwellers to the principal provincial cities such as Amiens, Poitiers, Nantes, Lille, Mulhouse, Strasbourg, Besançon, Carcassonne and Clermont-Ferrand. By June 1933, the network consisted of no less than 126 different lines with interconnecting routes extending over a total of 200,000 kilometres and carrying more than 36,000 passengers every day in a combined fleet of 800 buses. At every stop, an oval, stove-enamelled sign was erected, bearing the double chevron motif and the words '*Arrêt des Autobus*'. Typically, the whole venture was supported by a massive publicity campaign. Other companies quickly followed suit in other areas, using the same Citroën buses, so that these vehicles ultimately became a familiar and trusted feature of French daily life. Thanks to André Citroën, France soon had a nationwide bus system so efficient and effective that the French national railway company, SNCF,

In 1932 Citroën opened the SA Transports Citroën, using a fleet of Citroën-built C6G autobuses to serve a wide network of inter-city bus routes across France. Even the bus-stop signs bore the double chevron badge.

was forced to put pressure on the government to limit further growth of public transport by road, both passenger and freight. Also in 1931, André Citroën completely re-equipped his Paris taxi company with a brand new fleet of more than 4,500 Type C4 taxis, to replace a similar number of the old B14 models which had been running since 1927. Instead of the familiar green-and-yellow livery, however, these new vehicles were painted maroon-and-black, with a central orange stripe around the bodywork, bearing the Citroën name.

That year – 1931 – saw the establishment in Paris of yet another enterprising and imaginative Citroën sales initiative. In addition to the two magnificent showrooms that he had previously created at the Place de l'Opéra and on the Champs-Elysées, to celebrate the twelfth anniversary of the commencement of production at the Quai de Javel, on 30 September André Citroën opened a third, much larger display of his products in a vast 15,000 square metre shed built of glass and steel, a former rail-freight warehouse rented from the SNCF, located at the Place d'Europe, next to the Gare Saint-Lazare. This Magasin d'Europe was not so much a showroom as an exhibition of Citroën design or museum of Citroën achievements. Over three hundred exhibits representing every single variation of all the different Citroën car and commercial vehicle models so far made were put on display, many of them set in tableaux depicting

Opened in October 1931, the Magasin d'Europe was more than merely the biggest car showroom ever seen in France. Located in a vast warehouse near the Gare Saint-Lazare in Paris, it amounted to a huge museum of Citroën achievements.

Besides the new cars exhibited for sale in the Magasin d'Europe, examples of every type of Citroën vehicle ever made were also displayed – over a hundred different vehicles!

their appropriate working situations and decorated with life-size waxwork models of their drivers and passengers. The autochenilles which had taken part in the Croisière Noire were put on show, of course, displayed against a lifelike background of an African jungle scene, complete with lions and tigers. Also to be seen were several vehicles cut completely in two to demonstrate the workings of their engines and transmissions, plus numerous other exhibits explaining technical matters, such as the various stages involved in assembling a typical Citroën car. The Magasin also offered a cinema for the showing of Citroën films, a library and gallery for the display of Citroën publications, posters, photographs and other publicity material, a shop selling models and children's toys and a café-bar and restaurant where the customer could relax and recover from this intensive educational experience.

It was from the Gare Saint-Lazare that, one week later, André Citroën set out on his third and final visit to the USA, the source of his methods and the wellspring of his inspiration. In 1927 he had observed that, 'just as in the past painters and sculptors had travelled to Rome, the birthplace of contemporary art, today the engineers of the future must go to America, the birthplace of modern industrial culture'. But this time, Citroën returned to his spiritual homeland, not as a pupil of American methods, but as a professor, having been invited to address the Eighth Congress of American Heavy Industries, meeting at Columbia University in New York. Arriving there with his wife on board the North German Lloyd liner *Europa* on 13 October 1931, he made straight for Washington, where, the following day, accompanied by the French Ambassador Paul Claudel, he was received at the White House by President Hoover. The President had already met Citroën twice before; the first time being some twelve years previously, when, as Minister of Supply during the First World War, he had visited the munitions factory at the Quai de Javel; and the second, also in France, as Minister of Commerce, in 1923.

Evidently, the beleaguered President was particularly eager to renew his acquaintanceship with Citroën. So severe was the economic situation in America that in 1929, the combined output of the US automobile industry had actually fallen below that of France, which continued to be regarded by the Americans as a land of plenty – indeed, of gold, since the majority of its citizens still preferred to hold their savings in gold coins and bullion. Doubtless, Hoover hoped that the French motor magnate would be bringing with him some ideas on how to remedy the situation. Although he was not to be disappointed, the ideas that Citroën delivered then – and later at the congress – were not quite what he had anticipated.

While in Washington that day, Citroën was also welcomed by the National Geographical Society, which held a grand reception in his honour. During the ceremonies, he was made a life member of the society, an honour which had also been bestowed on G.-M. Haardt in 1930, when the leader of the Citroën Central African Mission had visited Washington to present the film of the Croisière Noire. As we saw in Chapter Seven, at that very moment, on the other side of the globe, Haardt was being held a virtual prisoner by a despotic Chinese warlord, along with the other members of the Citroën Central Asian Expedition, including the writer and photographer Maynard Owen Williams, who was travelling with the party as the official representative of the National Geographical Society. Later, his reports appeared in the Society's famous journal.

On returning to New York, Citroën went on to take part in three days of formal engagements as a member of an official French government trade and industry mission sent to promote better economic cooperation with the USA – a delegation which also included the Socialist Prime Minister and Foreign Secretary Pierre Laval. At that point in time, of course, Laval had not yet been recognised as the significant figure in French history that he was later to become. In the course of his long political career, which included three spells as premier, the opportunistic and avaricious Pierre Laval moved steadily from left to right, until he finally abandoned his Socialist origins during the German Occupation of France to play, with Nazi support, a dominant role in the collaborationist Vichy government, acting as chief Minister of State and Maréchal Pétain's deputy and heir-apparent. After the war, he was found guilty of treason for his part in abolishing the democratic constitution of the Third Republic, and was executed by firing squad at Fresnes prison on 5 October 1945.

On 15 October 1931, the Frenchmen visited Wall Street, where they found the bankers floundering in a mood of deep pessimism, despite the fact that the President had recently announced that a return to prosperity was 'just around the corner'. On 16 October, they attended a luncheon hosted by leading figures from the US automobile industry, then visited City Hall, where they were welcomed by the Mayor, Jimmy Walker. And on 17 October, they made a tour of New York in a motorcade of limousines escorted by police motorcycle outriders, with sirens wailing and the Stars and Stripes and the *Tricolore* flying side by side. This was the first time that Citroën had seen the recently-constructed Empire State Building, which, rising to 1,250 feet, dwarfed the 984 foot-high Eiffel Tower, previously the tallest man-made structure in the world. And from the viewing platform at its summit, he could see many more skyscrapers springing up all over Manhattan, including that veritable cathedral of Art Deco, the Chrysler Building. To Citroën, these pinnacles symbolised the dynamic, thrusting energy of American capitalism, which even then was far outreaching the achievements of European industry and commerce.

Here, the sky was the limit, even in the depths of an economic depression! In his eyes, New York, with its well-dressed crowds, incessant motor traffic and colourful neon signs illuminated night and day, seemed even more prosperous, vibrant and exciting than on his last trip. Where was the misery and poverty that he had heard so much about? Where were the soup kitchens? What had happened to the unending queues of unemployed hunger marchers pictured in the newspapers and cinema newsreels? Unfortunately, they had not disappeared; instead, they were encamped out of view in the Hoovervilles or shanty towns on the outskirts of the city, well away from the sightseeing tour arranged by the New Yorkers for their distinguished French visitors.

Moving to Philadelphia for a meeting with Edward G. Budd on 19 October, Citroën experienced a similar situation in the Pennsylvanian state capital. Not only that; he also found similar pro-German attitudes in the questions put to him by the journalists who interviewed him at press conferences. At that time, of course, French troops were still occupying the Ruhr to extract the unpaid reparations due from the Germans under the terms of the Treaty of Versailles, in the form of coal and steel.

Many Americans – especially those of German extraction, like the majority of the citizens of Philadelphia – could not understand why France was pursuing this matter, so long after hostilities had ended. To answer these questions more fully and explain the French point of view, on 19 October the *Saturday Evening Post* and then on 26 October the *New York Times* each carried long articles written by Citroën, giving his impressions of the current situation in the American car industry, together with his views on the state of international trade.

Measures to revive demand, including the abolition of tariff barriers and the creation of a free trade community within the international motor industry, was the theme that André Citroën addressed in his speech to the Congress of American Major Industries, delivered on 21 October before an audience including Walter P. Chrysler, President of the Chrysler Corporation, and many of the other important personalities on the American automotive and financial scene. Also present was the German industrialist Heinrich Thyssen, paymaster to the Nazi Party, who was there to argue on Hitler's behalf the case for the revision of the Treaty of Versailles and the ending of the payment of reparations to France.

Speaking in clear but less than fluent English, Citroën began by observing that the automobile was no longer a sign of affluence but actually a source of wealth in its own right. In fact, the value of the 35,600,000 cars so far constructed and in service around the world was now twice that of all the gold ever extracted from the earth during the entire course of human history, Citroën contended. Moreover, since 1914 the average price of cars sold in the USA had actually diminished by 25 per cent, whereas the cost of living had increased by 50 per cent over the same period. The spectacular economic progress achieved by the automobile industry, and which had already contributed so much to the prosperity and wellbeing of mankind, had occurred because constructors had united to combine their efforts and expertise, first in the USA and then throughout the rest of the world, he maintained.

Citroën then went on to astonish the Americans by proposing an extension of this cooperation. What he suggested was no less than alliance of the world's five principal automobile producers within the framework of an international society of motor manufacturers and traders, which would have the sole right to supply the market represented by the remaining 107 non-producing countries. As well as introducing a progressively penal rate of taxation on vehicles older than seven years, to ensure a constant renewal of the market, the member countries of this alliance would agree to remove all import barriers and other restrictions to trade. The result, Citroën claimed, would be a more rapid and harmonious motorisation of the world. This arrangement, he suggested, would serve to bring down prices and boost sales by eliminating the costs involved in paying customs duties, or in financing the overseas production facilities intended to overcome such customs barriers, and also in avoiding the unnecessary marketing expenses involved when selling in competitive situations. The proposed cartel, he declared, would achieve annual savings of approximately $80 million through the elimination of costly competition. The money saved could be ploughed back into improving roads and the general motor transport infrastructure, which would have a further beneficial economic effect, he believed. And to add a further impetus to the introduction of the car in underdeveloped, non-industrialised areas, Citroën proposed that these countries should be given large quantities of used cars from the richer nations as a gift.

Propounded in a country where laissez-faire economics and unrestricted market forces were then considered a virtue next to godliness, the dynamic Frenchman's progressive ideas fell on the proverbial stony ground. Indeed Citroën's proposals were considered so unholy as to be tantamount to corruption, since they touched upon a particularly sensitive spot in the corporate pysche of American business. When establishing his company in 1903, Henry Ford had been forced to embark on a long legal battle against a cartel of twenty-six other American car-makers, the Association of Licenced Automobile Manufacturers, which, when he refused to join their number, began an action for patent infringements against him. In 1911, his lone, obstinate crusade against this Motor Trust was finally vindicated. In a historic legal decision which made Ford's reputation as an American folk hero, his appeal in the Selden Patent lawsuit was upheld by the Supreme Court, and the US motor industry as a whole was liberated from what was widely regarded as a shameless conspiracy to limit its freedom of action. Memories were long, and Citroën's suggestions served only to reawaken fears of the dangers of such cartels.

The Americans need hardly have worried on that score. Free trade and the removal of international tariff barriers was a matter dear to André Citroën's heart. His British factory at Slough had been opened specifically to sidestep such restrictions and gain access to a market denied to his French-built cars. But after having shown initial promise, its existence had recently become a heavy liability. At the first sign of the onset of the Depression there in 1929, sales had plummeted to an embarrassingly low and thoroughly uneconomic level. Now output was a mere 10 per cent of what it had been at its height five years earlier – and as a result of a somewhat insular and chauvinistic 'Buy British' campaign currently being mounted by the motor trade in the United Kingdom, it was still falling.

To avoid this virtual boycott, Citroën Cars Ltd had been obliged to embark on a long-running publicity and marketing campaign to play down its French connections, by stressing the British content of its products and highlighting the financial contribution that the company was making to the British economy and exchequer. This public relations campaign began with a press release issued in September 1930, announcing the relaunch of the C4 and C6 range with suitably Anglicised names such as the Chiltern and Clarendon saloons, and with prices drastically reduced by up to 25 per cent throughout the range. It culminated in a letter to the Editor of the *Daily Mail*, signed by André Citroën and published on 27 April 1932, in which he expressed regrets at unhelpful, narrow-minded interpretations of the 'Buy British' slogan. Commenting on the contrast between official expressions of welcome towards foreign manufacturers, who had earlier been invited to establish subsidiaries here by the British government, and the actual trading situation now arising from this misguided policy, Citroën revealed that he had expended over £5,400,000 on supplies, wages and salaries, rents, customs duties and other expenses in the UK during the previous eight years.

In today's money values, this sum represents an investment of over £114 million. Although built partly from materials bought in Britain, and assembled totally by British labour directed by British brains, his products were being ostracised, Citroën complained. The boycott was not just a folly from a business point of view, it was also unfair, unsporting and thoroughly un-British!

Meanwhile, back in the USA, Citroën's tour ended with a visit to Henry Ford in Detroit, made on 24 and 25 October 1931. Here, in a ceremonial display of friendship and accord, the two motor magnates exchanged not just ritual handshakes but examples of their latest products: André presented Henry with a splendid C6 G saloon – as American-looking as any truly American car – and received a Model A open tourer in return. Altogether, over the two-day period, Citroën spent six hours alone with Ford, touring the factory, which was then still in full operation, and inspecting the innermost secrets of the Dearborn design offices and research laboratories, including, most probably, the new V8 engine that Ford was to reveal to the world just five months later, at the end of March the following year. Doubtless, the pair also toured the Greenfield Museum and Model Village that Ford had created just a couple of miles from his factory two years earlier, in association with his mentor, Thomas Edison. Opened by President Hoover in 1929, this, the world's first theme park, was already regarded as a national monument, a permanent re-creation of the rural, craft-based way of life of eighteenth- and nineteenth-century America that Ford's industrial and transport revolution was already sweeping away forever.

This time, the atmosphere at Dearborn was clearly more amicable than on his earlier visit there in 1924. But despite the public displays of mutual congratulation and reciprocated esteem, it is doubtful that, privately, the American welcomed with open arms Citroën's attempts to emulate his success. From Ford's point of view, Citroën had now become a serious rival, if not actually a threat. With Sir Percival Perry back at the helm again, his British interests were sailing ahead once more, thanks to the opening of a brand new factory, modelled on the Rouge plant, at Dagenham. But his French operations, founded at Bordeaux in 1913 but relocated in 1925 to Asnières on the outskirts of Paris, remained the lame duck of his worldwide empire, with disappointing sales. For this situation, Ford blamed the Citroën firm more than any other of his French competitors, since none other had gone so far in imitating his methods and copying his ideas. For his part, Citroën could hardly have forgotten Henry Ford's erstwhile publishing activities. Having spread to Europe ten years earlier, this anti-Semitic propaganda was currently being revived by the

Perhaps the two most important and influential men in the history of the mass-produced automobile: André Citroën and Henry Ford together at Dearborn, USA, in October 1931.

A meeting of minds? André Citroën opens the bonnet of his latest car, the C6G, to show his American host exactly how an automobile should be built.

Nazis and republished in Germany by Dr Goebbels. Even so, Citroën could not help feeling a purely professional admiration and respect for the American pioneer, who was his senior by fifteen years. Just like the American, he also lived solely for his business, and his principal interest lay in constantly improving and enlarging his factories.

The historic official pictures of them shaking hands showed the superficial contrast between these two tycoons, the greatest industrial personalities of their era: on one hand, the short, rotund, genial Frenchman, bald and bespectacled; and on the other, the sombrely-dressed, silver-haired American patriarch, tall, gaunt and austere. But what the photographs did not reveal, of course, were the deep differences of thinking that separated the two men. The forefather of the twentieth century, but somehow not quite a member of it himself, Henry Ford was a curiously erratic and capricious character for so successful an industrialist and businessman. A dual personality, full of contradictions and given to unpredictable swings of enthusiasm, he ruled his empire with intrigue and intimidation rather than by intellect. A homespun, rocking-chair philosopher and philanthropist, he believed in pacifism, teetotalism and reincarnation. As an inventor and engineer, his work was sometimes nothing less than cranky – and yet his espousal of the bio-sciences (he foresaw the use of biomass fuels and grew soya beans to make plastic components for his cars) was truly visionary. Throughout his career as a manufacturer, he believed that the foundation stone on which American democracy and prosperity was properly based was not the factory but the family-run farm. And yet, as a factory-owner himself, he sought to restrict the liberty of Ford personnel through the infamous 'social engineering' policies enforced by his Sociological Department, which attempted to control every aspect of his employees' lives, at work and at play.

For his own recreation, Ford enjoyed nothing more than to make expeditions into the forests with friends such as Thomas Edison, Harvey Firestone and the naturalist John Burroughs, sleeping out in a fleet of elaborately-equipped, chaffeur-driven camping cars. In this rural idyll, these 'vagabonds' would whittle hickory walking sticks, chop logs, do a little birdwatching, sing folk songs around a campfire like Boy Scouts and join with the local farmers in old-time country dancing. It is impossible to imagine a lifestyle less like that of the sophisticated, cosmopolitan André Citroën, whose customary haunts were casinos, racecourses and five-star hotels, and whose only interest in ornithology lay in observing the feathers adorning the high-kicking showgirls at the *Folies Bergère*.

André Citroën was not the only French motor manufacturer to seek inspiration at the feet of Henry Ford. Louis Renault had also made the trip to Dearborn, in 1912. Unlike Citroën, however, Renault had been unable to converse with Ford in English. Even so, there had been no need for an interpreter, for so well did the two master-mechanics understand each other that they had communicated by sign language while poring over blue-prints and prototypes. Renault and Ford were two of a kind, both being practical, pragmatic inventors who had become businessmen through force of circumstances, building up vast companies from nothing through sheer hard toil, much of it hands-on manual labour at the work bench, forge or lathe. Both came from farming or peasant backgrounds and neither had enjoyed the benefit of formal engineering training or, in Ford's case, of higher education of any sort, as had the sophisticated *haut bourgeois* socialite, André Citroën. He was a technocrat and entrepreneur who, initially at least, had entered the motor industry not through an obsession with automobiles, but because he thought they offered interesting commercial opportunities!

Nevertheless, Henry Ford's achievements must have seemed hugely impressive to the visiting Frenchman. During the twenty-seven years that had passed since Ford had sold his first car in 1903, he had produced more than 18,400,000 vehicles – over 17,600,000 in the USA alone. By this point in time, it had taken Citroën twelve years to make just over half a million (576,880) cars, a figure that paled into insignificance compared with the total of 14,250,000 vehicles produced during the same period by Ford's factories in the USA, Canada and Great Britain. Even so, André Citroën had already produced at least a hundred thousand more cars than Renault, his closest European competitor, had managed to build in thirty-two years of business. However, although Citroën also operated on the grand scale established by his American hero, producing a limited range of standardised cars in large numbers while refusing to diversify horizontally into other areas or markets, both he and Renault lacked the huge and almost insatiable American market which sustained Henry Ford's expansion. Working without the benefit of this enormous domestic demand, Citroën was overly dependent on the success of his export business. Louis Renault, on the other hand, never once made the mistake of putting all his eggs in one basket and took care to spread his risk by diversifying widely; not just by supplying a broader spectrum of the motor-car market, from popular run-abouts through to luxury limousines, heavy lorries and even military tanks and armoured vehicles, but also by engaging in other heavy engineering activities including the production of railway, aircraft and marine engines. Moreover, Renault financed his expansion and diversification purely from his profits and, despising bankers and stockbrokers, avoided using so much as a sou of borrowed money; in fact, he retained 98 per cent control of his firm until he was dispossessed of it entirely at the end of the Second World War.

Shortly after returning to Europe from New York on 27 October 1931, Citroën broadcast a radio message to the citizens of America, thanking his friends and hosts for their marvellous welcome and hospitality. Transmitted from Paris on 28 November 1931, and relayed nationwide across the USA, the message spoke of the ever-tightening bonds of friendship which, 'for many years have united me to your vast and noble country'. Expressing his admiration for all that he had seen, including Henry Ford's magnificent factories and the famous skyline of New York, Citroën avowed the hope that thanks to the limitless energy of the American people, the US economy would soon recover from the present difficult situation and resume maximum production. For his own part, Citroën announced that he would continue to follow the example of the American automobile industry in raising quality while reducing prices – but without lowering salaries. In fact, to help alleviate the unemployment situation, he had just reduced the prices of his vehicles by 10 per cent, right across the board.

Knowing that they were also listening in, Citroën went on to address a few words to his colleagues presently working abroad: firstly, his Technical Director Guillot, the engineers Dufresne and Jullien, and various other commercial personnel, including Charles Rocherand, currently in the USA; and secondly, all the members of the Citroën Central Asian Expedition, presently isolated in the heart of Asia, at Ourumchi in Chinese Turkestan. 'Excuse me if I take this opportunity to express to these men my congratulations for the results [they have] already obtained, and my heart-felt wishes for the continued success of their marvellous trip. In particular, may I congratulate the chief of the Mission, my friend and collaborator of twenty years, Georges-Marie Haardt,' André Citroën concluded, before introducing the Citroën Orchestra. Comprising 100 musicians drawn from among the employees of the Quai de Javel factory, this band then rounded off the broadcast with a stirring performance of the '*Marseillaise*' and the 'Star-Spangled Banner'.

While returning to France across the Atlantic with Pierre Laval and his party on board the luxury liner *Ile-de-France*, André Citroën had time to take stock of the situation and make his plans for the future. Sheltered by the palatial comforts of this floating grand hotel from the sea of troubles inundating the business world, with his usual optimism he came to the conclusion that the tide of economic crisis was now on the turn, and that good times lay ahead once more. The inevitable process of motorisation which, in reality, had hardly begun outside the USA and Western Europe was sure to continue unabated throughout the rest of the world, he was convinced. With luck, France and continental Europe would escape the worst effects of the slump altogether – and, if so, as the Henry Ford of France, he would be the first to benefit. Meanwhile, instead of retreating into a defensive mode and cutting back his operations, he decided that he would fight off falling sales by lowering prices and actually increasing production, in an all-out bid to enlarge his market at the expense of his less efficient competitors. Ironically, within a month of Citroën's visit, Henry Ford shut down his factories and laid off his workers without pay. That winter, four men were killed and many more injured when police fired on demonstrators marching to Ford's home, which was surrounded by barbed wire fences and protected by a force of private guards armed with machine guns.

Citroën's positive, aggressive, marketing-orientated strategy was entirely characteristic of the man. He had already proved that, given the chance to buy a superior product at a competitive price, the public would always recognise quality and value for money and reward him with its long-term loyalty. Some manufacturers considered that their responsibilities ended at the factory gate with the delivery of a motor car, but not Citroën. For him, the ideal of customer service and satisfaction was the true motive force of all economic activity. From the very outset of his career, he had made it the paramount priority in all his business dealings. He had been the first motor car-maker in the world to offer motorists a year's unconditional guarantee against all manufacturing defects, a step taken in 1929. Indeed, he had been the first to create a nationwide dealer network to care for his customers and their cars, long after they had left the factory. Now he would extend this policy of after-sales service by offering his customers inexpensive motor insurance for their Citroën vehicles, diversifying not for the sake of diversification, but merely with the aim of promoting sales of his cars. Accordingly, the Société des Assurances Citroën opened for business on 15 January 1932, with premiums 25 per cent lower than those currently being charged by existing French motor insurance companies, a development which caused a furore both in financial circles and the motor trade. To competitors such as Renault, who accused him of price-cutting, Citroën replied that, because his products were manifestly stronger and safer than average, they represented a lower actuarial risk.

Once again, Citroën's unorthodox methods were causing concern in certain quarters, if not outright offence. However, it would be misleading to call these opponents of change the *ancien régime*. Under the stresses of the worsening economic and political situation, a curious sociological fault-line was opening up throughout French society, similar to that which had polarised the nation during the Dreyfus affair thirty-five years earlier. Once again, the split was occurring not along lines of class, status, education and political allegiance, but down a philosophical divide. On the one hand were the progressives who saw change and innovation as the only way out of existing difficulties, and on the other lay the traditionalists who opposed any change in the status quo that would undermine French culture and alter the French way of life. This was particularly so in regard to the status of women, a cause which Citroën espoused. At that time, there was no universal suffrage in France, and unlike their Anglo-Saxon counterparts, French women enjoyed few legal rights. By promoting his cars as '*les voitures de la femme*', Citroën aroused the disapproval of chauvinistic males opposed to female emancipation. Throughout the twenties and thirties, the racy publicity produced by Pierre Louÿs invariably depicted Citroën cars being driven by short-haired, short-skirted models, typical of the flat-chested, freethinking flappers who so outraged reactionary public opinion. '*La femme moderne ne circule qu'en Citroën,*' proclaimed these advertisements and posters. Identified with such moral degeneracy, André Citroën became the *bête noire* of conformists and reactionaries. Even then, personal preference in the matter of automobiles provided a totem pole of social and political attitudes, and the double chevron badge grew to be thought of as a symbol of the avant-garde. From that point onwards – and for a long time afterwards – the more liberal, nonconformist sections of French society

Photographed in Provence by Pierre Louÿs, a stylish top-of-the-range example of the C6G, a special coach-built faux-cabriolet, built in 1932. The mannequin was English!

tended to choose Citroëns, while the conservatives – the *fonctionnaires* of officialdom, for example – bought Peugeots and Renaults instead.

For his own part, André Citroën believed that despite the apparent failure of the capitalist system in America, a change in Europe towards an industrialised, consumerised society on the American pattern was unavoidable. Ever the idealistic Utopian, he considered that the forward march of history was inevitable. Progress was unstoppable; there could be no standing still, not even in a slump. What was the point of shutting down his factories and making people unemployed? To relieve the situation and avoid hardship and unrest, it was vital to keep up production at all costs and so provide his employees with meaningful and constructive work.

Moreover, by now his own personal wish to be recognised not merely as a manufacturing and marketing innovator but as a genuine pioneer of automobile design had become more of an obsession than an ambition. Conscious of the more adventurous type of cars that were emerging from smaller specialist manufacturers and coachbuilders, he decided that time had come to be more radical in the styling and engineering of his products – and during his visit to the Budd Corporation in Philadelphia, he had seen a secret new development that promised exactly the kind of revolutionary technical breakthrough that he had been seeking for so long. What he had in mind was nothing short of a revolution in the design and construction of the popular, mass-produced automobile – a front-wheel-drive car so technically advanced that, when it finally appeared, it would be hailed as being at least five, if not ten, years ahead of its

The C4G saloon, introduced at the Paris Salon motor show in 1932. Although bigger and better then the AC4 which it replaced (it was equipped with the famous Moteur Flottant or Floating Power flexible engine mounting system) it was otherwise entirely orthodox in conception and construction.

time. In the event, it proved so successful that it remained in production for almost twenty-five years.

But before this adventurous new vehicle could be introduced, a further stopgap range of conventional rear-wheel-drive cars would be required. These three models, the four-cylinder 8CV and 10CV, and the six-cylinder 15CV saloons, were duly introduced at the Paris Motor Show in the autumn of 1932. The first Citroëns to carry the double chevron emblem on their radiator grilles like a heraldic motif on a shield (from the spring of 1933 onwards: previously, the Citroën emblem had been confined to a small, blue-and-yellow enamelled badge mounted on the top of the radiator shell) these cars were simply re-engineered versions of the old C4 and C6 designs, fitted with new high-strength mono-piece bodies constructed using the latest technology supplied by Budd. Even so, they were well received by the public. Ultimately, no less than sixty-nine different versions were available within the range. Over 95,000 examples were sold by the end of 1935, so reversing the fall in sales experienced in 1931 and 1932, and enabling Citroën to recover a 45 per cent share of the French volume market during 1933.

Eventually, this range became known as the 'Rosalie Series', in honour of the 8CV example nicknamed '*Petite Rosalie*' which, driven by the racing driver Cesar Marchand on the Montlhéry test track in March 1933, clocked up close on

Now at the height of his popularity and prestige, André Citroën welcomes the President of France, M. Albert Lebrun, to the Automobiles Citroën stand at the 1932 Paris motor show.

In 1931 the Citroën firm entered the motor sport arena for the first time, to win a series of sensational world endurance records in conjunction with the oil and lubricant manufacturers, Yacco. A succession of cars took part between 1931 and 1934, all called 'Rosalie' after the title of a current pop-song. This is the most famous, 'Petite Rosalie'.

Following 'Petite Rosalie's 300,000 km endurance run (which smashed 106 world and 191 international records), on 27 July 1933 André Citroën made a broadcast speech, offering a prize of 3 million francs to any competitor who could surpass this achievement by New Year's Day 1935. The prize was never claimed.

200,000 miles in 134 days at an average speed of 57.8 mph during a non-stop endurance trial organised by the Yacco Oil Company.

In doing so, it broke 106 world records and set standards unbeaten for thirty years. In fact, during the thirties, a succession of no less than ten of these record-breaking Citroën-powered, Yacco-sponsored cars took to the track; although easily the most famous, 'Petite Rosalie', was actually the third.

Hitherto, André Citroën had played no part in competitive motor sport, not because he disapproved of racing, but because his cars were simply not of the right size or type to compete with the Bugattis, Delages and Sunbeam-Talbots which then dominated the French motor racing scene. But endurance tests like this were a different matter. As had been demonstrated by an earlier series of long-distance runs staged by Voisin, endurance records were even better than racing victories in proving the quality and reliability of a motor car marque before the eyes of the ordinary motoring public. So when the Yacco company suggested a joint venture to publicise its lubricating oils, he was delighted to cooperate by providing vehicles and technical assistance. The success of this *coup de publicité* led to ambitious plans for further marathon endurance runs, including participation in the Monte-Carlo Rally. As a first step, in February 1934 a Citroën bus was entered in this famous event. Driven by François Lecot, it covered the 2,456 kilometres from Warsaw to Monte-Carlo inside 60 hours without incurring penalties, while carrying a load of ten passengers sleeping in couchettes – all of them veterans of the Croisière Noire expedition!

The tenth and last of the record-breaking Citroëns to run under the Yacco colours was actually a diesel-engined car. Known as the 'Yacco Speciale' rather than the 'Rosalie Ten', between 22 and 31 July 1937 this vehicle successfully completed a 20,000 kilometre run at an average speed of 109.54 k.p.h., again at the Montlhéry track, so culminating a research and development initiative begun by André Citroën himself some five years earlier, in 1932. In fact, Citroën had first revealed his interest in compression-ignition engines when delivering his address at the American conference in 1931: 'Speaking of exports, I should add that the research work at present under way . . . may in the near future open up markets in the colonies where petrol supplies are costly and difficult to provide and where the use of indigenous fuels such as oils and alcohol could greatly facilitate the development of the automobile,' he had announced.

Of course, Citroën was by no means alone in realising the potential of the diesel engine for automotive use, though clearly for very different reasons from those which have led to its new-found acceptance in passenger cars in recent years. Other automotive engineers in other countries shared his views at that point. Thus, by the time of the 'Rosalie Ten' run in 1937, the small, high-revving passenger-car diesel engine, although not exactly commonplace, was certainly no longer a novelty, for an example had been introduced by Mercedes-Benz on its 220D saloon in early 1936. But, in reality, as promised at the American congress, Automobile Citroën's practical involvement with the diesel engine had actually reached the stage of a working prototype as early as 1933. Moreover, progress was such that, twelve months later, during the summer of 1934, an example of

On test at the Montlhery track in July 1935, a 10A saloon fitted with the experimental Ricardo-Citroën diesel engine. Pictured are René Wisner of Automobiles Citroën and Archie Ferguson of Ricardo (wearing the trilby hat).

Citroën's first diesel engine, a 1,750 cc unit, was being tested at Montlhéry, fitted in examples of the Type 10CV saloon. Within a year, commercial examples of this car were being sold on the open market in France, six months earlier than the arrival of the Mercedes example, and in much greater numbers than their German counterparts. Clearly, thanks to the foresight of its founder, the Double Chevron firm also deserves to be recognised as a diesel pioneer, on equal terms alongside the three-pointed star of Mercedes-Benz – yet hitherto, it has always been accepted by motoring historians that its German rival was the principal world leader in this important area of automotive technology.

From information that has recently come to light in England, it is now known that André Citroën began to examine the possibility of producing a range of economical, long-lasting diesel engines for his range of taxis, lorries and other commercial vehicles as early as November 1932. That month, he sent Maurice Sainturat (the chief of his engine design department) on a fact-finding mission to Shoreham-by-Sea, on the south coast of England, with a view to initiating a joint research and development programme with the British engineering firm Ricardo & Company, with which he had first collaborated in 1925. The founder of the Ricardo firm, the distinguished engineer, scientist and inventor Sir Harry Ricardo (1885–1974) was one of that small band of British engineering thinkers who worked to investigate the theoretical principles of the internal combustion engine in the years immediately before and after the First World War. Born in the year that the first motor car appeared, he devoted his talents to automobile and aircraft engine design, designing the engines for the Mark V tank, the R100 airship and the Triumph-Ricardo motorcycle, as well as making many other valuable contributions to progress in transport engineering.

The greater part of Sir Harry's engineering work was entirely theoretical, but in the course of his experiments into combustion chamber swirl, he invented a device with a specific practical application – the Ricardo Comet cylinder head. Originally intended for use on heavy trucks and buses, this patented Ricardo technology permitted petrol engines to run at higher compression ratios and to be converted to run on the compression-ignition principle, thus opening up the possibility of small, high-speed diesel engines suitable for use in light commercial vehicles and passenger cars.

On returning to Paris, Sainturat reported favourably to his *chef* at the Quai de Javel, and accordingly, a licensing agreement was duly drawn up in March 1933. The following July, a dedicated Diesel Department was established at Citroën's Bureau d'Etudes, or research office, in Paris, headed by René Wisner, a talented engineer who happened also to have been the former heavyweight boxing champion of the French Army and a member of the French team in the 1926 Olympic Games. Then, on 18 October 1933, André Citroën made a visit to England to inspect personally the facilities at Ricardo's Bridge Works at Shoreham. Apparently, during lunch he entertained staff in the works canteen by performing a series of amusing conjuring tricks with matches!

In view of the environmental considerations that preoccupy engine designers nowadays, it is interesting to note that, during the development of the prototype of the Ricardo-Citroën diesel engine, the overriding obsession on the part of André Citroën himself was not so much the reduction of fuel costs as the elimination of smoke. As a committed non-smoker, André Citroën was one of the first industrialists to ban cigarette smoking throughout his factories and offices, and his views extended to his products also. During the development programme, engineers from Paris were repeatedly sent to London to observe the exhaust emissions from the AEC buses equipped with the Ricardo Comet diesel engine that ran on the streets of the British capital.

Citroën and Ricardo soon became good friends, and often played backgammon together during the Englishman's visits to Paris. A witness to these meetings was the British engineer J.H. Pitchford, later to become the Managing Director of the Ricardo firm, who was then based at Citroën's Bureau d'Etudes as manager and technical coordinator of the project, and who thus had frequent, friendly contacts himself with André Citroën. According to Jack Pitchford, 'Citroën was a charming man, always agreeable, approachable and amusing, totally without pretension and absolutely democratic in his relationships with his employees and associates.'

In fact, the whole Anglo-French collaboration seems to have been particularly

For many years until his death in 1935, André Citroën paid for the floodlighting of the Place de la Concorde and the Arc de Triomphe entirely as a gift to the people of Paris, in addition to his famous illuminations on the Eiffel Tower, inaugurated in 1925.

amicable and successful, for Wisner was also an anglophile who spoke fluent English. In a letter to Sir Harry dated 5 February 1934, André Citroën recorded his complete satisfaction at the results being obtained from an experimental single-cylinder engine by then under test at Shoreham. And in a similar letter dated 24 July 1934, he again commented on the good results being obtained from 'our first diesel engine' – a prototype overhead-valve four-cylinder engine constructed at the Quai de Javel. On 19 July 1934, René Wisner wrote to Sir Harry from Paris announcing that this first 75 × 100 mm engine had satisfactorily completed a programme of bench tests in Citroën's research laboratories, and that he was now proceeding to install the motor in a taxi to undertake road trials. 'The engine functions with perfect silence from 250 rpm up to 3,500 rpm and seems to demonstrate all the qualities required from a passenger car engine,' Wisner reported. Various photographs in the Ricardo archives taken in July 1935 show three of these Rosalie 10CV saloons fitted with the 1,750 cc diesel engine under test at Montlhéry, with René Wisner and Archie Ferguson (Ricardo's chief draughtsman) standing nearby.

On 25 March 1935, René Wisner wrote again to Sir Harry with the news that Automobiles Citroën had decided to put into production two further diesel engines, both of which the company intended to exhibit at the Paris Salon later that year. But on this occasion, the good news was tempered by sad tidings: 'You will be sorry to learn that Monsieur Citroën is gravely ill and has entered hospital for treatment,' Wisner reported.

CHAPTER TEN

The Final Gamble

From his father, Citroën had inherited an emotional disposition not uncommon among Jewish men: although warm, cheerful, sensitive, energetic and optimistic he was also impatient and impetuous, often reacting rashly and incautiously to events. However, his optimism was certainly not of the fatuously hopeful, daydreaming kind. Citroën was a realist, not a dreamer, and his expectations were always rationally based in the philosophy of scientific humanism, which holds that there is a consistent thread of progress and improvement to be discerned in the history of mankind. If there was a flaw in his personality, it was in his gambler's assessment of risk. He continually refused to countenance failure, never made provision for defeat and always declined to concern himself with what, these days, is referred to among business men as the 'downside' of an investment decision. If he considered that something was worth doing, or ought to be done as a matter of principle, he did it without delay, making up his mind quickly, with the minimum of discussion and deliberation. And having done so, he boldly embarked on his course of action with his eyes set firmly on the horizon and with never so much as a backward glance to count the cost or assess the consequences of failure.

Motivated by this progressive philosophy, even in the depths of the Depression André Citroën refused to be depressed. Despite a continual contraction in the French car market and a consequent reduction in his own sales, he and his company seemed to be surviving the hard times, confounding the critics who believed that he was nothing more than a brash adventurer whose success was just a flash in the pan, and who had predicted that he would be the first casualty of the economic downturn. Although the spectacular progress of Automobiles Citroën had been momentarily stalled, its engine was far from worn out by the strain of twelve years of rapid growth, and was merely ticking over in readiness for the next burst of acceleration.

At the peak of the good times in 1929, annual French automobile production had hit a total of roughly 250,000 vehicles, of which approximately 40 per cent had been made by Citroën. In 1930, it fell back to 225,000, and then again in 1931 to 200,000, with Citroën's share falling to 35 per cent. By 1932, it was down to 170,000. But due to the success of his new commercial vehicle range, Citroën's contribution to the rapidly-expanding vehicle population of France was not just holding fast but actually increasing, albeit slightly. By the end of 1932, there were around 1,700,000 cars, lorries and buses running on the roads there, of which no less than 500,000 (29.5 per cent) bore the double chevron

Among the last of Citroën's conventional rear-wheel-drive models was the six-cylinder 15CV saloon of 1933.

badge. Six years earlier, in 1926, there had been only 600,000 vehicles, of which 175,000 (29 per cent) were Citroëns.

Consequently, at the turn of the new decade, having reached his fifty-second birthday and about to be promoted to the rank of Grand Officier in the Légion d'Honneur, André Citroën had good cause to look back over his past achievements with a certain degree of pride and satisfaction. Yet increasingly, he found himself discontented with his reputation as the Henry Ford of France. Far better to be thought of as the poor man's Ettore Bugatti, he believed! Clearly, if he was to stay ahead of his rivals, he would have to outdistance them not just in quantity of production but in quality of design. He had never been the kind of manufacturer who was content to aim for the lowest common denominator among his clientele. But from now on, he would aim to reach the highest common factor in their aspirations, he avowed, by producing a car with an advanced specification that offered them a degree of performance and technical sophistication hitherto unknown in a mass-produced vehicle. Despite the short-term position, there was no long-term reason to postpone plans for this revolutionary new car, he considered. The time had come to take his biggest ever gamble. Not only would he launch the new model as soon as possible, he would abandon all his existing models to concentrate his resources entirely on the production of this one, unproven design.

The car that André Citroën envisaged – the immortal Traction Avant – was to be quite unlike anything that he had produced before, a truly 'clean sheet' design so dramatically new in every respect that its appearance would send shock waves reverberating round the motoring world. Intended to give him a five-year lead over his rivals, it remained in production for almost twenty-five. Even when its production ceased in 1957, it was still thought by many experts to be technically superior to many other mass-produced popular cars then on the market. Indeed, Citroën's 'new concept in motoring' proved to be so innovative and conceptually advanced that it is still recognised by engineers and designers today as being the one design that, above all others, set the pattern and standards of the modern family car. For the very first time on a mass-produced vehicle, such avant-garde features as monocoque chassisless construction, front-wheel-drive, automatic transmission, independent front suspension, hydraulic brakes and (later) rack and pinion steering were to be combined in a long, low-slung, all-steel bodyshell, embodying the latest notions of graceful, streamlined styling. Rapid and responsive to drive, spacious and comfortable to ride in and affordable to own and run, it was also to be an outstandingly reliable and economical vehicle, priced well within the means of the typical business or professional motorist. The intention was that it would be capable of cruising safely at 60 mph while returning an average fuel consumption of no less than

One of the first publicity pictures taken of the revolutionary new 7CV Traction Avant in early 1934. The first mass-produced car in the world to offer front-wheel-drive, chassis-less monocoque construction and hydraulic brakes simultaneously, the Traction Avant continued in production for over twenty years and set the technical pattern of the modern family saloon.

Early examples of the Traction Avant on the production line at the newly reconstructed Quai de Javel factory in late 1934. The one-piece integral monocoque body, still minus engine and transmission, can clearly be seen.

An interesting technical feature of the Traction Avant was its compact engine and transmission unit. This 'Bloc Moteur' could be withdrawn entirely for maintenance or replacement simply by removing four large nuts from the studs protruding forward from the body shell, after first detaching the wings and bonnet.

30 mpg – a standard of performance and economy previously unheard of at that time. And whereas all of Citroën's previous cars except the first were related closely to their predecessors, the Traction Avant had nothing in common with any existing model. There was no inheritance of design, construction or components whatsoever; every single part was new and different. At a stroke, the Traction Avant made all other cars – Citroëns included – out of date.

There was, of course, nothing new in the idea of the front-wheel-drive car; already, numerous examples had been produced in limited numbers by various small, specialist firms, chief among them Cord and Ruxton in the USA, DKW and Adler in Germany, Alvis in Great Britain and Tracta in France. What distinguished Citroën's courage and audacity in adopting the principle was that although its use eventually become standard practice in the design of family cars and was ultimately adopted universally by all the major volume manufacturers, back in the thirties when the Traction Avant was launched, he stood alone in abandoning rear-wheel-drive entirely throughout his range. Even by the time that the 2CV appeared in 1948, Automobiles Citroën was still unique in making only front-wheel-drive cars, and indeed, it continued to be so for many years after the war.

Despite the fact that both Renault and Peugeot considered front-wheel-drive to be not just technically unfeasible but actually undesirable, Citroën knew that the principle offered drivers a far higher standard of stability and safety. Firstly, from the handling and roadholding point of view, it obviously made more sense for the engine to pull the car through a bend, as a horse pulls a cart, instead of pushing it from behind, providing of course that the problem of transmitting that power to the front wheels could be solved. But secondly, by eliminating the

The first example of the Roadster version of the 7CV Traction Avant, this car, built in May 1934, was presented by André Citroën to his daughter Jacqueline, then aged nineteen.

propshaft tunnel to the rear and lowering both the floorline and the centre of gravity, a much more spacious, stable and aerodynamically efficient body shape could also be achieved.

When cornering in a front-wheel-drive car, the driving force of the car is exerted in the direction of the turn, to maintain the correct trajectory through a curve. In a rear-wheel-drive car, however, the force is exerted along the fore and aft axis of the vehicle, in the general direction being followed at the time, rather than into the curve. In other words, the driving force imparted by the rear wheels is exerted crosswise to the required direction being followed by the front or steered axle. It therefore follows that, for the same vehicle speed and for the same degree of grip provided by the tyres, a front-wheel-drive car can withstand a greater centrifugal force without loss of tyre adhesion and directional stability. This means that it can go into a turn at a higher speed without risk of skidding, or corner more safely on slippery surfaces.

To complicate matters, these centrifugal forces are magnified by factors such as the camber of the road and side winds, so that the vehicle tends to drift sideways in a turn, without necessarily losing grip and skidding. To counteract this drift, the driver must make constant steering corrections to preserve balance and maintain the set course. Moreover, as this drifting effect is greatest on the driven wheels, in a rear-wheel-drive car the back axle tends to break contact with the road first, before the front or steering axle, and the driver can only correct this slide by harsh or violent movements of the steering wheel, turning it from lock to lock, a manoeuvre that calls for experience and skill. On a front-wheel-drive car, however, the driver can correct drift easily and gently by constant, slight adjustments of the steering wheel, a technique requiring much less experience and skill. The end result is that, all things being equal, the front-wheel-drive car is far easier to control and thus inherently safer than its rear-wheel-drive counterpart, allowing even the most clumsy novice driver to drive at speed with confidence.

Precisely how and when Citroën gave his staff the green light to begin work on the Traction Avant project has never been established. But the veteran designer Jean Daninos (who worked at the Quai de Javel between 1932 and 1935 before going on to found his own Facel Vega marque) recalled that: 'One day [in 1932] the boss called us together to show us a small low-slung front-wheel-drive saloon from Germany – an Adler Trumpf. He had been offered the manufacturing rights to this car, but chose instead to produce his own FWD [front-wheel-drive] vehicle from scratch. 'This is what I want my next car to look like,' he told us. 'In future, Citroën customers must be able to step down into their vehicles, instead of climbing up into them like passengers clambering aboard a stage coach.' Clearly, the chance to be able to make such a dramatic advertising claim greatly appealed to André Citroën's highly developed sense of marketing and publicity priorities.

Daninos and his fellow engineers were sceptical. Achieving this look would mean much more than merely designing a new body, they pointed out. To switch to front-wheel-drive would mean that a complete new engine, power train and suspension system would have to be developed. But André Citroën was adamant; the challenge of being the first major volume manufacturer to adopt front-wheel-drive was irresistible.

As we have seen, during his trip to the United States in 1931, Citroën had once again visited the Budd Corporation in Philadelphia, the source of the all-steel body-building technology that he had been using under licence since 1924. Here, Edward G. Budd had showed him a front-wheel-drive prototype designed by Joseph Ledwinka and William J. Muller (who had created both the Ruxton and the Cord) which had been produced primarily to demonstrate a novel, chassisless monocoque bodyshell that Budd's engineers had developed. Hitherto, cars had always been constructed by bolting the body onto a separate chassis frame, in a way that derived directly from the age of the horse and cart. Budd's unitary construction process allowed this heavy chassis frame to be completely eliminated, however. By welding up the sheet-steel panels of the body in such a way that their own prestressed shape provided sufficient strength and stiffness, the resulting monocoque itself could carry the loads imposed by the engine and transmission, as well as the weight of the driver and passengers.

Inspecting the Budd prototype, André Citroën realised that here, at last, was a way to make the mass production of a front-wheel-drive car a practical proposition. Because the body itself would be capable of holding engine, transmission and suspension together, it would be possible to get the car's weight, centre of gravity and ride height down to the levels he desired. Better still, it also promised a harmonic solution to the many diverse engineering and construction problems that ensue when cars are both powered and steered by the same front axle.

To realise this front-wheel-drive project, codenamed 'PV' ('*Petite Voiture*'), Citroën began to recruit a top-level design and development team, employing the very best talents from within the company as well as engaging leading engineers and design consultants from without. Working under his Chief Engineer Maurice Broglie, this special task force operated in total secrecy from a hide-out in the old Mors premises in the Rue du Théâtre, not far from the Quai de Javel but far enough away from routine activities at the Citroën factory for its movements to go undetected by insiders and outsiders alike.

The highly experienced Citroën old hand Maurice Sainturat was given responsibility for developing the engine, Maurice Julien was asked to design the novel torsion-bar independent suspension, and Raoul Cuinet, assisted by Jean Daninos and Pierre Franchiset, was given the job of designing and engineering a new chassisless bodyshell along the principles already developed by the Budd company. Jean-Albert Grégoire, a leading independent expert and front-wheel-drive pioneer, took on the contract to supply the driveshaft couplings, and Flaminio Bertoni, an Italian sculptor who had never designed a car before, was engaged for the task of styling the bodywork and designing the interior and exterior details. His work included the superb, instantly recognisable frontal aspect of the Traction Avant, distinguished by its impressive grille emblazoned with double chevrons (introduced also on the Rosalie models) that was the car's most characteristic visual feature.

Another interesting personality involved in the project as a consultant was the amateur engineer and designer Dimitri Sensaud de Lavaud. Born in Spain in 1884, Sensaud de Lavaud had amassed a huge fortune from his family's coffee plantations in Brazil, which enabled him to indulge in his hobby of inventing mechanical devices, largely by paying others to make his ideas work. One of these inventions was an infinitely variable automatic transmission system, in which the conventional gearbox and clutch were replaced by a hydraulic turbine, or torque converter. In effect, this relieved the driver from the work of changing gear by constantly adjusting the power output of the engine to match the resistance encountered by the wheels, without human intervention. The advantages of this system, which had been used successfully by Voisin as early as 1925, impressed André Citroën enormously. Personally, he disliked the physical effort of driving, and wherever possible he always sought to make the task of controlling his cars as easy as he could – and so the notion of fitting the turbine to the Traction Avant and eliminating the gearshift altogether was a highly attractive proposition, since so many of his potential customers would be inexperienced drivers, new to motoring.

Over-optimistic as ever, Citroën planned to launch his new car in the autumn of 1934, and set a breakneck timetable for the design and development of the Traction Avant. Even today, with the benefit of computer-aided design techniques, the cycle of producing and testing a new model normally takes a minimum of five years. His advisers had predicted that at least six years of intensive work would be required before the Traction Avant could be offered to the public, but *le patron* insisted that this was far too long to wait, and that the car must be on the market within four years.

But by the spring of 1933, it was clear that the project was well behind schedule and that certain vital technical teething troubles had still not been overcome. Realising that fresh ideas and energies were required to make a breakthrough, André Citroën began a headhunt for new talent and consulted his friend Gabriel Voisin for suggestions. As it happened, Voisin not only knew of just such a person, he had already collaborated with this designer on a front-wheel-drive project of his own, some three years previously. Even more fortuitously, the individual concerned was actually looking for a job.

Remembering the debt that he owed to Citroën for the success of his own entry into the motor industry twenty-three years earlier, Voisin passed on the name, and in doing so he repaid his friend more than a thousandfold. For it was on Voisin's recommendation that André Citroën duly appointed the brilliant engineer André Lefebvre as overall manager for the PV project, giving him carte blanche to get the car ready on time.

As the subsequent events of motoring history clearly show, in placing his confidence in Lefebvre, Citroën assured not only the future of the Traction Avant but the future of his marque. For, over the following twenty-five years, Lefebvre went on to create a whole succession of radical, innovative and unconventional cars and gain for Automobiles Citroën the worldwide reputation for advanced design which it still enjoys today.

Distinguished as the only automobile designer ever to compete in motor racing at the highest level, Lefebvre was the archetypal engineer-artist, interested only in creating cars, and completely unconcerned with the trifling matters of administrative detail, office politics or personal prestige that motivate lesser talents. A tall, dark, handsome, lordly figure who drank nothing but water and champagne, his whole life was one long love affair with the automobile, punctuated by innumerable shorter liaisons with a procession of pretty women. Born near Paris in 1894, he trained to be an aircraft designer at Paris's Ecole Supérieure d'Aéronautique, and on the outbreak of war he began his career in 1915 with Voisin, designing and building bombers for the French Air Force. After the war, when Voisin transferred his attention from aviation to the automobile business, Lefebvre moved with him, and was later partly responsible for designing a series of highly original racing cars, one of which he drove in the 1923 Grand Prix de l'Automobile Club de France at Tours, finishing fifth. In the wake of the Wall Street crash of 1929, the market for luxury cars collapsed, and Voisin was forced to sell off his business to Belgian interests when Citroën failed to find the money to complete a takeover. Although André Lefebvre and Gabriel Voisin were obliged to part company, the pair were to remain close friends for the rest of their lives, consulting each other on every technical and automotive issue.

For the next two years, Lefebvre spent an unproductive and uncongenial stint with Renault, where he attempted to interest his new boss in the proposals for a

An unsung genius of motor car design, André Citroën's protégé André Lefebvre. Principal designer of the Citroën Traction Avant, he later went on to create the 2CV and DS19. The only automobile motor engineer ever to compete in motor racing at the highest level, Lefebvre finished fifth in the 1923 Grand Prix de l'Automobile Club de France at Tours, driving an experimental Voisin which he had helped to design.

front-wheel-drive car which he had produced while working with Voisin. Alas, Louis Renault had rejected his suggestions out of hand as being idiotic: 'I won't waste five minutes on such nonsense,' Renault is said to have told him. Being opposites in every conceivable way, inevitably the two men quarrelled, and Lefebvre walked out – as luck would have it, straight into a job with Renault's greatest rival. In common with others who had made the transition from Billancourt to the Quai de Javel, Lefebvre soon discovered that he had moved from an empire to a republic.

Immediately upon arrival at the Citroën works, on 12 March 1933, Lefebvre identified the problem areas and set about finding solutions, toiling round the clock. By June a definitive working prototype had been produced, working to the original design brief and thus combining many contributions, not least those of André Citroën himself.

Even so, many snags remained to be ironed out before the car was ready to enter series production. Firstly, Gregoire's Tracta constant velocity driveshaft joints proved unreliable and eventually had to be replaced by Glaenzer type units. Constant velocity joints were required to solve the problem of transmitting power from the gear box 'around the corner' to the wheels when the steering was angled at a lock. Without them, it was impossible for the wheels to revolve smoothly at a constant speed when rounding corners.

But secondly and far more alarmingly, Sensaud de Lavaud's automatic 'turbine' transmission turned out to be a total failure on the Traction Avant, except when cruising on flat roads. Under heavy load while climbing hills the oil in the torque converter overheated to boiling point – 'an excellent device for frying chips but useless as a gearbox', was Lefebvre's sardonic comment. Nevertheless, André Citroën refused at first to consider abandoning the idea, since it had worked quite satisfactorily when tested on his rear-wheel-drive models during the course of 1932. It was not until a car broke down at an important demonstration one year later (in February 1934 – see Chapter Nine) that he changed his mind at the very last moment and instructed Lefebvre to replace it with an orthodox clutch and a three-speed synchromesh gearbox, so that the large stock of cars so far completed could be sold without risk of incurring a catastrophic level of warranty claims.

The engineers had foreseen the inevitability of this volte-face, of course, and had made their provisions. Thus, the work was accomplished within a couple of weeks by installing a new, conventional mechanism within the casing of the old turbine. Lefebvre himself designed the gear selector mechanism incorporating the unusual 'mustard spoon' dashboard-mounted lever that was one of the Traction Avant's most idiosyncratic features. Later, Citroën's detractors claimed that the episode of the Sensaud de Lavaud automatic transmission was proof of his ignorance, impracticality and naivety in technical matters. Yet the British motoring journalist W.F. Bradley, continental correspondent of *The Autocar*, reported that he had driven almost ten thousand kilometres in a conventional Rosalie model fitted with this device, without experiencing problems of any kind. In this case then surely any initial incompatibility between the Turbine and the Traction's front-wheel-drive configuration could have been ironed out with further development. But the necessary time and money could not be found.

Solving these complex engineering problems would have been enough of a challenge for even the biggest American car companies of that era, yet for André Lefebvre and his team there were other equally pressing difficulties to be dealt with on the manufacturing and production-engineering side. For while they were struggling to perfect the Traction Avant, André Citroën had embarked on another, equally ambitious, parallel project that imposed far greater demands on the human and financial resources of his company than the design and development of a new car.

From the moment of their very first meeting almost fifty years earlier, as schoolboys at the Lycee Condorcet, relations between André Citroën and Louis Renault had never been cordial. But early in 1932, Citroën received an unexpected and quite unprecedented invitation from his greatest competitor, to inspect the expansion and improvements that Renault had recently carried out at his factory at Billancourt, further down the Seine from the Quai de Javel. It was an offer that Citroën could not refuse; nothing interested him more than the sight of a car production line in full flow and the chance to see, at last, the innermost workings of his rival's establishment must have been just too good to miss. To his great alarm, Citroën discovered that the Renault factory had expanded to such an extent that it now overflowed across the banks of the Seine to encompass the Ile de Séguin. Covering 250 acres and employing 32,000 workers plus 15,000 machine tools it was now the largest industrial complex in France, an economic concentration greater than the town of Chartres. Citroën could make his rounds of the Quai de Javel on foot within a morning, but Renault's territory was now so huge that it was necessary to use a car to tour the Billancourt installations, which were not confined solely to car manufacturing.

After the visit, quite uncharacteristically, Louis Renault invited André Citroën to dine with him at Maxims restaurant. Situated in the rue Royale, just off the Place de la Concorde in Paris, this was the unofficial club of the senior figures in the French car making and racing fraternity, often frequented by Citroën and his friends, but not normally one of Renault's haunts. Despite his great prestige as founding father of the French automobile industry, he was not the convivial, socializing type and always avoided the receptions, parties and banquets that appealed so much to André Citroën. Described by a biographer as a crotchety character, 'always in bad humour, irritable, tense and even more aggressive because of his natural shyness', he did not enjoy the public responsibilities incumbent on his position. Nor did he relish his duties as a major employer. An instinctive autocrat and conservative, whose individualism was of the reclusive, introverted kind, Renault lacked the benign, progressive paternalism that characterised Citroën. Indeed, he deplored the radical, leftish political and social trends of contemporary France, a state of affairs that he regarded as anarchistic and degenerate.

However, in the course of the banter and false bonhomie that normally accompanies such encounters between men of incompatible personalities and philosophies, Renault reiterated a proposal that had first been suggested some years earlier by his nephew and right-hand-man, Francois Lehideux. In future, the two men should give up their rivalry and enter into a partnership. As one of France's oldest-established car manufacturers and the acknowledged leader in matters of design and construction, he, Renault, would produce the cars while Citroën, the super-salesman and publicity expert, would market and distribute them. Once again, the proposal was refused, point blank. The assertion that Renault's cars were technically superior to his own was demonstrably false and hardly worth the trouble of refuting, Citroën considered; the implication that he, personally, was more of a showman than a serious engineer and industrialist was quite unacceptable and amounted to a challenge that he simply could not ignore.

With G.-M. Haardt no longer alive to restrain his foolhardy optimism, Citroën took up the gauntlet that Renault had thrown down. Now was the time to settle the argument once and for all. The new Traction Avant would show who was the better engineer, of course. But in order to prove that he was also the better businessman, he too would have to build a brand new factory, even bigger and better than his arch-rival's, to replace the by now outdated facilities at the Quai de Javel: an ultra-modern factory in which he could produce his ultra-modern car with the maximum efficiency and profitability. Accordingly, following a year's careful preparation, in the period between April and July 1933, a third of the entire Quai de Javel site was torn down and reconstructed to provide a vast, modern press shop and assembly hall, equipped with the very latest tools and machinery from America. Three years of normal building work were telescoped into six months of frantic, non-stop activity: 12,500 tonnes of steelwork was erected (more than that contained in the Eiffel Tower), 1,800 concrete piles were sunk, and 323,000 square feet of floorspace laid down. Even more remarkably, this massive reconstruction programme took place with minimal disruption of routine production; for most of the time, the assembly line continued to turn out cars at the rate of 400 vehicles per day. The whole undertaking was a triumph of industrial planning and organisation.

However, for more than a month of that time, the Quai de Javel was closed for an altogether different reason. Between 29 March and 5 May 1933, a strike took place throughout Citroën's Paris factories, the third and longest that the firm experienced under André Citroën's leadership. In the light of the worsening economic situation, that spring, the French government introduced a number of deflationary measures intended to reduce the cost of living by 10 per cent. Accordingly, Citroën proposed a corresponding reduction in wage and salary levels throughout his company. Already, the number of employees had been reduced from a high-point of 35,000 in 1929 down to 18,000 in early 1933, through rationalisation and efficiency measures as well as a severe diminution in demand. Fearful of further job losses, the militant trade unions responded by threatening a strike. To forestall this (and also to take advantage of a situation which actually favoured its rebuilding plans), the management decided on a lock-out. For the duration, a state of siege existed, with the factory guarded by the police. But behind the barricades and picketlines, the reconstruction work went on uninterrupted.

Indeed, during the course of 1932, the Citroën firm had experienced a catastrophic fall in sales, and production had plunged to 48,000 units, half the level seen at the peak just three years earlier. The explanation was not merely the overall economic situation, of course. By now, rumours had begun to circulate in France that André Citroën was about to launch a sensational new car, and this caused customers to put off purchasing the current Rosalie models in anticipation of better things to come. Moreover, this caution was compounded by murmurs of a more worrying sort, concerning not just the financial condition of the double chevron marque, but also the health and wealth of its founder. Was not André Citroën suddenly looking somewhat tired and gaunt of late, and not at all the familiar, rotund, happy-go-lucky figure of renown? Did he not seem so much thinner and frailer recently, as if weighed down by insupportable responsibilities? What was causing this change in his appearance – ill health, business problems, money worries, or perhaps all three? In truth, André Citroën was now working under intolerable pressures. As he grew older, his life became ever more difficult, not least because so many of the trusted friends and advisers of his own generation who had supported him in the early days of his career had now disappeared from the scene. First Eknayan, then Guillot, and lastly and most tragically of all, the irreplaceable Haardt had all died one by one, leaving him to face the world alone. And although the supply of cash had always been a problem, by now the lack of it was becoming a matter of grave concern. The huge profits of 100 million francs recorded in 1926 had evaporated into debts of 75 million francs in 1929 and 125 million francs in 1930.

Apart from these financial difficulties, there were other worrying developments on the political front. Recent events in Central Europe – where Citroën had intended to make his next great thrust of expansion – showed that his plans were about to be thwarted, not by a rival motor magnate, but by another far more sinister opponent with territorial ambitions. On 30 January 1933, Adolf Hitler, whose views on 'the Jewish question' were already well known in France, was appointed Reichskanzler in Germany. That night, the Nazi Party celebrated its triumph by staging a torchlight procession of stormtroopers through the streets of Berlin. As the parade passed the French embassy in the Pariserplatz, the massed bands began to play the old Prussian war song '*Siegreich wollen wir Frankreich schlagen*' ('Triumphant, we will defeat France'), throwing down a calculated insult and challenge to the old enemy. All who could read the omens knew then that war was inevitable. As early as 1922, Hitler had sworn that, on gaining power, 'the annihilation of the Jews will be my first and foremost task'. Sure enough, within two months of gaining power, he decreed a boycott of Jewish businesses throughout Germany. Before the year was out, the Nazis had not only banned trade unions and enacted a range of oppressive measures intended solely to persecute the Jews, but they had also constructed numerous

Although André Citroën's work brought him into contact with many of the world's most important political and industrial personalities, he preferred the company of creative, artistic people. Here, Charlie Chaplin joins the Citroën family on their winter-sports holiday at St Moritz in January 1932.

concentration camps to imprison without trial any dissidents, Jews or Gentiles alike, who opposed their racist policies. In the words of the historian Alan Bullock: 'the gutter had come to power . . . and street gangs had seized control of the resources of a great modern state'.

Anticipating this persecution, Citroën refused to attend the 1933 Berlin Motor Show held in February, one month after Hitler's takeover of power. Here, with typical panache, Automobiles Citroën had already arranged to stage an impressive presence and had built a huge stand and hospitality centre, the Club Citroën, which dominated the event. Apparently, Adolf Hitler – no novice in such propaganda methods himself – noticed the effectiveness of Citroën's publicity with displeasure and gave orders that such a display by a foreign maker (and most particularly a Jewish one) was never to be repeated in the Reich.

Thus, the Führer must have been infuriated when, despite his disapproval, Citroën dared to press on with his plans to expand in a German-speaking territory by setting up a full-scale sales network in the Saar, the much fought-over region lying next to Alsace-Lorraine on the Franco–German border, which had been under French control since the end of the First World War. However, the venture lasted only two years. In 1935, a referendum among the population decided that the region should be returned to Germany, and Automobiles Citroën was obliged to retreat. Since 1933, it had been Nazi policy that '*Deutsche Volk fahrt Deutsche Wagen*' ('German people drive German cars'), and by means of bureaucratic controls and import regulations the German authorities hindered the activities of foreign manufacturers, making the sales of Citroën and other French cars virtually impossible in the Saar as well as east of the Rhine. That same year, the Citroën factory at Cologne, opened in 1927, was closed down.

By late 1933, André Citroën's financial position – never exactly secure, even at the high point in his fortunes – was worsening by the day, and a race against time had begun to get the new car on to the market as quickly as possible, in order to revive sales and improve the company's cash flow. This meant that staff on the Traction Avant project were regularly working ten hours a day, seven days a week. At one point, Roger Prud'homme, chief engineer of the test workshop, was obliged to remind Citroën that his men were exhausted by the effort and needed a weekend off to rest. 'My dear Prud'homme,' Citroën remarked, 'It's no longer a matter of days, but of hours.' 'In that case, m'sieu, we shall be here on Sunday as usual,' came the reply.

Surely, the extraordinary loyalty and devotion that Citroën inspired among his staff and associates distinguishes him as one of the most remarkable leaders ever to command a major enterprise, industrial or military, and explains how he was able to achieve so much within a relatively short time; indeed, the whole process of the rise and fall of Automobiles Citroën under his direction took place within a period of only fifteen years. Unlike Henry Ford and Louis Renault, who were both cold, calculating and authoritarian in their relationships with subordinates, André Citroën was a considerate, sensitive and humane man who trusted and respected his employees, treating them generously, if not as equals, then certainly as fellow human beings – an attitude unknown both at Billancourt and Detroit. He was never dictatorial; what other bosses could only achieve by issuing orders or threatening sanctions from above, he could obtain by walking casually among his staff, chatting to them on their own level, recognising individuals by name and giving them all a cheerful smile and a warm handshake. Somehow, he was able to communicate his own enthusiasm for the job in hand and to inspire everyone involved with his own confidence in the future. In doing so, he created the unique Citroën *esprit de corps* – a mystique or quasi-religion, the temple of which was the Quai de Javel.

It was always characteristic of Citroën to thank his colleagues personally for services rendered by offering them his hospitality, and over the years the tradition of an annual celebration in the form of a lavish thanksgiving banquet had grown up at the Quai de Javel. All who had made a special contribution in any one year were invited from both within the Citroën organisation and without. As the company expanded, these gatherings steadily outgrew each successive venue, until the point arrived when it became difficult to find a place in Paris large enough in which to hold the festivities. The dinner of 1933, held on Sunday 8 October, was a particularly crowded affair. As no less than 6,333 guests were invited to the celebrations (which also marked the inauguration of the rebuilt Javel factory), there was little alternative but to stage the event in the vast vehicle-delivery hall of the new plant, which was over 250 metres long. Once again, André Citroën showed his mastery of planning and organisation. In spite of the gargantuan scale of the feast and the enormity of the task of catering adequately for so many hungry *convives*, no detail was overlooked. Even the matches and cigars presented to every guest were embossed with the double chevron badge.

While the band of the Garde Républicaine and the Orchestre Citroën played suitably festive music in the background, the diners seated at 120 long tables, each bearing fifty *couverts*, enjoyed a four-course meal of gastronomic pretensions and proportions, accompanied by three fine wines of excellent vintage, and followed, of course, by champagne, coffee and liqueurs. For those who are interested in matters of cuisine, the menu comprised *crème de princesse* soup, *jambon en croûte* and *poularde Strasbourgeoise*, followed by salad, cheese and fruit and, finally, an icecream dessert moulded in the shape of the *Petite Rosalie* record-breaking car.

At two higher tables placed along the length of the hall sat *le patron* and a further 180, from the worlds of politics, diplomacy, finance, education, journalism and sport. Present were such dignitaries as Louis Serre, the Minister of Commerce in the government recently formed by Edouard Daladier, General Gourard, the military governor of Paris, M. Fiquet, the President of the Paris City Council, Baron Petiet, the president of the French equivalent of the Society of Motor Manufacturers and Traders, Prince Axel of Denmark, and even the tennis stars Borotra and Lacoste. Also gathered there were senior figures from the international motor and aeronautical industries, including, from Great Britain, Daniel Metz and General Swinton of Citroën Cars Ltd and, from France, the industrialists Louis Breguet, Marcel Michelin, Gaston Chausson and Louis Renault, who was seated at Citroën's right hand.

When all had eaten their fill, the President of the National Chamber of Automobile Commerce, M. Raymond Mole, rose to salute their host, speaking also on behalf of the 15,000 car dealers of France that he represented. No one had done more to promote and advance the cause of the motor car in Europe than André Citroën, M. Mole rightly claimed. He had been the first car-maker to take whole-page advertisements in the daily papers, and the first to write his name in the sky, 'a name that was also inscribed in the sands of Africa and imprinted for ever in the wildernesses of Asia; a name that scintillated in letters of light, illuminating the night sky of Paris; and a name, moreover, that when carried along the roads from place to place and from country to country covered every day a distance equivalent to several circuits of the globe.'

Replying to the toast, André Citroën returned to the theme that he had developed in his speech in America. 'The automobile is no longer a luxury but has become an indispensible tool of work,' he claimed. 'Its development has now entered a popular, democratic phase, in which it has become essential for the transport of both goods and people alike. That is why we may be confident that its manufacture will become the great industrial and economic driving force of the future, central to the creation of wealth and the improvement of human well-being throughout the world.'

If this prediction seems self-evident today, it should be remembered that, although it was no longer confined to those who could afford to employ a chauffeur, motoring was still an activity very much the preserve of the ruling classes. Given the prevailing circumstances, in the early thirties, most car manufacturers in Europe were extremely cautious about the prospects of expanding car ownership throughout society as a whole. In England, a forecast prepared by the Society of Motor Manufacturers and Traders in 1926 had concluded that, as no family or individual with an annual income of less than £450 (about £25,000 in today's currency) could afford to buy and run a car, out of a total of 4,700,000 such recipients of incomes, no less than 3,940,000 could be discounted as potential motorists, leaving a maximum market of only 760,000 households. But of course, just as incomes were rising, the price of cars was falling in real terms – between 1924 and 1936, the cost of car ownership in Great Britain was halved. Yet this was an economic trend that only men of vision like André Citroën had the imagination to foresee. Indeed, even in the early thirties, when many countries had no roads at all, he was already prophesying the congestion that the success of the motor car would bring to the world's great cities. Alone among contemporary motor manufacturers, he pointed out that to overcome the greatest obstacle to the future development of the automobile industry, the first priority was to develop an infrastructure of ring roads, underground parking places and other traffic control measures that would prevent damage to the urban environment.

The celebrations concluded with a spectacular firework display. Reinvigorated by all they had seen, heard, eaten and drunk, Citroën's guests returned to their duties to continue their good work in the cause of the double chevron marque, their energy and enthusiasm rekindled by contact with the dynamic motor magnate. Truly, this banquet was the high point in André Citroën's career – the event that marked the zenith in the fortunes of the Citroën firm. Who among those jubilant guests could have foreseen the cruel come-uppance that fate had in store for their genial and generous host, and how, within a year, his gambler's luck would change so adversely?

With the new factory completed and in operation, it was now time to put it to its intended purpose: the production of the revolutionary Traction Avant, and ultimately, so it was planned, in massive numbers of more than a thousand vehicles a day, an incredible target for that time. It appears that, after several false starts, by June 1933 a definitive design and working prototype had been arrived at and approved, so that Messrs Cuinet and Franchiset were able to set out for the Budd company in the USA some time early in November 1933, carrying with them the plans required to order tooling for the bodywork. Even as they sailed across the Atlantic, revisions to the design were still being telegraphed daily to their boat! Three weeks later, they returned with a new colleague, the American Dennis Kendall, who was to supervise the installation of machinery and the opening of the production line.

So it happened that on 24 March 1934, almost exactly one year after the arrival of André Lefebvre at the Quai de Javel, the top-secret Traction Avant car was first unveiled by its creator, at a gathering of forty leading concessionnaires. Three weeks later, on 18 April, it was revealed to the press at the Magasin d'Europe. By May 1934, the first cars were on sale in France at the price of 17,700 francs, no more than had been charged for the by now obsolete Rosalie models which they were to supersede.

Rushed into production ahead of time to drum up sales, frankly, the Traction Avant – initially called the 'Citroën Sept' – was woefully underdeveloped and poorly built, so much so that the first owners were put into the position of being unpaid test drivers, liable to experience endless breakdowns. The brakes, driveshafts and torsion-bar suspension of the early production models all gave trouble, and the workload of Lefebvre's hard-pressed team actually increased as they struggled round the clock to solve a succession of unforeseen on-road problems.

For example, on 8 June 1934, André Citroën staged a Concours d'Elégance in the Bois de Boulogne, an event that he was particularly fond of holding, since it provided an opportunity to combine automobile glitz with feminine glamour. Seven immaculately groomed Traction Avant cars took part in the parade, each driven by a notable society beauty: four saloons, one Bordeaux-red car driven by Mlle Ginette Loubet, one navy-blue car driven by Mlle de Korsak and two white cars driven by Mlle Arlette Morel and Mme Françoise Spitzer; two cabriolets, a pearl-grey example driven by Mme Robert Fenwick and another painted beige, driven by the Comtesse de Caraman-Chimay, and finally, a black faux-cabriolet with the Baroness de Rothschild at the wheel. But when, after the prizegiving, it was time for the cars to move off, none could do so. The brakes on all of them had overheated and locked solid. While his mechanics worked unobtrusively to free the cars, André Citroën stepped forward to distract the attention of the crowd by making an amusing impromptu speech.

In spite of all these difficulties, the car received a rapturous welcome from press and public alike. In its edition of 19 April, the influential French motoring magazine *l'Auto Journal* declared: 'The front-wheel-drive Citroën 7 . . . is so up-to-the-minute, so audacious, so rich in original technical solutions, so different to all that had been done before that it truly deserves the epiphet "sensational".' The *Journal* then went on to praise André Citroën for having introduced, in the midst of a period of unprecedented crisis, 'a car so truly French in the elegance of its engineering and its finesse of styling and design. If France is ever to recapture its pre-eminence as a car producer in overseas markets, it requires the existence of such an advanced vehicle, truly sensational in the way that it combines a high technical specification with a modest price,' the *Journal* patriotically concluded.

The existence of the Traction Avant was revealed to British motorists in the 8 May issue of *The Motor*, some six weeks after its first public appearance in France. In an article entitled 'A car we could not overturn', *The Motor*'s journalists

The Traction Avant's first appearance at the Paris Salon motor show, October 1934. No less than ten different versions were exhibited, including three examples of a fabulous new model, the 22CV, which never entered volume production.

During the first half of 1934 the Citroën firm continued to build conventional cars concurrently with the Traction Avant. Among the most expensive of these rear-wheel-drive models was this special six-cylinder Grand Luxe 15CV sports saloon, fitted with an all-alloy coachbuilt body. Note that, in common with every Citroën built from January 1934 onwards, this car has double chevrons fixed to its radiator grille. Initially adopted for the Traction Avant, this characteristic motif became the marque's principal identifying feature.

praised the Traction Avant's 'extraordinary stability' and 'exceptional road-holding and riding comfort'. Noting that it was a streamlined saloon without conventional leaf-springs, frame or front axle, and that its weight was reduced by novel construction, the article concluded: 'this interesting car represents a courageous attack upon current automobile problems and the ingenuity and ability shown by its builders are worthy of the highest praise'. *The Autocar* echoed this verdict, saying in its road test published on 1 February 1935 that 'the car can . . . be driven at amazing speeds over a pot-holed surface that you would not take at more than a cautious 20 mph in the average car'.

In June, the Traction Avant was entered in its first competition event, an automobile version of the Tour de France. Driven by François Lecot, who had been entrusted with pre-production testing of the prototype in North Africa, one of the first 7CV examples to come off the assembly line covered over 5,000 kilometres through France and Belgium within seventy-seven hours. This achievement Lecot promptly repeated by driving the 5,400 kilometres from Paris to Moscow and back non-stop in forty-eight hours, no mean feat considering the roads of the time. A former racing cyclist-turned-rally driver, Lecot's talents had first attracted the attention of André Citroën when he drove a Citroën bus in the Monte-Carlo Rally earlier that year.

At the Paris Salon motor show which opened on 3 October 1934, the full

The cabriolet version of the proposed 22CV, seen here on the Paris Salon stand alongside its massive 90 hp 3,822 cc V8 engine. All traces of these prototypes disappeared during the war when they were destroyed on the instructions of the new Citroën management.

Described in Citroën's publicity material as the fastest, safest production vehicle in the world, the 22CV (seen here in saloon form) was Citroën's final riposte to Henry Ford. Three examples are believed to have been sold commercially before the Citroën firm crashed. Where are they now?

In September 1934 a larger 1,911 cc engine was introduced on the Traction Avant. Gradually improved by various minor modifications, this engine remained in service until 1981, being used to power the Citroën Type H van long after production of the Traction Avant ceased in 1957.

extent of the proposed Traction Avant range was revealed in its entirety before record crowds. Replacing the three versions previously introduced (the 7A series light saloon, fixed-head coupé and roadster powered by a 1,303 cc 7CV engine), there were to be a further three similar cars powered by a more effective 1,529 cc engine (7B series), three more powered by a 1,628 cc high-performance engine (7C series), plus nine new models powered by a 1,911 cc 11CV engine. This 11A series comprised three short-wheelbase cars, a four-seater light saloon, a fixed-head coupé and a roadster, all similar in style and dimensions to those of the 7 series; a standard-wheelbase six-seater saloon (the 11 Normale), a cabriolet, a fixed-head coupé and a coupé-de-ville; and, finally, two long-wheelbase versions, a nine-seater family saloon and a commercial saloon featuring a fully-opening tailgate.

And as if this huge choice of fifteen different bodywork and engine combinations were not enough, to crown his Traction Avant range Citroën also proposed to offer a further six high-performance, super-deluxe cars (a normal saloon, a family saloon, a roadster, a fixed-head coupé, and a coupé-de-ville) powered by a monster 3,820 cc V8 engine capable not just of reaching 140 kph but of maintaining such high speeds safely and surely for hours on end. Doubtless, this engine was inspired by Henry Ford's V8, introduced in 1932, which Citroën had previewed at Detroit in 1931. Three prototypes of the 22CV were exhibited at the 1934 Paris Motor Show, but none were ever built in series production.

For by then it was all too late. The financial collapse of Automobiles Citroën had become inescapable. That year, there would be no great banquets, parties or celebrations. A little over two months later, on 21 December 1934, as a result of legal action taken by an impatient minor creditor, the company was forced into liquidation, to be taken over by its chief creditor, the Michelin tyre firm, to which Citroën had already pledged his own personal shareholding. Thus, having lost both his fortune, his company and, indeed, his name, André Citroën was never to see his optimism vindicated by the resounding success of his 'new concept in motoring' or by the long line of avant-garde designs which followed it.

Ironically, the Citroën Traction Avant was a gamble that paid off for everyone except its creator. Still acknowleged by discerning drivers today for its exceptional stability and exemplary handling and road-holding, it quickly became a legend. Indeed, its rapid commercial success allowed the company's new owners to repay all Citroën's remaining liabilities and debts within two years of acquiring control.

Judged today to be a masterpiece of automobile design and construction, with only minor modifications it remained in production for almost a quarter of a century, during which time more than 759,000 examples of its many different variants were produced, while its original 11CV engine continued to be manufactured until 1981, so setting a record for the continuous production of a single automobile component unbroken to this day.

Louis Renault was to have the last word in the contest. It is reputed that, voicing his regrets at his rival's bad luck, he said: 'The only dirty trick I ever played on André Citroën was to show him my new factory on the Ile de Séguin. After that he ruined himself trying to do in three months what it had taken me thirty years to accomplish.' Later, Renault made another telling remark. Speaking to the French motoring journalist Charles Faroux, he said: 'Citroën did us all a lot of good. He stopped us from falling asleep. We had to stay on our toes constantly just to keep up with him.' Unfortunately, as Faroux pointed out, it is impossible to build anything durable and lasting with intelligence and audacity alone: 'The experience of centuries shows it is also necessary to add the cement provided by such qualities as level-headedness, prudence and restraint, plus that very rare material known simply as common sense.'

CHAPTER ELEVEN

Citroën Pressé

Sixty years after Citroën's demise, the questions raised by the affair continue to exercise the best brains of leading business schools and management consultancies. For the whole débâcle was – and remains – a textbook case of the all too familiar situation that occurs when a successful, expanding company grows beyond the capacities of its founder to control it. Can the buccaneering style of individual initiative and enterprise essential to the establishment of a business ever be reconciled with the high degree of stability, responsibility and probity called for in the management of a large industrial corporation? Was the Citroën affair a typical failure of financial administration of the type continually encountered by thousands of businesses – a routine cash flow crisis played out on a grand scale? Or was it a unique, monumental example of over-trading, caused entirely by André Citroën's energetic, over-optimistic personality, and which could and would have easily been avoided by a more sober entrepreneur in his position?

With the wisdom of hindsight, it is hard to escape the conclusion that André Citroën was a man carried to fame and fortune by a freak wave of prosperity, but

Citroën the family man enjoys a game of backgammon with his wife in their apartment at the rue Octave-Feuillet in Paris.

The 7B Traction Avant Roadster, photographed by Pierre Louys beside the Dordogne in 1934. The peace and tranquillity in the affairs of the Citroën firm suggested by this portrait were to be short-lived.

who, when the tide turned, was then drowned in an attempt to swim against the current of events. There is no doubt that, although he was certainly no despot in the tradition of so many of the industrial autocrats of his era, he ran his business in a individualistic way, to please his own inclinations. But he was never guilty of reckless incompetence or irresponsibility, as some commentators have suggested. However, instead of pursuing the quest for profits simply for the sake of profits, a path that he considered sterile and ultimately unproductive, he preferred to follow his own personal interests and intuition in his business affairs. With Citroën, it was always adventure and innovation at any price. Rather than merely making money, he was interested in making better cars, building them up to a standard, not down to a price. And as we have already seen, his cavalier attitude to finance and those who provided it was revealed as early as 1924 by his famous pronouncement, 'the moment an idea is right, its price becomes of no importance'. For Citroën, money was simply the lubricant that oiled his industrial machine, and as long as there was a plentiful supply in the sump to keep things moving, it didn't matter where it came from or where it went.

It seems that Automobiles Citroën was under financial pressure and at odds with the banks from the very start of its activities. Although André Citroën had made substantial profits from his munitions business during the First World War, these were subsequently taxed by French government at the penal rate of 90 per cent and therefore did not extend to covering the costs of starting up a major motor-manufacturing business from scratch. Thus Citroën was obliged to look beyond his network of family and friends such as Eknayan for further working capital and to finance his new venture on credit. In contrast to Renault, he had no hesitation in incurring substantial debts and would never allow his plans to be postponed by a shortage of cash. But in a country ravaged by war, burdened by huge international debts and preoccupied with the problems of economic and industrial reconstruction, finance for such enterprises was hard to come by. In their corporate history of the Ford company 1915–1933, Allan Nevins and Frank Ernest Hill reveal that, in an attempt to overcome these early financial difficulties, in the summer of 1919 André Citroën approached Henry Ford with an astonishing offer of partnership. 'He had laid down a programme for building 30,000 units the next year and had booked orders for 14,000. But . . . the banks had stopped his credit', the American historians relate. 'He telegraphed to Charles Sorensen Chez Fordson in Dearborn: 'Willing to accept any financial cooperation with Ford, whether partnership or as sleeping partner or formation of limited company. Shall soon be absolute master of French market and will also make very big exportations.' The requirements of the business were ten million dollars, Citroen claimed. To gain Ford's backing, he was prepared to come at once to Dearborn with all his papers. But Sorenson (Henry Ford's chief lieutenant) crushed his hopes in ten words: 'Impossible to secure Mr Ford's aid in financing your company,' he cabled in a curt reply. An individualist himself, Ford had no interest in a tie-up with any other manufacturer in any other country, and certainly not with Citroën in France.

Undeterred by this rebuff, André Citroën fought on alone and overcame his problems temporarily. But such was the rapid rate of growth that he encouraged that in 1924, although remaining under his absolute control, it proved necessary for his privately-owned firm to 'go public' and be incorporated as a limited-liability company, the Société Anonyme André Citroën, with a share capital of 100 million francs, double that existing at the start. Indeed, so great was the furious pace of expansion forced by the dynamic Citroën that, by 1926, to finance the launch of the new B14, a further substantial injection of capital was required. However, to retain his independence, instead of approaching the banks, this time Citroën made a direct appeal to the public by means of advertisements in the press, and quickly raised a loan of 250 million francs with interest fixed at 7½ per cent, which gave these lucky private investors an exceptionally generous return on their money for that era.

Even so, this subscription proved insufficient to finance the company's progress, and in 1927, to fund the launch of the C4, it was once again necessary to increase the share capital to 300 million francs; and then, one year later, to 400 million francs. To get hold of this kind of money, Citroën had no alternative but to take the conventional financial route. And so it was that, in 1928, the old established, Jewish-owned merchant banking firm Lazard Frères arrived at the Quai de Javel, in the person of its President Pierre David-Weill. (The David-Weill and Citroën families were eventually united in marriage when André's son

Maxime married Pierre David-Weill's daughter Antoinette. Similarly, his daughter Jacqueline married Paul-André de Saint-Sauveur, son of the boss of the Schneider industrial company, a major shareholder in Automobiles Citroën.)

Naturally, in return for its support, made in the form of loans and a substantial shareholding, the bank insisted on a measure of involvement in the running of the Citroën company, nominating its own representatives to sit on the board of directors. By 1929, there were four such placemen: David-Weill, Paul Frantzen, Raymond Phillippe and André Meyer. And although Citroën remained president and G.-M. Haardt vice-president, Frantzen had taken over from Haardt as managing director with day-to-day control of all aspects of administration. By this point, around 20 per cent of Automobiles Citroën was owned by business and institutional investors as opposed to private shareholders and Citroën family interests, the two principal outside parties being Lazards and the Schneider industrial group, run by Armand de Saint-Sauveur. Even so, Citroën's own personal shareholding was such that he remained in overall control of his affairs, at least in theory.

But in practice, things were rather different. In the interests of rationalisation and economy, and to establish a greater measure of financial control over Automobiles Citroën and its extravagant patron, the bankers began to make sweeping changes in the way that the company was managed and directed, cutting this, squeezing that and reorganising everything. Citroën soon found out

Madame Citroën photographed in March 1930 at the start of the Paris–Cannes rally organised by the Automobile Club Feminin de France of which she was a prominent member. The name and role of the large gentleman is unknown. As was her custom, Mme Citroën is wearing a tweed suit and cloche hat by Chanel.

that his hands were being tied by red tape and that his freedom to make his own decisions was being severely restricted by the dead hand of cost-accountancy. In his view, officialdom and bureacracy had descended on the Quai de Javel, stifling its former spirit of enterprise and creativity and adversely affecting the morale of its workforce. Indeed, industrial disputes and petty strikes, hitherto unknown at the Citroën factories, were already rife. Despite the growth and expansion that was taking place, and which they readily sanctioned, all that the bankers were interested in were short-term returns, he complained; the Lazard men had no overall vision or long-term objectives other than in maintaining the security and profitability of their loans.

By November 1930, he had had enough of this interference, which, he considered, was creating conflicts that threatened the efficiency of his factory and the quality of his products. In a bold and defiant memorandum, he insisted that, henceforth, the two most senior managers appointed by the bank – the Managing Director Paul Frantzen and the Finance Chief Witold Chaminsky – would report directly to him, and that budgetary and cost-control matters would be supervised by a new financial secretariat which he would personally supervise. It was, in effect, a *coup d'état,* overthrowing the influence and control of Lazard Frères. When his action was approved by a vote of confidence at the annual general meeting of shareholders on 4 December, André Citroën was once again complete master in his own house. Now he was free to put into action the revolutionary plans that he had been hatching for so long, assisted by his faithful *ancien régime,* Haardt, Mannheimer, Schwab and Pommier, who were returned to the board of directors forthwith.

Apparently, the divorce was accepted by the bankers as 'a divergence of views' of the kind inevitable when, after a short honeymoon, both marriage partners discover that, apart from a superficial need for each other's company, they share no common interests and are incompatible in outlook and temperament. Indeed, Lazard Frères had profited greatly from their short-lived partnership with Automobiles Citroën, since within that two-year relationship their shareholding in the firm had trebled in value. Yet even so, despite the civilised expressions of regret, another black mark had been deposited permanently in Citroën's account with the French banking fraternity.

There were certainly no hard feelings on Citroën's part. Indeed, he liked and respected the Lazard men as human beings. They were not villains or robbers, out to cheat him; it was just that as bankers – like all bankers, in his experience – they had little vision or imagination. Despite their large art collections, they were not creative people; they did not understand or recognise creativity; nor did they appreciate that, in a trading business, the trust and goodwill that comes from harmonious human relationships ultimately counts far more than figures on a balance sheet. And, most assuredly, they did not know the difference between a good car and a merely mediocre one. 'The banks are only interested in lending short-term to make their own long-term gains. It is not a good economic system,' Citroën had observed with rueful acuity in 1926.

Following the departure of the Lazard administration, three years of unfettered activity took place at Automobiles Citroën, during which time the Traction Avant was developed and the Quai de Javel factory was completely modernised and rebuilt. Between 1931 and 1933, the output of the French automobile industry fell by 20 per cent (Citroën's own by 33 per cent), and the number of car producers in France dropped from 90 to 28. No less than 118 banks went bust. But in the midst of this economic crisis of unprecedented severity, with his sales revenues plunging like a bucket down a bottomless well, Citroën spent more freely than ever before. When the tragic and untimely death of G.-M. Haardt in March 1932 left him alone at the driving seat, the company roared ahead at full speed, completely out of control. There was no one left on board with a sufficiently powerful restraining influence over *le patron* to reduce the throttle and apply the brakes.

The inevitable result was that, on 28 February 1934, Automobiles Citroën ran headlong into a severe financial crisis. On this date, Citroën was due to make a repayment of 50 million francs in long-term borrowings and interest to his financiers, but as the hour grew nearer it became clear that he could only raise a tenth of that amount. When his clearing bankers, the Bank of France, refused to extend further short-term credit to tide him over, he had only one alternative in order to avoid default – to call on the generosity of the Double Chevron

An aerial view of the Quai de Javel factory, after its reconstruction in 1933. The huge delivery hall in which André Citroën held his great banquet in October 1933 can be seen lying crosswise behind the administrative building which faced the River Seine.

organisation. A sort of informal whip-round was held, and the money was cobbled together by contributions and donations from his dealers and concessionnaires, who never once throughout the crisis had doubts in Citroën's abilities to make good. All would be well when the Traction Avant was ready for sale, of that Citroën was certain. The new car was bound to be a huge success and would quickly restore his fortunes. Not only would his greatest gamble get him out of his present embarrassment, but it would keep him in funds for years to come. No one else had anything like it. It was so advanced that it would take his rivals ages to produce a vehicle which could compete with it.

So confident was he of its virtues that he decided it was time to play his trump card. At the end of February 1934, he invited several bankers and financiers to a secret preview, a month or so before the car's existence was revealed to the press, to demonstrate the asset that would clear his debts. Unfortunately, far from being a triumph, the event was a disaster. The automatic gearbox failed, and the car broke down. Not being technical men, open to a rational explanation of the problem, the bankers went away unimpressed, even more disinclined than ever to lend money on this foolhardy venture. Bitterly disappointed, Citroën conceded defeat and allowed the integrity of his 'new concept in motoring' to be compromised, ordering the *Bureau d'Etudes* to produce a manual gearbox in time for the scheduled press demonstration three weeks later.

By now, the rumours were spreading fast throughout the motor industry and beyond: André Citroën was in trouble. With the dire shortage of money at the Quai de Javel common knowledge, all his skills in propaganda and public relations were called upon to persuade his creditors to hold off in their demands for payment. Exhausted by the physical and mental effort of keeping the show on the road, Citroën grew thinner and paler by the day; to those who saw him in his few public appearances at that time, he seemed but a shadow of his former self. For the first time in his life, his optimistic expectations had been severely shaken.

And on the wider political and economic scene, a parallel crisis continued to mount. The forces of reaction were now on the march throughout Europe – not just in Germany but in France and England too. On 6 February 1934, street-fighting had broken out in Paris when 40,000 demonstrators from the various Fascist leagues – principally the Action Française and the Croix de Feu – marched on the Chamber of Deputies in an attempt to overthrow the Republic. The *coup d'état* was only averted when the police opened fire on the crowd in the Place de la Concorde; sixteen demonstrators and one policeman were killed and over two thousand participants in the battle seriously wounded. A week later, the Communists staged a counter-demonstration and called a token general strike. Although the Third Republic was saved, the government headed by Edouard Daladier fell, to be replaced by an equally short-lived administration led by Gaston Domergue. Playing out his own personal drama against this backdrop of political and social turmoil, Citroën was filled with feelings of apprehension. Looking forward, he had apocalyptic forebodings of an impending disaster in Europe, as destructive as the events of 1914–18, and possibly even worse than that for Jews like himself. Looking back, he was haunted by the spectre of his father's financial disgrace and suicide in circumstances all too similar to his own.

To make matters worse, another financial scandal had recently blown up to fan the flames of anti-Semitism: the Stavisky affair, in which a shady financier of Ukrainian Jewish origins, Serge Stavisky, had floated a loan worth millions of francs secured on worthless bonds, apparently with the complicity of certain high-ranking politicians and government officials. The fraud was seized upon by the demagogues of the far right as an excuse to stage another major political drama. Once again, as in the Dreyfus case, the affair provided a focus for popular discontent, and all the old conservative, provincial Catholic suspicions and prejudices against such diverse targets as Freemasonry, high society, cosmopolitan intellectuals, Protestant progressives, international Jewry and the Americans were given a thorough airing.

Caught up in the midst of this social instability and political chaos, André Citroën was forced to the conclusion that only one viable course of action remained open to him. If he was to save his firm, he had no alternative but to appeal for help from old Edouard Michelin, patriarch of the Michelin tyre firm which now ranked as his largest trade creditor. He had known the Michelin family for almost thirty years, since his days with Mors, and Edouard, now aged seventy-five, had visited the Quai de Javel as recently as 1928. In fact, the Michelin firm of Clermont Ferrand had been the sole suppliers of wheels and tyres to Automobiles Citroën from the outset and although this business had been very profitable in the past, by now it was owed a very large sum indeed for goods delivered but not yet paid for. In 1929, at the height of his success, Citroën had negotiated an agreement with the Michelin firm, giving him a discount of 10 per cent on all wheels and tyres supplied, provided that his output continued to exceed eighty thousand vehicles a year. The following year, production fell below this figure and remained there, but the discount was offered and taken nonetheless in the expectancy that sales would shortly revive, allowing the shortfall to be made up according to the terms of the deal. So it was that Citroën's debt to the Michelin men mounted inexorably throughout the early thirties.

Still a family-owned concern, the Michelin tyre company had its origins in the 1830s when the Englishwoman Elizabeth Pugh-Barker, niece of Charles Mackintosh (who first discovered the secret of dissolving natural rubber in benzine) married Edouard Daubrée, the part-owner of an agricultural machinery business in the Auvergne. Elizabeth brought with her to France the know-how for making toy rubber balls and other domestic articles, and by 1863 the Michelin company was fully established as a manufacturer of rubber ware. By 1888 it had grown large enough to be incorporated as a limited company or Société Anonyme.

In 1891, Edouard and André Michelin (actually the grandsons of M. Daubrée's partner Aristide Barbier) patented the world's first detachable pneumatic cycle tyre, following up this invention four years later with a similar tyre for cars. A development of John Dunlop's idea, the Michelin demountable tyre consisted of a flexible rubber inner tube containing air under high pressure, protected by an outer canvas cover coated with hard rubber into which a tread was moulded. This cover had wire rings bonded into its inner edges, allowing the tyre to be secured reliably, but not permanently, to the wheel rims. Now it was possible to ride and drive on a cushion of air, instead of a solid, circular block of rubber – and, if it punctured, to rapidly remove and repair it.

Enterprising and astute, the Michelin brothers prospered greatly in the motor car boom which took place before and after the First World War, and soon became figures of great importance in the emerging French automobile industry. Despite being cunning and secretive (so much so that they were known in Paris as 'the old foxes of the Auvergne'), they were certainly not backward or old-fashioned in their outlook. On the contrary, like a good many other entrepreneurs from a rural background, they proved to be extremely go-ahead in their business methods, and embraced modern technology with enthusiasm. And although they were secretive to the point of paranoia, they also possessed a flair for publicity rivalling that of André Citroën himself. In 1898, they created their famous Michelin Man trademark, Monsieur Bibendum, and then went on to launch their renowned series of road maps and restaurant guides which, with their coveted stars, still represent the ultimate test of the cuisine and accommodation provided for business motorists and tourists travelling on the roads of Europe today.

By 1934, André had died, leaving his younger brother Edouard (1859–1940) in sole charge, at an age when most other men would have long since retired. Edouard was assisted by a deputy, his son Pierre, and by his *homme de confiance* (right-hand man), a certain Pierre-Jules Boulanger, who, unlike most of the Michelin management hierarchy, was not actually a member of the family. In response to Citroën's appeal, Edouard promptly sent these two lieutenants to Paris, accompanied by engineers from Michelin's own Bureau d'Etudes, to inspect the factories and examine the Traction Avant. Fortunately for Citroën, unlike the bankers, the Michelin men were technically competent and could recognise a good car when they saw it. In fact, they were deeply impressed by the vehicle, and soon gave their thumbs-up to the rescue scheme. The outcome was that Edouard Michelin agreed to advance Citroën a short-term loan in addition to the existing debt, on condition that he was given an option to buy the company and that Citroën offered up his own personal shareholding in Automobiles Citroën as security. Moreover, Citroën was obliged to undertake not to leave the company and attempt to set up a rival firm in partnership with Ettore Bugatti or the Americans, with whom he was rumoured to be having secret discussions. He was also required to allow the Michelin men to assume a role in the management of the company, in order to implement immediately a programme of drastic economies and redundancies within the Citroën organisation and to set up a system of quality control to overcome the evident manufacturing deficiencies affecting the sale and production of the Traction Avant.

Edouard Michelin (who rarely ventured far from his base at Clermont Ferrand) visited André Citroën at the Quai de Javel in June 1934. On Citroën's left is M. Michelin's son-in-law, M. Bourdon.

The resulting *Super-Contrôle* (Inspection Department), headed by the Michelin engineer M. Antoine Hermet, which for many years remained a unique quality-control facility among the world's motor manufacturers, was undoubtedly one of the factors most responsible for the subsequent renaissance in the reputation of Automobiles Citroën.

By July 1934, André Citroën had put together his own refinancing proposals, involving a further injection of capital totalling 180 million francs, a third provided by the banks, a third by his dealers and concessionaires and a third by the French government, from public funds. But despite the reassuring presence of the Michelins on the scene as *de facto* guarantors, after much deliberation, both the banks and the government, under its new premier, Pierre-Etienne Flandin (later Foreign Minister in the Vichy regime), turned down the scheme and refused to participate. The Socialist Opposition, led by Leon Blum and Jules Moch, demanded nationalisation, saying that the matter was 'One of the most painful crises of modern capitalism'. Yet despite the ever-rising tide of unemployment and industrial unrest, there were to be no New Deal-style State rescue schemes on offer in France. Aware that Flandin was a man of the right and, moreover, a friend and frequent social guest of Louis Renault, many political observers detected in the decision a sinister undercurrent of hostility

Throughout their careers, the two great French motor magnates André Citroën and Louis Renault repeatedly clashed head-on in a duel of industrial strength that was depicted on the cover of the French illustrated magazine Vu *in January 1935. In fact, their rivalry had begun when they were schoolboys at the same Lycée.*

and anti-Semitism towards Citroën personally. Undoubtedly, old scores were being settled by those of influence and authority whom Citroën had offended in the past. Even among newspaper comment and public gossip, more than a trace of *Schadenfreude* was evident. What had happened to all Citroën's personal wealth? Why had he no savings or financial reserves of his own to throw into the balance? Had he not gambled it all away at Deauville or lost it on the horses? Had he not admitted that he never really cared how much the croupiers raked off him? Too bad. He should have been more prudent, more cautious and have put something away for a rainy day. The fact of the matter was that André Citroën's flamboyant free-spending style of business, so in tune with the spirit of the twenties, now seemed to strike a discordant note in the austere atmosphere of the thirties.

For the next few months, a sort of hiatus or creditor's moratorium held sway, as all involved held off from further action in the hope not just of saving their investment but also of preventing large-scale unemployment and precipitating a general crisis of confidence in the French motor industry – a scenario which could only benefit foreign manufacturers and lead, perhaps, to a takeover of Automobiles Citroën by the Americans. Indeed, the French were worried that American interests might seize control of their entire motor industry, just as the

Americans had wrested away their early lead in aeronautical engineering and air travel.

However, at the end of November 1934, a small creditor by the name of Jean Ostheimer, owner of the Compagnie Franco-Américaine des Jantes en Bois, a supplier of Bakelite steering wheels, which was owed only 60,000 old francs, lost patience and put in the equivalent of a winding-up petition in the French commercial courts. Under French law, the Société Anonyme André Citroën was then required to deposit a statement of its financial situation at the Financial Tribunal of Paris. Unable to prove its solvency, on 21 December 1934 the company was adjudged bankrupt and a state of judicial liquidation (receivership) declared. Nominated as *juge-commissaire* to administer this liquidation and prepare a report was a certain President Piketty, assisted by three liquidators. Simultaneously, a creditors' committee was formed, comprising Pierre Michelin, Paul Frantzen (representing Lazard Frères) and a M. Ducastel of le Comptoir Sidérurgique, another large creditor. In the mean time, while the receivers went about their work, to safeguard the assets and protect the 20,000 jobs still provided by the company, Automobiles Citroën was allowed to continue in production at its previous level of trading. (A few months later, Jean Ostheimer sold his business to the Michelin family. His reward was an appointment as managing director of the Michelin Tyre Company's US subsidiary.)

In one of his last public appearances, André Citroën greets Francois Lecot and his Traction Avant at the finish of the Paris–Moscow–Paris run on 4 October 1934.

Early in the New Year, Maurice Dollfus, Managing Director of the newly-formed Matford company (created by a merger between Henry Ford's French interests and the old established Mathis car firm) wrote to Ford's European supremo in London, Sir Percival Perry, informing him of these momentous developments in the French motor industry. 'You will have heard by now that Citroën has gone bust . . . but there is no doubt that it will be revived,' Dollfus reported. 'I can see what Citroën is aiming at – that is to make an arrangement with his creditors and start afresh again, having left behind him the unbearable weight of his liabilities. But I am confident that he will not succeed in doing that,' Dollfus stated. 'Ultimately, this Citroën business will turn out to be a good thing for us, but for the time being it has upset the apple cart to such an extent that there is no possibility of selling cars in France at present under normal conditions. . . . On the whole it can be said that Citroën, although he has been largely instrumental in [pioneering] the diffusion [mass marketing] of automobiles in France, has unquestionably been the greatest disturbing factor on the French market. When a new Citroën business is formed, it will have to be conducted on more reasonable lines,' Dollfus continued, adding that he was having to watch the financial position of all his own suppliers very carefully in the light of the Citroën bankruptcy, since most were Matford suppliers also. 'I will keep you posted on the situation, because it has a very far-reaching effect, not only in France but in other European countries where [Ford] has interests,' Dollfus concluded.

Thus, fearful of the repercussions that the débâcle would have on their own fragile trading positions, the entire European and American motor industry closed ranks to witness André Citroën's collapse. The great gambler had rocked the boat once too often with his crazy ideas and over-ambitious innovations. In these turbulent economic times, who among other motor manufacturers would be rash enough to risk his own skin by jumping into unknown waters in order to save such an incorrigible adventurer and individualist?

And that is how, in a series of moves begun in January and finalised one year later in December 1935, prompted and encouraged by the French government, the Michelin family took over Automobiles Citroën lock, stock and barrel, acquiring a 57 per cent controlling interest in its share capital in exchange for an agreement to assume responsibility for paying off all its debts. Actually, the French Government had earlier proposed a take-over of Citroën by Renault, but this course of action was unacceptable to the principals of both firms! In return for the surrender of André Citroën's own personal shareholding (ceded along with his other rights and privileges on 15 January 1935), it was further agreed that he would be indemnified against personal bankruptcy. Although Citroën was allowed to remain as titular head of the firm as chairman following the judgement of the court, he was forced to relinquish all executive control to Pierre Michelin and P.-J. Boulanger.

In effect, in one great gulp, Automobiles Citroën and its founder had been swallowed up by Monsieur Bibendum, the Michelin Man.

For the next forty years, its destiny was to rest in very different hands. Normally, when car manufacturers fail financially and are taken over, it is by former rivals who lose no time in making changes, enforcing new principles and

Monsieur Bibendum, the immortal mascot of the Michelin tyre firm which swallowed up the Citroën company in 1935. Looking even more rotund and well-fed, the corpulent Michelin Man is still very much alive as an advertising trademark today.

eradicating old established practices. But in this case, there was no such clash of interests. Michelin was merely a creditor and not a competitor, and with no previous car-making experience, it had no preconceived philosophy about the rights and wrongs of car construction. Otherwise, on gaining control, the Michelin men might easily have put a stop to any further work on Citroën's new Traction Avant and returned to producing conventional cars, treating their new acquisition as simply a safe, captive market for their tyres.

But Michelin was itself a pioneering, research-orientated company, run by a farsighted management which encouraged new ideas. Indeed, at the time of the takeover it had already embarked on a course of research that was to lead inevitably to a truly revolutionary breakthrough in the technology of transportation – the steel-belt radial tyre, the technical principles of which were then in the course of being mastered by Michelin's scientists. Moreover, to market such advanced concepts as the low-profile Pilote tyre which it had already developed to the point of production, the Michelin company needed the cooperation of an innovative car-maker; one which would help it get its new products on the road, by producing, in due course, a range of advanced vehicles with suspension and steering characteristics specifically designed to exploit and demonstrate the advantages of Michelin tyre knowhow.

Nevertheless, the new Michelin management brought with it from Clermont-Ferrand a very different style of management from that which had existed under André Citroën's rule. Austere, frugal and highly secretive, it fostered the high-quality standards of design, engineering and production that André Citroën had established, but suppressed entirely the extravagant advertising and promotion that had characterised the firm in earlier days. From then on, and throughout the forties, fifties and sixties, an iron curtain descended around the Quai de Javel as impenetrable as any that ever shrouded the USSR. The spirit of André Citroën the pioneering innovator survived; the ghost of Citroën the flamboyant self-publicist was exorcised.

The final chapter in the life of André Citroën was not, alas, a happy one. By now his health was deteriorating visibly by the day, so much so that after the Christmas and New Year holidays of 1934/5, he received a message from Pierre Michelin suggesting that it was no longer necessary for him to come to his office at the Quai de Javel. In fact, in the circumstances, it might be best for all concerned if he remained at home to rest. Far from aiding Citroën's recovery from illness, the suggestion – or was it an order? – came as a mortal blow. On reading the note, he broke down in the presence of his wife, devastated at the thought of being excluded from his beloved factories, the creation of which had been his life's work and, for the past fifteen years, his sole *raison d'être*. Once such a noted bon vivant, Citroën had lost his appetite long ago, but now he found that he could not eat at all. Weakened to the point of invalidity, and with his spiritual energy and will to survive virtually extinguished, on 18 January 1935 he was admitted to a private clinic in the rue Georges-Bizet, where a malignant tumour of the stomach was diagnosed. All efforts by the doctors and surgeons to defeat the cancer (a course of treatment which culminated in a major operation performed on 9 May) proved unsuccessful. At 9 a.m. on Wednesday 3 July 1935, André Citroën passed away. He was seven months short of his fifty-seventh birthday.

All who heard of his demise were conscious that he had suffered a terrible injustice. Having built up Europe's largest car company from nothing, he had been left with nothing. Some said that he had died of a broken heart, the victim of political duplicity and treachery; others, less condemning, believed that his death was the inevitable result of the mental and physical exhaustion brought about by months of prolonged, and ultimately futile, efforts to save his firm. Whichever was correct, it all amounted to the same thing, as his devoted colleagues, collaborators and employees recognised. Throughout the following day, they solemnly filed by in their thousands, in tribute to their friend and patron, as his body lay in state on a catafalque placed in the great hall of the Citroën office building, before the vast glass window that had been installed in the rebuilding of the Quai de Javel, to give him a constant view of activities on the adjacent assembly line. On the coffin, draped with a black velvet cloth embroidered in silver thread with the double chevron badge, were placed his insignia as a Grand Officier of the Légion d'Honneur.

Citroën was buried on Friday 5 July at the nearby Montparnasse Cemetery, in a short religious ceremony conducted by the Chief Rabbi of Paris, Dr Weill. Here, after being borne through the streets of Paris from the Quai de Javel on a horse-drawn funeral carriage, followed by a long cortège of mourners walking

Thursday 4 July 1935: André Citroën's body rests on a catafalque in the entrance hall of the Quai de Javel factory as, one by one, his colleagues and employees file past to pay their last respects.

on foot, his body was laid to rest in the family tomb, alongside that of his daughter Solange, who had died as an infant ten years previously.

Among those present with his family at the graveside were the Barons Edouard, James and Henri de Rothschild, the military governor of Paris, General Gourard, representatives of the French government and the civilian administration of the City of Paris and of the French, American and British motor industries. Representing Citroën's British interests were his cousin Daniel Metz and General Sir Ernest Swinton.

Evidently, Citroën's passing was mourned almost as much in England as in France. In its obituary, published the previous day, *The Times* recorded that 'his death removes from the industrial world . . . one of the most striking personalities of post-war years'. The *Daily Telegraph* went further, saying that 'he was a man whose business achievements were astonishing. By sheer ability he succeeded in making his previously unknown name almost as famous as any in Europe. No enterprise was too great for André Citroën. An active brain impelled him to carry out one great commercial adventure after another. The greater the risk, the more the enterprise appealed to him.'

Just over two weeks after Citroën's funeral, at exactly thirty minutes past noon on 22 July 1935, a black 11CV Traction Avant moved off from the headquarters of the Automobile Club de France in the Place de la Concorde in Paris. The event marked the start of what must surely rank as the most severe test of man and machine ever undertaken in motoring history – the world's longest ever marathon run. At the wheel was François Lecot, a fifty-six-year-old hotel-keeper from Rochetaillée-sur-Saône near Lyons, who had already made a name for himself as an amateur rally driver in the service of the Citroën firm. But this time Lecot had embarked on a freelance mission that was to prove a unique and unrepeated feat of driving prowess, an ordeal of more than 250,000 miles, equivalent to over ten circuits of the globe.

Already that day, Lecot had spent eight-and a-half hours at the wheel and had driven 350 miles – yet there was still another 350 miles and nine hours of driving to go. The following day there would be a further 365 miles to cover . . . and the next . . . and the next . . . until an entire 365 consecutive days of almost non-stop round-the-clock driving had been endured. Every single day for the following year, the indefatigable Frenchman was to spend exactly eighteen hours at the wheel of his Citroën, following a gruelling schedule that allowed him just half an hour's rest at meal breaks by day and four hours' sleep at nights, while his car was serviced and repaired. Starting out at Rochetaillée at precisely 3.30 a.m. every day, his itinerary involved a daily 715 mile round trip, heading alternately either north to Paris and back via Saulieu, Auxerre, Sens and Fontainebleau or south to Monte-Carlo via Vienne, Montelimar, Orange and Avignon. Villagers living on his route could tell the time from his passing without looking at their watches. Every day, the Traction Avant went by at exactly the same time, dead on the dot, providing a time check as accurate as the pips on the wireless or the chime of the clock.

Needless to say, the idea behind this extraordinary venture had been hatched eighteen months earlier by André Citroën himself, when searching for a spectacular way to demonstrate the reliability and endurance of the Traction Avant. But after Citroën's demise, the new Michelin management, averse to such publicity stunts, promptly withdrew the offer of official Citroën backing and sponsorship. So Lecot decided to carry out the plan himself, at his own expense, raising the funds by mortgaging his hotel business. Monitored by relays of official scrutineers from the Automobile Club of France, who ensured that an absolute speed limit of 56 mph and an average speed of 40 mph for the duration was observed, the marathon was completed without mechanical problems of any kind, although the car was damaged slightly several times en route as a result of minor collisions and traffic accidents. A standard production model, Lecot's car was modified only by the fitting of a special anti-mist windscreen and the addition of a second left-foot accelerator pedal, to reduce leg fatigue. During the entire run, the robust 1,911 cc engine required only three major services, although its cylinder head was decoked ten times, due to the inferior quality of pre-war petrol and lubricants rather than any defect in the car. Its tyres were changed every 15,000 miles.

In fact, Lecot's trip involved a couple of excursions, just to break the monotony. In January 1936, he took a few days off to compete in the Monte-Carlo Rally, driving to the starting point at Lourenço in Portugal and back before returning home to resume his normal activities. Then, in June, he began a series of visits to the great European capitals, driving in turn from Paris to

Berlin, Amsterdam, Rome, Barcelona, Vienna and Copenhagen to clock up another ten thousand miles, but by July he was back to his old routine.

Lecot's epic marathon ended at Monte-Carlo on the evening of 24 July 1936, with exactly 400,000 kilometres (248,601 miles) on the clock. No other record-breaking attempt involving a single car driven continually by the same driver has ever come remotely near to equalling this achievement. Yet the feat was undertaken not for fame or huge financial gain, but solely as an act of homage to the Traction Avant's creator, André Citroën.

Twenty-three years later, on 9 October 1958, the Quai de Javel in Paris was officially renamed the Quai André Citroën as a permanent (if somewhat belated) tribute to the man who had created there one of France's most renowned and respected automobile companies. But of the factory building that he founded on the site, today there remains not a trace. It was closed as a production centre in 1974, and was demolished in 1983 to make way for a property development scheme. The demolition men took almost nine months to knock down and carry away what, fifty years earlier, André Citroën had constructed in less than five.

In recent years, attempts have been made to rehabilitate the reputation of France's greatest automobile pioneer, and to this end a park and exhibition centre has been created on part of the old Automobiles Citroën factory site, named the Parc André Citroën. From here, it is still possible for the pilgrim to catch a glimpse of the Eiffel Tower, that eternal symbol of French engineering prowess which had fascinated Citroën since boyhood and which had carried his name in lights. Under its shadow, both literally and metaphorically, he spent his whole working life. Surely, there exists no finer monument to André Citroën's towering genius than this world-famous structure, with which he was so closely associated. Like Gustave Eiffel's unique edifice, his achievement rose so much higher, and lasted so much longer, than everything else around it.

CHAPTER TWELVE

Citroën sans Citroën

Following André Citroën's demise, a strange, gloomy quietude settled over the Quai de Javel, according to the reports of various *anciens* (old boys) of the company. The factory brass band, la Fanfare Citroën, was disbanded, and the blasts of publicity that had constantly heralded the founder's name throughout his regime were silenced. All mention of him was forbidden within the environs of the company, and he was no longer referred to in official Citroën communications with the outside world. Even so, Citroën's personality was still to be felt around the place, like a ghost that haunts its former habitation and whose visitations are frequently sensed by the living but never discussed. It was to be three years before his right to an eternal presence there was officially acknowledged by the new management and he was symbolically reinstated by the placing of a small bust in the great entrance foyer of the Quai de Javel building.

The sheer glamour and panache of André Citroën's publicity methods is summed up by this stylish poster for the right-hand-drive version of the 7CV Traction Avant, produced and sold in the United Kingdom in 1935 as the Super-Modern Twelve. After the war, assembly of the Traction Avant by Citroën Cars Ltd at Slough continued until 1955.

... LA CARROSSERIE CITROËN
" TOUT-ACIER MONOCOQUE "

1925
LA PREMIÈRE
TOUT-ACIER

LA TOUT-ACIER
MONOPIÈCE

1935
LA TOUT-ACIER
MONOCOQUE

Si la forme change, la matière demeure : de l'acier, rien que de l'acier.

Depuis leur fondation, les Usines Citroën ont la hantise de faire solide.
Deux étapes capitales marquent les progrès accomplis :
1º La carrosserie " Tout-Acier " (1925) ;
2º La carrosserie " Tout-Acier Monocoque " (1934-35).

La carrosserie " Tout-Acier ", avant d'être " Monocoque ", était faite
de plaques d'acier soudées ensemble électriquement sur une armature
d'acier et boulonnées sur le cadre du châssis. Cet ensemble a fait ses
preuves et sa renommée est universelle. Cependant, si solide qu'il fût, il
comportait un assemblage (carrosserie et châssis).

*Following the Michelin take-over,
Citroën's sophisticated publicity was
immediately replaced by simpler, cheaper,
more factual material, such as this
example produced in late 1935. Pretty
girls and their pets were no longer to be
seen on Citroën posters and
advertisements. Even so, this press ad
gives credit to the huge technological
advances made in a mere ten years under
André Citroën's direction.*

By then, Citroën's great legacy, the Traction Avant, had proved itself to be a
rich inheritance. Thoroughly revised and improved – and, at last, properly
constructed – it had already gained the high reputation that it was to enjoy for
the remainder of its long career, and in consequence was selling extremely well.
So much so, in fact, that its popularity soon restored Automobiles Citroën's
output to former levels and rescued the company from its earlier financial
plight. In due course, the Citroën Traction Avant became one of the minor
export successes of the British motor industry. Known as the 'Light Fifteen', it
was manufactured in an Anglicised right-hand-drive form at Citroën Cars Ltd's
Slough factory, initially from 1935 to 1940 and again from 1945 to 1955, using a
high proportion of British-made components. Almost 16,000 of the 25,000
examples built there were exported throughout the Commonwealth (mainly to
Australia and South Africa), where its rugged construction and robust
performance over unsurfaced roads were considered superior to all other
comparable British-made vehicles, few of which had been designed to cope with
such conditions.

Under the shrewd control and direction of the Michelin men, the renaissance
of Automobiles Citroën continued in postwar years, so that it was soon
numbered once again among the biggest and most successful car companies in

André Citroën's legacy of advanced engineering lived on after the Michelin take-over. In 1938 the Michelin management introduced a new six-cylinder 15CV version of the Traction Avant, to take the place of the abandoned 22CV luxury car. Popularly known as 'la Reine de la Route', the 15-Six represented the height of performance and comfort among French Grand Routieres, until replaced by the DS19 in 1955. This is the seven-seater Familiale version, built in 1939.

France, second only to Renault, now a state-owned concern. Throughout the fifties and sixties, the double chevron firm introduced a long succession of highly advanced and innovative front-wheel-drive vehicles, all descending technically from the Traction Avant and designed by the team of highly gifted engineers recruited by André Citroën and headed by his protégé, André Lefebvre.

Finally, in the early seventies, Automobiles Citroën entered its third and present era. Wishing to concentrate its resources on the manufacture of tyres, the Michelin company entered into a series of negotiations and partnership arrangements with a number of other motor manufacturers including Fiat, with a view to divesting itself entirely of its accidental acquisition. These financial manoeuvres were eventually concluded in 1974 and ratified in 1976, when Automobiles Peugeot bought an 89.95 per cent interest in Citroën from Michelin and the other remaining shareholders. With French government backing and approval, the two famous marques – formerly bitter rivals – were then merged within the framework of a new management structure known as the PSA Group, entirely controlled by Peugeot interests. The intention was that the two partners would combine to provide mutual technical, financial and administrative support. But although sharing joint manufacturing facilities, they would maintain their own distinct character and identity, producing their own individual models (with certain common components), which would then be sold by autonomous distribution networks competing in every sector of the market. Thus the long-term survival of the Citroën marque was assured, albeit in the hands of a company whose management was entirely different in character and philosophy to the two regimes that had gone before.

So what then became of the reputation of the man who gave the Citroën firm its name? Why is it that although the double chevron marque lives on in the modern motoring world and is now more widely recognised around the globe than ever before, so little is generally known and understood about its eponymous creator?

Almost exactly five years after André Citroën's death, the premonitions that had so troubled him, his family and his Jewish friends during the last years of his life came to pass almost exactly as he had feared. In June 1940, the German Army returned once more to the outskirts of Paris, and this time, its blitzkrieg advance was not repelled. On Friday 12 June, an advance guard of the *Wehrmacht* goose-stepped down the Champs-Elysées and through the Arc de Triomphe in

André Citroën in happier times, on holiday at St Moritz in 1933. In the days before ski-lifts, the coming of the caterpillar car transformed winter-sports in the Alps. In fact, Citroën provided a fleet of these C-6 saloons equipped with half-tracks and skis for holiday-makers at the Swiss resort. During the summer, his autochenilles were also used to ferry bathers across the beach at Deauville, where he regularly rented a holiday villa.

an impromptu victory parade, while from the top of the Eiffel Tower and other public buildings the Swastika fluttered over a deserted Paris which had been declared an open city and from which the majority of its population had fled. Later that month, Adolf Hitler, accompanied by Hermann Goering and other members of the Nazi hierarchy, arrived on French soil to sign an armistice agreement between the French and German governments, a humiliating ceremony held on 22 June in the very same railway carriage, located in the Forest of Compiègne, in which Maréchal Foch had accepted the surrender of the German Army in 1918. An eyewitness spoke of the feelings of hate, scorn, revenge and triumph that passed across the Führer's face during the proceedings; newsreel pictures showed him stamping his foot in glee, elated at the defeat he had inflicted on the old enemy.

At dawn on 23 June, Hitler entered Paris in person, as much a tourist as a conqueror. Accompanied by his official architect Albert Speer, he briefly toured the sights of the city, to seek inspiration for the rebuilding of his own capital, Berlin, in a style commensurate with his grandiose ambitions. Standing at the hub of the Third Reich and at the centre of his New Europe, the rebuilt Berlin would eclipse even the magnificence of Paris and last for at least a thousand years. Serving as a model for the Führer's own architectural ambitions, the incomparable historic buildings of the French capital were mercifully spared from destruction, although many of its finest privately-owned art treasures (including those of the Rothschild, Seligman, Wildenstein, Stern and David-Weill families) soon found their way into the possession of the failed painter-turned-dictator and his Nazi henchmen.

For the next four years, a state of military occupation existed throughout the northern half of France, including the entire western and southern coasts and the eastern *départements* bordering Germany, while the remaining territory was governed by a nominally French administration, based at Vichy and headed by the elderly reactionary, Maréchal Pétain. A hero of the First World War, now in his mid-eighties, Pétain was the very same figure who was to have been André Citroën's guest of honour at the inauguration of the trans-Saharan travel company in 1925. In the occupied zone, a state of martial law was imposed, and all civilian matters – legal, commercial and industrial – were placed under ultimate German military control. This meant that the unwelcome presence of a German *Verwalter* (administrator) was forced upon the Citroën factories, where the production of cars promptly ceased. However, Citroën's new Managing Director Pierre Jules Boulanger was a Gaullist who despised both the Nazis and the Vichy regime and refused to cooperate directly with the German authorities, avoiding all contact with the occupiers beyond that which was essential to ensure the continuance of the Citroën firm and to protect the livelihood of its workforce. A distinguished and much-decorated First World War veteran, he was convinced that the *Wehrmacht*'s stay would be short, and by a variety of ploys he steadfastly resisted all pressure to assist the Axis war effort. By breaking all records for slowness of production, he ensured that only a minimal quantity of lorries left the Quai de Javel assembly line to join the German transport fleet, a stand that led to his name appearing on the Gestapo's notorious blacklist of sixty-seven prominent Frenchmen who were known to be hostile to the Reich. Consequently, Boulanger spent the war under constant threat of being arrested and deported to Germany should the Allies suddenly invade or a civil uprising break out in occupied France.

Boulanger's anti-collaborationist stand was not typical of all French industrial bosses, however. As the maker of France's first tank, in 1918, Louis Renault continued to manufacture military vehicles for the *Wehrmacht*, which led to the destruction of his factories in repeated bombing raids by the RAF and USAAF during the Second World War, beginning with an attack on the Billancourt plant made during the night of 3 March 1942. After the Liberation, he was arrested on charges of collaboration, but died in prison while awaiting trial. His firm was then nationalised by the French government as the Régie Renault. Nor was Boulanger's attitude typical of the local politicians and government officials who administered France during the Vichy regime. Many welcomed the end of the musical-chair politics of the Third Republic and the fall of the radical left, and offered no resistance to the Nazi's persecution of the Jews and Bolsheviks, which began in France almost from the very moment of capitulation.

Hitherto, France had been the birthplace of Jewish emancipation in Europe, home of the Declaration of Human Rights and a country in which Jews were permitted to reach the highest levels of power in public administration and politics, including the office of prime minister. In 1940, however, the République Française became the Etat Français, and the cry 'Liberté, Egalité, Fraternité' was officially replaced by 'Travail, Famille, Patrie'. Renouncing all the established democratic institutions of the Third Republic, the Vichy government introduced a number of authoritarian measures in the so-called Free Zone, including a *Statut des Juifs*, intended to eliminate Jews from all positions of influence in French national life. Throughout the Occupation, no Jew could hold a job in the Vichy-controlled armed forces or civil service, or in journalism, publishing, the cinema, the theatre or the other media industries. A second *Statut* passed in 1941 set a quota of a mere 2–3 per cent for Jewish membership of the medical, law and teaching professions. In the Occupied Zone, the anti-Semitic measures introduced were even more oppressive – almost as draconian, indeed, as in Germany. As a prelude, in September 1941 an anti-Semitic exhibition, '*Le Juif et la France*' was staged at the Palais Berlitz in Paris, with the specific aim of arousing xenophobic feelings against naturalised Jews and encouraging denunciations and betrayals. Then, from May 1942 onwards, Jews of all occupations and classes were required to wear a yellow Star of David badge, to carry special identity cards and, if they were shopkeepers, to declare their racial origins with a window poster announcing 'Jewish business'. All were subject to arbitrary fines and the systematic confiscation of their property, forbidden to queue for food or other rationed goods, excluded from using certain communal facilities such as restaurants, cinemas and libraries and even public telephone kiosks, and forced to travel in separate carriages on the Paris metro and other trains.

Finally, in Paris during the night of 16/17 July 1942, 15,000 Jewish citizens, including 4,000 children, were rounded up and herded into an old cycling stadium, the Vélodrome d'Hiver, before being sent on to a special concentration camp established at Drancy on the outskirts of the city. This was nothing more than a staging post in the journey that led inevitably to Auschwitz. In the course of the remaining years of the war, over 75,000 Jews – not foreigners, aliens and refugees, but bona fide French citizens (in fact, 30 per cent of the entire French Jewish population) – were deported to Germany. This persecution was conducted not only by the Gestapo but also by French internal security agencies such as the Police aux Questions Juives and, later, the Milice, or Militia, an autonomous, paramilitary political police force modelled on the SS, whose actions reflected both enthusiastic support of Hitler's racist policies imposed on Paris and Vichy from Berlin and also a deeply-rooted, indigenous anti-Semitism. Protected from deportation by her connections with the influential Saint-Sauveur family, Madame Citroën remained in Paris and survived the Occupation, unlike many of her relations in the Citroën and Bingen families who became victims of the concentration camps. Her daughter Jacqueline had converted to catholicism on marrying Paul-Andre de Saint-Sauveur who, of course, was classed as an Aryan. Her sons Maxime and Bernard escaped to England to join the Free French Forces. Bernard served with distinction in an RAF bomber squadron and was eventually awarded the rank of Commandeur in the Legion d'Honneur, military class. Her brother, Jacques Bingen, became a hero of the Resistance, taking his own life by swallowing a cyanide capsule after being captured by the Germans, so as to avoid betraying secret information under torture by the Gestapo.

This 'Final Solution' in France was precisely the catastrophe that André Citroën had long foreseen and feared, but from which he, at least, had been spared. But not completely. During the German invasion of France, on 3 June 1940 the *Luftwaffe* staged a bombing attack on the Citroën factory, while carrying out Operation Paula, an air offensive intended to destroy the French Air Force and to intimidate the population of Paris. This attack, which included raids on key targets such as airfields, railway junctions, radio transmitters and other communications and industrial centres in the Paris region, was to have unfortunate long-term consequences for the Double Chevron firm and for the reputation of its founder. Although the Quai de Javel factory itself was only slightly damaged, the adjacent Lutetia administrative building housing the company's technical and administrative archive was completely destroyed by a bomb. With it were lost all the documentary records of product design, production and sales during the André Citroën era, together with other papers and correspondence relating to Citroën's business affairs. It can therefore be argued that, intentionally or otherwise, by attacking the factory he created and destroying its archives, the Nazis damaged André Citroën's standing in the eyes of posterity, by depriving historians of documentary evidence relating to many of the technical advances that he originated during his career. The material discovered in the Ricardo archives concerning the development of the diesel engine (a subject about which little was hitherto known in France) is a case in point.

In truth, André Citroën was the victim of his own rebounding publicity and propaganda, and as his life drew to its premature close, his fame turned from renown to notoriety. Portrayed – indeed, caricatured – in the popular press as a frivolous, feckless dilettante, he was depicted principally as a showman and socialite, and his great industrial achievements were overlooked, lost in a welter of inaccurate, sensationalist or downright scandalous reporting that concentrated on the more controversial aspects of his social life. But after his death, popular interest in Citroën as a personality died also, and no longer the target of journalists, cartoonists and gossip columnists, his celebrity status was abruptly withdrawn. Forgotten by the press, his international fame rapidly diminished, and for the following five decades his memory was kept alive only by motoring enthusiasts and connoisseurs. Thus, in postwar years at least, very little has been written about André Citroën – and scarcely more about his cars – in French, let alone in English.

Clearly, as one of the world's most famous 'missing persons', his reputation is long overdue for reassessment and rehabilitation. The conclusion must be that, like many other of history's most productive and creative characters, he was a creature of paradoxes – a complex, enigmatic personality who displayed a puzzling mixture of contradictory traits. A brilliant engineer and manufacturing technologist, he was uninterested in practical mechanics and avoided the detailed aspects of car design and development. A devoted family man who enjoyed a stable marriage and conducted his private life with discretion, he was by no means a puritan, and deserved his reputation as a bon vivant. A socialite who regularly dined among presidents and princes and danced with the kings and queens of the entertainment world, he was not a snob; classless, cosmopolitan, kindly and humane, he was equally at home when eating in a working man's bistro or chatting among his employees at the factory canteen. Recognised in America and Great Britain as a figure of worldwide importance, in France he was regarded as an outsider, and in some circles, even as a troublemaker. And – easily the most baffling contradiction of all – although he ranked as one of the world's greatest ever promoters and champions of the automobile, he actually disliked driving, and rarely took to the wheel of a motor car.

Again, for a man who loved to take a chance, Citroën was remarkably untainted by the get-rich-quick, casino-culture mentality, which prizes short-term business windfalls above long-term gains. But that he was a compulsive gambler there can be no doubt. Although he spent relatively little on the material rewards which motivate other rich and successful men, for his own pleasure and relaxation he enjoyed nothing more than playing baccarat or roulette, often winning or losing very large sums indeed with a casual, carefree, easy-come, easy-go disregard for the bourgeois conventions of thrift and caution. As he so often remarked himself, had he not been a gambler, ready to take the kind of risks that other men avoided, he would never have achieved such fame and fortune. By defying the conventional rules of the game of business, backing his hunches against the odds, much as he did at the green baize tables of the Deauville casino, he won his bet to revolutionise the motor car industry, but in the process lost his bid for personal survival.

Even so, despite his unfortunate downfall, he accomplished four industrial feats of lasting importance and significance. Firstly, in opening at the Quai de Javel France's first truly large-scale, volume-production manufacturing enterprise, André Citroën helped to win perhaps the greatest battle of the First World War, the vital fight to increase the output of munitions. He then went on to help establish, through the example of his great car factory, the solid foundations upon which the industrialisation of France was eventually to be based. At the beginning of the nineteenth century, France had been the second largest trading nation in the world, but a hundred years later it had fallen to fourth in the international league, to become principally an exporter of agricultural produce, foodstuffs, wine, spirits, perfume, fashions and other luxury goods rather than a supplier of manufactured products. More than any other entrepreneur and industrialist of his generation, André Citroën helped to reverse this trend. By establishing among France's politicians, industrialists and educators a profound appreciation of the economic benefits that can flow from a sound investment in science and technology, his work assisted in creating a far more sympathetic understanding of, and attitude towards, large-scale industrial investment and productivity in his country than existed across the Channel.

Secondly, in founding Automobiles Citroën he created not just the largest car company in France but Europe's first truly international automobile concern, a business which continues to thrive and prosper today, albeit under the wings of its erstwhile rival Peugeot. And by establishing a tradition of engineering excellence and innovation, he began that long succession of radical products which gave the double chevron marque the worldwide reputation for technical quality and originality which it still enjoys today. The train of thinking begun with the Type A and continued with the Traction Avant can be traced onwards through a long line of seminally important cars such as the Citroën 2CV, DS and GS, to the models currently being built by Automobiles Citroën today. But more important still, over the past sixty years the influence of the radical thinking he encouraged at the Quai de Javel has spilled out over and beyond the bounds of the Citroën company to infuse the entire French motor industry, and thus to secure his country's status as one of the four most important and successful automobile producers in the modern world. Its present position, based on uncompromising principles of advanced design, high-quality engineering and sophisticated manufacturing technology, can be traced directly to the tradition of excellence established by André Citroën. The end result is that, thanks principally to this farsighted investment in superior technical education and advanced design and technology, the French automobile industry, of which Citroën was so prominent a progenitor, is today the equal of its German, Japanese and American counterparts in technical excellence, but has completely overtaken that of the United Kingdom, by every measurable yardstick of achievement. As other commentators have already remarked, Citroën's contemporaries in the British motor industry – leaders such as Herbert Austin and William Morris – never prized talent, integrity and originality among their engineers to the extent that he did. Six decades later, the consequences of this difference in attitude at the top are plain to see.

The long-standing competition between the Citroën and Renault firms continued for many years. The rivalry fought out on the streets and highways of France by the country's two biggest car producers is epitomised by this atmospheric photo taken on the boulevard de Clichy, Pigalle, in the early thirties. Here, in front of the Moulin Rouge cinema, in a locality once frequented by André Citroën, a 6CV Renault is outflanked and outnumbered by two Citroëns, a Type C2 Trefle and a C4F four-seater faux-cabriolet.

Thirdly, in producing the Traction Avant, André Citroën created the technical framework of the modern family car. By being the first manufacturer in the world to introduce simultaneously on a single model such advanced features as front-wheel-drive transmission, chassisless monocoque construction, hydraulic brakes and independent suspension, he defined the standards of quality, performance and security subsequently adopted – sometimes reluctantly – by the remainder of the international motor industry.

Fourthly, more so than any other individual before or after, André Citroën was responsible for the motorisation of Europe, a revolution not just of transportation but also of social mobility. In pioneering the popular car, Citroën began the process of emancipation that ultimately set its citizens free from the geographical and economic ties which, in the past, had bound them permanently to the place and station in life in which they were born, allowing them to follow their individual talents to a more prosperous and egalitarian future. Indeed, in so far as the destiny of mankind is actually guided by the work of industrialists, engineers, scientists and technologists rather than the more loudly praised efforts of politicians, philosophers, artists and writers, then Citroën can surely be counted as one of the founding fathers of modern Europe and a figure of major significance in the history of the twentieth century. As a dedicated internationalist, he refused to acknowledge divisions of nationality, class or creed, nor would he acknowledge any of the other boundaries, conventions or constraints that might limit the scope of his inventiveness. Only mediocrity and shortsightedness were foreign to him. In the modern phrase, he was surely one of the greatest 'makers and shakers' of his generation.

Although he belonged to a race long renowned as traders, merchants, bankers and financiers, André Citroën believed that real and lasting wealth could only be achieved by the creative process of inventing, designing and manufacturing new products, and never merely by seeking profit for the sake of profit alone. As an industrialist, engineer and entrepreneur, he applied technology in a truly imaginative way, producing an inexhaustible fund of original yet practicable ideas which, with his remarkable flair and expertise, he was able to put into commercial effect. But whether his achievements were energised by a courageous yet mistaken assessment of risk or, as some have claimed, simply by blind, facile optimism is a question for the reader to judge, bearing in mind that, in fairness, the same could be said of any ambitious entrepreneur whose plans go awry due to an unforeseen, indeed unpredictable, change of economic circumstances.

The fact remains that this individualistic and iconoclastic personality was unique among the automobile barons of his era. No other motor-magnate dared to make so great a leap, or risk so hard a fall, in the cause of progress. Continually throughout his career, he pointed the route forward and dictated the pace of change, confounding the caution and cynicism of those rivals who copied him, without ever catching up. Wherever André Citroën led, inevitably the rest were forced to follow in his footsteps, even long after he himself had departed from the scene.

APPENDICES

The Cars of the André Citroën Era

Type	Capacity	Available From	To	Production
REAR WHEEL DRIVE				
A	4cyl 1327cc	June 1919	Dec 1921	24,093
B-2	4cyl 1453cc	June 1921	Oct 1925	89,841
B-2 Caddy Sport	4cyl 1453cc	Oct 1922	Oct 1923	[300]
C2 & C3	4cyl 856cc	May 1922	May 1926	80,759
B-10	4cyl 1453cc	June 1922	Oct 1925	[inc in B2]
B-12	4cyl 1453cc	Oct 1925	Oct 1926	28,700
B-14	4cyl 1539cc	Oct 1926	Jan 1927	119,467
B-14F	4cyl 1539cc	Jan 1927	Oct 1927	[inc in B14]
B-14G	4cyl 1539cc	Oct 1927	Oct 1928	[inc in B14]
AC-4	4cyl 1628cc	Oct 1928	Oct 1929	[inc in C4]
C-4	4cyl 1628cc	Oct 1929	Oct 1930	243,068
C-4F	4cyl 1628cc	Oct 1930	Oct 1931	[inc in C4]
C-4G	4cyl 1767cc	Oct 1931	Oct 1932	[inc in C4]
AC-6	6cyl 2442cc	Oct 1928	Oct 1929	61,273
C-6E	6cyl 2442cc	Jan 1929	Oct 1929	[inc in AC6]
C-6F	6cyl 2442cc	Oct 1929	Oct 1931	[inc in AC6]
C-6G	6cyl 2650cc	Oct 1931	Oct 1932	[inc in AC6]
8CV	4cyl 1453cc	Oct 1932	May 1934	38,835
10CV	4cyl 1767cc	Oct 1932	May 1934	49,249
10CV-Legere	4cyl 1767cc	Oct 1932	May 1934	[inc in 10CV]
15CV	6cyl 2650cc	Oct 1932	May 1934	7,228
15CV-Legere	6cyl 2650cc	Oct 1932	May 1934	[inc in 15CV]

Front Wheel Drive – Traction Avant

Type	Capacity	Available From	To	Production
7A	4cyl 1298cc	May 1934	Jun 1934	7,000
7B	4cyl 1628cc	Jun 1934	Dec 1934	20,620
7S	4cyl 1911cc	Jun 1934	Oct 1934	1,500
7C	4cyl 1628cc	Dec 1934	Mar 1939	61,669
11	4cyl 1911cc	Sep 1934	Jan 1937	18,000
11L	4cyl 1911cc	Sep 1934	Jan 1937	37,100
22	8cyl 3822cc	(Paris Salon 1934 only)		nil

Traction Avant Production

7CV – all production during 1934 & 1935	35,074
11CV – all production during 1934 & 1935	10,995
All Traction Avant types during 1934 & 1935	46,069

OTHER CITROËN MODELS AVAILABLE BETWEEN 1935 AND 1939

Type	Capacity	Available From	To	Production
11BL	4cyl 1911cc	Jan 1937	Mar 1939	40,400
11B	4cyl 1911cc	Jan 1937	Mar 1939	24,800
7C'Eco'	4cyl 1628cc	Mar 1939	Sep 1939	7,800
11BL'Perfo'	4cyl 1911cc	Mar 1939	Sep 1939	22,500
11B'Perfo'	4cyl 1911cc	Mar 1939	Sep 1939	9,350
15	6cyl 2867cc	Apr 1938	Sep 1939	2,000
7UA*	4cyl 1628cc	Jan 1935	Jul 1938	7,260
11UA*	4cyl 1911cc	Jan 1935	Jul 1938	7,400

* Modified Rosalie Type 10CV & 15CV bodies with Traction Avant engines installed in reversed position to drive rear axle.

EUROPEAN CAR PRODUCTION – MAJOR MANUFACTURERS 1919–35

Year	Citroën	Renault	Peugeot	Fiat	Ford GB	Total UK
1919	2,810	2,456	500	1,973	12,175	
1920	12,244	18,700	770	6,584	46,362	
1921	10,993	5,883	6,327	8,988	31,955	
1922	21,025	8,177	7,615	10,466	27,303	
1923	32,678	21,124	10,996	13,629	30,596	73,000
1924	55,387	32,542	14,832	23,310	27,497	117,000
1925	61,487	44,836	20,724	37,054	22,271	132,000
1926	50,404	47,657	23,753	23,363	21,859	153,000
1927	76,077	40,221	21,276	44,404	12,558	165,000
1928	72,356	55,884	25,652	42,694	6,685	165,000
1929	102,891	54,117	31,292	42,780	25,756	182,000
1930	77,788	46,956	43,303	32,219	27,861	170,000
1931	71,932	41,128	33,322	16,419	24,152	159,000
1932	48,027	43,215	28,317	19,680	25,571	171,000
1933	71,472	49,964	36,178	29,646	52,561	221,000
1934	56,123	56,220	35,617	31,507	53,613	257,000
1935	30,759	58,050	41,829	31,735	66,605	312,000
Total	854,453	627,130	382,303	416,451	515,380	

Note: UK figures represent combined total production of private cars only. No figures for individual manufacturers (i.e., Austin and Morris) are available.

Sources: individual companies and Society of Motor Manufacturers and Traders

Citroën 10 hp type A - 1919

Engine: 4 cylinders in line with side valves and removable cylinder head.
2 crankshaft main bearings.
Thermo-syphon cooling – no water pump or fan.
Horizontal Solex carburettor.
Magneto ignition.
Electric self-starter.
Cubic capacity 1,327cc.
Bore 65mm. Stroke 100mm.
Output 18 bhp at 2,100 rpm.
French fiscal rating 8CV.

Transmission: Rear wheel drive, 3 forward speeds plus reverse. Single dry disc clutch.

Suspension: Single inverted quarter elliptic springs at front axle; superimposed double quarter elliptic springs at rear axle.

Steering: Irreversible worm-screw and sector.

Brakes: Pedal operated transmission brake; hand operated wheel brake, acting on rear drums only.

Tyres: Michelin 710mm x 90mm high pressure on solid disc pressed-steel wheels.

Chassis dimensions:
Normal chassis:
3wheelbase 2,83m; track 1.19m; length 4.00m; width 1.41m; height 1,75m
Short chassis:
wheelbase 2,55m; length 3,40m

Weight: Normal chassis   810kg
Short chassis   680kg

Performance: Maximum speed – 65km/hr (40.4 mph)

Fuel consumption: 7.5 litres per 100 km (37 mpg)

Production: 24,093 units including commercial variant

Versions built:
Long chassis: Torpedo (4 seater open tourer); Conduite Intérieure (4 seater limousine); Coupe de Ville (2 seater plus driver) Torpedo Sport; Camionnette (van); Camion (light platform truck)

Short chassis: Torpedo (3 seater open tourer); Conduite Intérieure (3 seater limousine); Coupe de Ville (2 seater plus driver) Camionnette (van)

10HP Type B2; available from June 1921 to June 1922, plus 10HP Type B10; available from June 1922 to September 1925

Citroën B 2 coupé de ville - 1923

Engine: 4 cylinders in line with side valves and removable cylinder head.
2 crankshaft main bearings.
Thermo-syphon cooling.
Horizontal Solex carburettor
Magneto ignition
Electric self-starter
Cubic capacity 1,452cc
Bore 68mm. Stroke 100mm. Output 20 bhp at 2,100 rpm
French fiscal rating 9CV

Transmission: Rear wheel drive, 3 forward speeds plus reverse. Single dry disc clutch.

Suspension: Single inverted quarter elliptic springs at front axle; double quarter elliptic springs at rear axle. Friction dampers on later models.

Steering: Irreversible worm-screw and sector.

Brakes: Pedal operated transmission brake. Hand operated wheel brake, acting on rear drums only.

Tyres: Michelin 710mm x 90mm high pressure (4kg) on solid disc pressed-steel wheels. From 1924, Michelin Confort 730mm x 130mm low pressure (2.2kg)

Chassis dimensions:

Wheelbase	2.83m	(tourer body)
Track	1.19m	
Length	4.00m	
Width	1.41m	
Height	1.75m	

Kerb weight:

B2 tourer	810kg	
B2 saloon	1,020kg	
B10 tourer	1,010kg	
B10 saloon	1,220kg	

Performance: Maximum speed – 72km/hr (44.7 mph)

Fuel consumption: 8 litres per 100 km (35.3 mpg)

Production: 89,841 units including commercial variants

B2 Versions built: Torpedo (open tourer) – 3 and 4 seater; Conduite Intérieure (limousine); Coupe de Ville; Luxury landaulette; Landaulet/Taxi; Camionnette (van); Voiture de livraison (pick-up); Normande (farmer's wagonette); Boulangere (delivery van); Torpedo Caddy Sport

B10 Versions built: Torpedo (4 seater open tourer)

All steel body: Conduite Intérieure (4 seater 6 light saloon) bodies only

Citroën 5 cv type C - 1922

Engine: 4 cylinders in line with side valves and removable cylinder head.
2 crankshaft main bearings.
Thermo-syphon cooling.
Horizontal Solex carburettor
Magneto ignition
Electric self-starter
Cubic capacity 856cc
Bore 55mm. Stroke 90mm
Output 11bhp at 2,100 rpm
French fiscal rating 5CV

Transmission: Rear wheel drive, 3 forward speeds plus reverse. Single dry disc clutch.

Suspension: Single inverted quarter elliptic springs at front axle; double quarter elliptic springs at rear axle.

Steering: Irreversible worm-wheel and sector.

Brakes: Pedal operated transmission brake. Hand operated wheel brake, acting on rear drums only.

Tyres: Michelin 650mm x 80mm high pressure (4kg) on solid disc pressed-steel wheels.

Chassis dimensions:

Wheelbase	2.25m
Track	1.18m
Length	3.20m
Width	1.40m
Height	1.55m

Kerb weight: 543kg

Performance: Maximum speed – 60kph (37.3 mph)

Fuel consumption: 5 litres per 100 km (56.5 mpg)

Versions built: Torpedo C2 (2 seater open tourer); Torpedo C3 (3 seater open tourer – Trefle or Cloverleaf); Cabriolet C2 & C3; Camionette C2 & C3

Production: 80,759 inc 32,567 commercial.

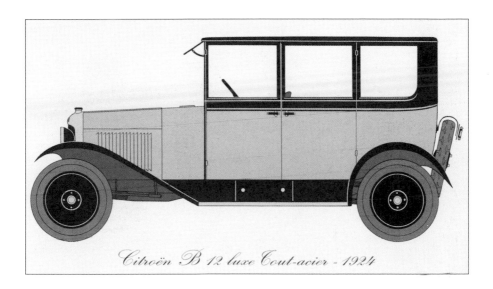

Citroën B 12 luxe Tout-acier - 1924

Engine: 4 cylinders in line with side valves and removable cylinder head.
2 crankshaft main bearings.
Thermo-syphon cooling.
Horizontal Solex carburettor
Magneto ignition
Capacity 1,452cc
Bore 68mm. Stroke 100mm
Output 20 bhp at 2,100 rpm
French fiscal rating 9CV

Transmission: Rear wheel drive, 3 forward speeds plus reverse. Single dry disc clutch. Banjo-type one-piece rear axle.

Suspension: Semi-elliptic springs at front axle; Quarter-elliptic springs with friction dampers at rear axle.

Steering: Irreversible worm-screw and sector.

Brakes: Pedal operated drum brakes on all four wheels.

Tyres: Michelin Confort 730mm x 130 mm low pressure on solid disc pressed-steel wheels.

Chassis dimensions:

Wheelbase	2.87m	(saloon body)
Track	1.22m	
Length	4.10m	
Width	1.41m	
Height	1.83m	

Performance: Maximum speed – 75kph (46.6 mph)

Fuel consumption: 8.5 litres per 100 km (33.2 mph)

Production: 38,381 units

Versions built: Torpedo (all-steel 4 seater open tourer); Torpedo Commercial (drop-down rear door); Conduite Intérieure (all-steel 4 seater, 6 light limousine); Cabriolet (coachbuilt 3 seater); Coupe de Ville (coachbuilt 2 seater plus driver); Landaulet (ditto); Taxi (ditto); Camionnette (van); Normande; Boulangere; Ambulance

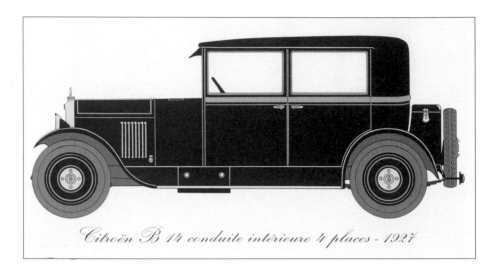

Citroën B 14 conduite intérieure 4 places - 1927

Engine: 4 cylinders in line with side valves and removable cylinder head.
2 crankshaft main bearings.
Thermo-syphon water cooling.
Horizontal Solex carburettor
Magneto ignition
Capacity 1,539cc
Bore 70mm. Stroke 100mm
Output 22 bhp at 2,300 rpm
French fiscal rating 9CV

Transmission: Rear wheel drive, 3 forward speeds plus reverse. Single dry disc clutch plate. Gleason banjo-type rear axle.

Suspension: Semi-elliptic front springs with friction dampers.
Superimposed quarter-elliptic rear springs with friction dampers.
Steering: Irreversible worm-wheel and sector.

Brakes: Pedal operated drum brakes on all four wheels, assisted by Westinghouse vacuum servo on B14F & B14G. Lever operated hand brake acting on rear wheels.

Tyres: Michelin Confort 730mm x 130 mm low pressure on solid disc pressed-steel wheels with nickel plated hub caps.

Chassis dimensions:
Wheelbase 2.87m (saloon body)
Track   1.23m

Length	4.10m
Width	1.41m
Height	1.83m

Kerb weight: 1,150kg

Performance: Maximum speed – 80kph
(49.7 mph)

Fuel consumption: 8.5 litres per 100 km
(33.2 mpg)

Production: 119,467 units not including commercial derivatives.

Versions built: Torpedo (4 seater open tourer)

B14 & B14F
Conduite Intérieure (4 door, 6 light saloon); Coach (2 door, 4 light saloon); Cabriolet (2 or 4 seater versions); Coupe de Ville (2 seater plus driver); Taxi Conduite Intérieure (4 seater plus driver); Taxi/Landaulet (2 seater plus driver); Torpedo Commercial Camionnette (van); Normande; Boulangere; Camion (lorry)

Plus B14G
Berline (4 door, 4 light, 4 seat saloon); Familiale (4 door, 6 light, 7 seat saloon); Cabriolet Decapotable (2 or 4 seat drop-head coupe); Faux Cabriolet (2 or 4 seat fixed-head coupe)

Citroën C 4 conduite intérieure 5 places - 1929

Engine: 4 cylinders in line with side valves and removable cylinder head.
3 crankshaft main bearings.
Water cooling with pump and radiator fan
Horizontal Solex carburettor.
Coil and distributor ignition.
Cubic capacity 1,628cc
Bore 72mm. Stroke 100mm
Output 30 bhp at 3,000 rpm
French fiscal rating 9CV

Transmission: Rear wheel drive.
3 forward speeds plus reverse
Single dry disc clutch.
Gleason banjo-type rear axle.

Suspension: Four semi-elliptic springs set obliquely to the chassis axis, all with friction dampers.

Steering: Irreversible worm-screw and sector.

Brakes: Pedal operated drum brakes on all four wheels, assisted by Westinghouse vacuum servo. Lever operated hand brake acting on transmission.

Tyres: Michelin Confort 13 x 45 low pressure on solid disc pressed-steel wheels with chromed hub caps.

Chassis dimensions:

Wheelbase	2.85m (saloon)
Track	1.32m
Length	4.10m
Width	1.58m
Height	1.74m

Kerb weight: 180kg

Performance: Maximum speed – 90kph (55.9 mph)

Fuel consumption: 9 litres per 100 km (31.4 mpg)

Production: 243,068 units of all types

Versions built: Berline (4 seat, 4 light saloon); Conduite Intérieure (4 seat, 6 light saloon); Familiale (7 seat, 6 light saloon); Cabriolet Decapotable (2 or 4 seater drophead); Faux Cabriolet (2 or 4 seater fixed head); Torpedo (4 or 7 seat open tourer); Torpedo Commercial; Conduite Intérieure; Commercial; Taxi Decapotable; Camionnette (van)

Plus C4F
Roadster; Coupe Landaulet; Berline Large (width 1.70m, track 1.42m); Conduite Intérieure Large (ditto)

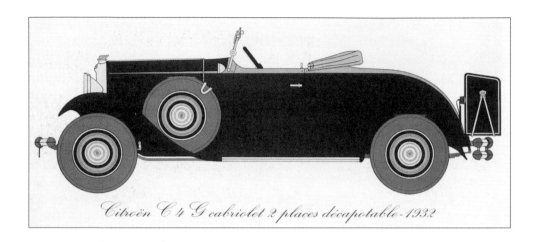

Citroën C 4 G cabriolet 2 places décapotable-1932

Engine: 4 cylinders in line with side valves and removable cylinder head.
3 crankshaft main bearings.
Water cooling with pump and radiator fan
Horizontal Solex carburettor.
Coil and distributor ignition.
Cubic capacity 1,767cc.
Bore 75mm. Stroke 100mm.
32 bhp at 2,700 rpm.
French fiscal rating 10CV.

Transmission: See AC4.

Suspension: See AC4

Steering: See AC4

Brakes: See AC4

Tyres: Michelin Confort 13 x 45 low pressure on solid disc pressed-steel wheels with chromed hub caps.

Chassis dimensions:

Wheelbase	2.78m (standard)
Track	1.34m (standard)
Length	4.10m
Width	1.58m
Height	1.74m

Kerb weight: 1,200kg (standard)

Performance: Maximum speed – 95kph (69 mph)

Fuel consumption: 9 litres per 100 km (31.4 mpg)

Production: see C4

Versions built: Berline; Conduite Intérieure; Familial; Commercial; Roadster; Cabriolet; Faux; Cabriolet; Torpedo; Torpedo Familial; Torpedo; Commercial; Conduite Intérieure; Commercial; Coupe Landaulet

(All but Commercial versions also available in Grand Luxe specification)

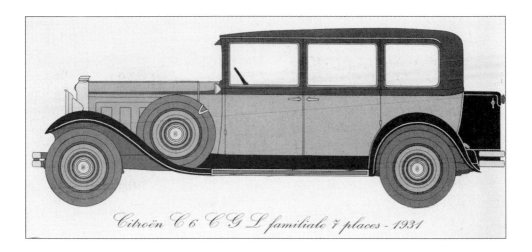

Citroën C 6 C G L familiale 7 places - 1931

Engine: 6 cylinders in line with side valves and removable cylinder head.
3 crankshaft main bearings.
Water cooling with pump and radiator fan
Horizontal Solex carburettor.
Coil and distributor ignition
Cubic capacity 2,442cc
Bore 72mm. Stroke 100mm
Output 42 bhp at 3,000 rpm
French fiscal rating 14CV

Transmission: Rear wheel drive, 3 forward speeds plus reverse. Single dry disc clutch. Gleason banjo-type rear axle.

Suspension: Four semi-elliptic springs with friction dampers.

Steering: Adjustable worm-wheel and sector.

Brakes: Pedal operated drum brakes on all four wheels, acting by rods and cables, assisted by Westinghouse vacuum servo. Lever operated hand brake acting on rear wheels.

Tyres: Michelin Confort 14 x 45 low pressure on solid disc pressed-steel wheels with chromed hub caps.

Chassis dimensions:
Wheelbase   2.95m (saloon grand tourisme)
Track   1.32m

Kerb weight: 1,275kg

Performance: Maximum speed – 105kph (65.2 mph)

Fuel consumption: 14 litres per 100 km (20.2 mpg)

Production: 61,273 units of all types

Versions built: Berline Luxe

AC6 & C6F
Berline Grand Tourisme; Conduite Intérieure Luxe; Familial Luxe; Cabriolet Decapotable (2 or 4 seater); Faux Cabriolet (2 or 4 seater); Torpedo, Torpedo Grand Tourisme; Torpedo Familial, Coupe de Ville; Roadster, Camionnette (van) Camion

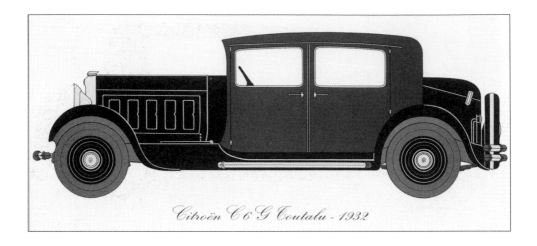

Citroën C 6 G Toutalu - 1932

Engine: 6 cylinders in line with side valves and removable cylinder head.
3 crankshaft main bearings.
Water cooling with pump and radiator fan
Horizontal Solex carburettor
Coil and distributor ignition
Cubic capacity 2,650cc
Bore 75mm. Stroke 100mm
Output 50 bhp at 3,000 rpm
French fiscal rating 14CV

Chassis dimensions:

Wheelbase	2.96m (standard)
Track	1.42m (standard)
Length	4.60m

Width	1.70m
Height	1.74m

Kerb weight: 1,380kg (standard)

Performance: Maximum speed – 110km/hr (68.4 mph)

Fuel consumption: 15 litres per 100 km (18.8 mpg)

Production: see C6

Versions built: see C6 plus:
Coachbuilt Berline Toutalu (all-alloy);
Coachbuilt Drophead Coupe by Sical

Citroën 8 A berline - 1932

Engine: 4 cylinders in line with side valves and removable cylinder head. 3 crankshaft main bearings. Water cooling with pump and radiator fan Horizontal Solex carburettor Coil and distributor ignition Capacity 1,452cc Bore 68mm Stroke 100mm Output 32 bhp at 3,200 rpm French fiscal rating 8CV

Transmission: Rear wheel drive. 3 forward speeds plus reverse. Single dry disc clutch. Gleason banjo-type rear axle. Optional free-wheel device.

Suspension: Four semi-elliptic springs, mounted in silent blocks. Friction dampers.

Steering: Hour-glass screw and sector.

Brakes: Bendix type pedal operated drum brakes on all four wheels. Lever operated hand brake acting on rear wheels.

Tyres: Michelin Super Confort 140 x 40 low pressure tyres on steel disc wheels with large-diameter chromed hub caps.

Chassis dimensions:

Wheelbase	2.70m
Track	1.34m
Length	4.24m
Width	1.62m
Height	1.67m

Carosserie: All steel 'Monopiece' unitary construction

Kerb weight: 1,165kg

Performance: Maximum speed – 90kph (55.9 mph)

Production: 38,835 units including commercial versions

Versions built: Berline (4 door, 4 light saloon); Berline Commercial (with rear door); Coach (7 different 2 door versions including cabriolet and faux cabriolet); Torpedo (4 door open tourer); Torpedo Commercial (with rear door); Camionnette (van)

Citroën 10 A conduite intérieure 5 places - 1934

Engine: 4 cylinders in line with side valves and removable cylinder head.
3 crankshaft main bearings.
Water cooling with pump and radiator fan
Horizontal Solex carburettor
Coil and distributor ignition
Cubic capacity 1,767cc
Bore 75mm. Stroke 100mm
Output 36 bhp at 3,200 rpm
French fiscal rating 10CV

Transmission: Rear wheel drive, 3 speeds plus reverse.
Single dry disc clutch.
Gleason banjo-type rear axle.
Optional free-wheel device

Suspension: 4 semi-elliptic leaf springs mounted in silent blocks. Initially, friction dampers, later, hydraulic shock absorbers. Final versions had torsion bar independent front suspension.

Steering: Hour-glass screw and sector.

Brakes: Bendix type pedal operated drum brakes on all four wheels. Lever operated hand brake acting on rear wheels.

Tyres: Michelin Super Confort 140 x 40 low pressure tyres on steel disc wheels with large-diameter chromed hub caps.

Chassis dimensions:

Wheelbase	3.00m
Track	1.42m
Width	1.72m
Height	1.69m

Note: Type 10CV Legere had same chassis/body dimensions as Type 8CV

Carosserie: All-steel 'Monopiece' unitary construction

Performance: Maximum speed – 100kph (62.1 mph)

Production: 49,249 units including commercial versions

Versions built: Berline (4 door, 4 light, 5 seat saloon)
Standard chassis Conduite Intérieure (6 light saloon); Commercial (2 different versions); Familial (6 light 7 seat saloon); Coach (5 different 2 door versions including cabriolet and faux cabriolet); Torpedo (3 different versions); Taxi (2 different versions); Camionnette (van); Camion (lorry)
Grand Luxe Coach (2 door 5 seat); Coach Toutalu (2 versions, all-alloy body); Roadster (2 seat with dickey); Legere Berline
Short chassis Torpedo Coach (7 different versions)

Citroën 15 AL coach - 1932

Engine: 6 cylinders in line with side valves and removable cylinder head.
3 crankshaft main bearings.
Water cooling with pump and radiator fan
Horizontal Solex carburettor
Coil and distributor ignition
Cubic capacity 2,650cc
Bore 75mm Stroke 100mm
Output 56 bhp at 3,200 rpm
French fiscal rating 10CV

Transmission: Rear wheel drive - 3 forward speeds plus reverse.
Single dry disc clutch.
Gleason banjo-type rear axle.
Optional free-wheel device

Suspension: 4 semi-elliptic springs mounted in silentblocks. Hydraulic shock absorbers. Final versions had torsion bar independent front suspension.

Steering: Hour-glass and sector

Brakes: Bendix type pedal operated drum brakes on all four wheels. Lever operated hand brake acting on rear wheels.

Tyres: Michelin Super Confort 160 x 40 low pressure on steel disc wheels with large-diameter chromed hub caps.

Chassis dimensions:
Wheelbase   3.15m
Track   1.42m

Width   1.72m
Height   1.70m

Note; 15V Legere had same chassis/body dimensions as 8CV with longer bonnet.

Carosserie All steel 'Monopiece' unitary construction

Performance: Maximum speed – 110kph (68.4 mph)

Production: 7,228 units including commercial versions

Versions built: Berline (4 door, 2 light, 5 seat saloon)

Standard chassis Conduite Intérieure (6 light, 5 seat saloon); Familial (6 light, 7 seat saloon); Torpedo (2 different versions); Coach (5 different 2 door versions including cabriolet and faux cabriolet)

Grand Luxe Berline; Conduite Intérieure (2 versions); Familial; Coach (4 different versions); Roadster; Coupe de Ville

Short chassis Berline

Leger Torpedo; Coach (7 different versions)
Note: In January 1934, all three Rosalie models (8CV,10CV & 15CV) were relaunched with a revised, semi-streamlined body featuring a sloped-back radiator shell, elongated chromed headlamp housings and enclosed front wings, in versions designated NH (Nouvel Habillage)

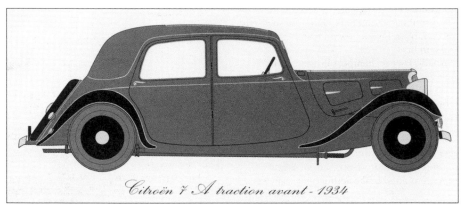

Citroën 7 A traction avant - 1934

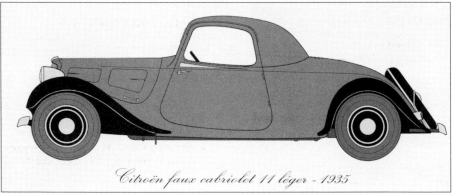

Citroën faux cabriolet 11 léger - 1935

Engine: 4 cylinders in line with overhead valves plus removable cylinder head and wet liners.
3 crankshaft main bearings.
Water cooling with pump and radiator fan
Downdraught Solex carburettor
Coil and distributor ignition

Characteristics

7A
   Cubic capacity 1,303cc
   Bore 72mm. Stroke 80mm
   Output 32 bhp at 3,500 rpm
   French fiscal rating 7CV

7B
   Cubic capacity 1,529cc
   Bore 78mm. Stroke 80mm
   Output 35 bhp at 3,500 rpm
   French fiscal rating 9CV

7C
   Cubic capacity 1,628cc
   Bore 72mm. Stroke 100mm
   Output 36 bhp at 3,800 rpm
   French fiscal rating 9CV

7S, 11AL & 11A
   Cubic capacity 1,911cc
   Bore 782mm Stroke 100mm
   Output 46 bhp at 3,800 rpm
   French fiscal rating 11CV

Transmission: Front wheel drive by cardan shafts. 3 forward speeds (2 synchronised) plus reverse. Single dry disc clutch.

Suspension: Fully independent at front, by longitudinal torsion bars; semi-independent at rear, by trailing axle with transverse torsion bars.
Initially, friction dampers but hydraulic telescopic type from April 1935 onwards

Steering: Initially, hour-glass worm and segment type, then from May 1936 onwards, rack and pinion.

Brakes: Lockheed hydraulically operated drum brakes on all four wheels. Lever & cable operated hand brake acting on rear wheels.

Tyres: Michelin Super Confort 140 x 40 on Michelin
Stop steel wheels with chromed hub caps.

Chassis dimensions:

Wheelbase	2.91m
Track	1.34m

7A, 7B,

Length	4.38m

7C, 7S, IIAL

Width	1.56m

(Legere type)

Height	1.52m

Chassis dimensions:

Wheelbase	3.09m (saloon)
	3.27m familial)
Track	1.46m

11A

Length	4.65m (saloon)
	4.85m (familial)
Width	1.76m

(Normale type)

Height	1.54m (saloon)
	1.58m (familial)

Carosserie All steel monocoque unitary construction

Kerb weight 900 kg (7A); 1025 kg (7C); 1100 kg (11A)

Performance:
Maximum speed: 95kph – 7A (59 mph)
100kph – 7B and 7C (62 mph)
110kph – 11A (68.4 mph)

Fuel consumption:
9 litres per 100 km – 7A & 7C (31.4 mpg)
10 litres per 100 km – 7B & 7S (28.2 mpg)
11 litres per 100 km – 11A (25.7 mpg)

Production during 1934 & 1935:
7CV – 35,074
11CV – 10,995

Total Traction Avant – 46,069

Versions built: 7A, 7B, 7C, 11AL; Berline (4 light 4/5 seat saloon)

(Legere type) Cabriolet (2 + 2 in dickey seat); Faux Cabriolet (2 + 2 in dickey seat)

11A
Berline (4 light 5/6 seats)

(Normale type)
Conduite Intérieure (6 light 5/6 seats); Familial (6 light 7/9 seats); Cabriolet Faux Cabriolet; Coupe de Ville (2 versions)

Sources and Bibliography

In French

Bellu, René. *Toutes les Citroën*, Paris, Editions J.-P. Delleville, 1979
Borge and Viasnoff. *La Traction Avant*, Paris, Balland, 1975
—. *La Album de la Traction*, Paris, Editions E/P/A, 1978
Citroën SA *Citroën 1919–1939*, Paris, Delpire, 1968
de Serres, Olivier. *Le Grand Livre de la Traction Avant*, Paris, Editions E/P/A, 1984
—. *Le Grand Livre Citroën, tous les modèles*, Paris, Editions E/P/A, 1988
Dumont, Pierre. *Quai de Javel, Quai André Citroën*, Paris, Editions E/P/A, 1978
Reiner, Sylvain. *La Tragédie d'André Citroën*, Paris, Amiot Dumont, 1954
Rocherand, Charles. *André Citroën, souvenir d'une collaboration*, Paris, Editions Lajeunesse, 1938
Rousseau, Jacques. *Histoire mondiale de l'Automobile*, Paris, Hachette, 1958
Sabates, Fabien. *Croisières Héroique Citroën*, Paris, Baschet, 1984
—. *Moi Citroën*, Paris, Rétroviseur, 1994
— and Schweitzer, Sylvie. *André Citroën: les Chevrons de la Gloire*, Paris, Editions E/P/A, 1980
Voisin, Gabriel. *Mes Mille et une Voitures*, Paris, La Table Ronde, 1962
Wolgensinger, Jacques. *Citroën 1919–1939*, Paris, Delpire, 1967
—. *André Citroën*, Paris, Flammarion, 1991

Automobiles Citroën publications and archive material:

Adieu à Javel (commemorative brochure, 1976)
Centenaire de la naissance d'André Citroën (commemorative brochure, 1978)
Dates (corporate history brochure, 1986)
En avant la traction ((commemorative brochure, 1984)
Généalogie (booklet, 1979)
Le Bulletin Citroën (company magazine, 1924–33)
Le Double Chevron (company magazine, 1965–86)
Les Jouets Citroën (commemorative brochure, 1978)
Publicité (corporate history brochure, 1986)

In English

Allan, Tony. *An American in Paris*, London, Bison Books & Linkline Publications, 1977
Beevors, A. and Cooper, A. *Paris After the Liberation*, London, Hamish Hamilton, 1994
Byrd, Richard E. *Antarctic Discovery*, London, Putnam, 1936
Cobban, Alfred. *A History of Modern France*, vol. 3, London, Pelican, 1965
Georgano, N. *The Complete Encyclopedia of Motor Cars*, London, Ebury Press, 1973
—. *Cars 1886–1930*, Gothenburg, Nordbok, 1985
—. *The World Guide to Automobiles*, London, Macdonald Orbis, 1987
Gregory, Alexis. *The Gilded Age: The Super-rich of the Edwardian Era*, London, Cassel, 1993
Haardt and Audouin-Dubreuil. *Across the Sahara by Motor Car*, London, Fisher & Unwin, 1924
—. *The Black Journey*, New York, Cosmopolitan, 1927
Johnson, Paul. *A History of the Jews*, London, Weidenfeld & Nicholson, 1987
Lacey, Robert. *Ford: The Men and the Machine*, Boston, Little, Brown, 1986
le Fevre, Georges. *An Eastern Odyssey (la Croisière Jaune)*, London, Gollancz, 1935

Nevins, A. and Hill, F. *Ford*, 3 vols, New York, Charles Scribner's Sons, 1957
Pryce-Jones, David. *Paris in the Third Reich*, London, Collins, 1981
Rhodes, A. *Louis Renault*, London, Cassell, 1969
Richardson, K. *The British Motor Industry 1896–1939*, London, MacMillan, 1977
Sedgewick, M. *Cars of the Thirties and Forties*, Gothenburg, Nordbok, 1979
Shirer, William. *The Rise and Fall of the Third Reich*, London, Secker & Warburg, 1960
—. *The Collapse of the Third Republic*, London, Heinemann/Secker & Warburg, 1970
Swinton, Major-General Sir Ernest. *Over my Shoulder*, Oxford, George Ronald, 1951
Wistrich, Robert S. *Anti-Semitism: The Longest Hatred*, London, Thames Mandarin, 1991
Wood, J. *Wheels of Misfortune: The Rise and Fall of the British Motor Industry*, London, Sidgwick & Jackson, 1988

Archives:

Ricardo Consulting Engineers Ltd
The Ford Motor Company, USA
The Royal National Lifeboat Institution
The Tank Museum
Royal Archives, Windsor Castle

Newspapers, magazines and periodicals:

Daily Mail
Daily Sketch
Daily Telegraph
Light Car & Cyclecar
Motor
National Geographic:
vol. XLV, no. 1 (January 1924); vol. XLIX, no. 6 (June 1926); vol. LIX, no. 6 (June 1931); vol. LX, no. 4 (October 1931); vol. LXI, no. 3 (March 1932); vol. LXII, no. 5 (November 1932)
New York Times
The Autocar
Times

Index

Albert 1st (King of Belgium) 103
Amschel, Meyer 8
Artault, Ernest 51
Audouin-Dubreuil, Louis 93, 105, 116, 126

Bacquet (General) 38
Baker, Josephine 51, 80
Bakst, Leon 30
Bechet, Sidney 80
Bedaux, Charles 185
Bendix, Vincent 136
Bertoni, Flaminio 172
Bettembourg (Commandant) 92, 105
Billancourt (Renault factory) xx, 175
Bingen, Giorgina 35
Bingen, Jacques 213
Blum, Leon 198
Boas, Andre 28
Bollée, Amédée 24
Boulanger, Pierre-Jules 197, 210, 211
Bradley, W.F. 68, 175
Brasier, Henri 31
Breguet, Louis 180
Broglie, Maurice 172
Brook Green (Hammersmith depot & show-
    rooms) 69, 89
Brull, Charles 105, 120
Budd, Edward G. 64, 159, 172
Bugatti, Ettore 73, 197
Byrd, Richard E. (Rear Admiral USN) 137,
    141

Capel, Arthur 'Boy' 35
Chaminsky, Witold 193
Chanel, Gabrielle 'Coco' 35, 84
Chaplin, Charlie 43
Chausson, Gaston 180
Chevalier, Maurice 30, 82
Chiang Kai-Shek (Marshal) 117
Chrysler, Walter 150
Citroën, Barend/Bernard 6, 7, 9
Citroën, Bernard (brother of André) 13, 28, 29,
    38
Citroën, Bernard (son of André) 21
Citroën, David 32
Citroën, Hugues 13, 28, 32, 41

Citroën, Jaqueline 192
Citroën, Levie 7
Citroën, Maxime 213
Citroen/Limoenman, Roelof 7
Citroen/Kleinmann, Masza 6
Citroen/Rooseboom, Netje 8
Condorcet (Lycée) 11, 23, 175
Congress of American Heavy Industries (8th)
    148
le Corbuiser 52, 78
Cuinet, Raoul 172, 181

Daladier, Edouarde 195
Daninos, Jean 171, 172
David-Weill, Pierre 191
Delaunay, Sonia 78
Devonshire House, London (Piccadilly show-
    rooms) 74
Disraeli, Benjamin 8
Dollfus, Maurice 201
Doumergue, Gaston 104, 195
Dreyfus, Alfred (Dreyfus affair) 19
Dufresne, Louis 51, 156
Dumont, Pierre 115
Duncan, Isadora 29

Ecole Polytechnique, Paris 16, 17, 19
Edison, Thomas 152, 155
Edward VII (as King or Prince of Wales) 30,
    32
Edward VIII (as Prince of Wales or Duke of
    Windsor) 79, 107, 110, 134, 136
Eiffel, Gustave (and Eiffel Tower) 12, 13, 76
Eknayan, Atanik 34, 39, 191
Estienne, Jean-Baptiste (General) 95, 100
Exposition (Grande Universelle de Paris, 1887)
    13
Exposition (des Arts Decoratif, Paris, 1925)
    76

Faroux, Charles 186
Ferguson, Archibald 165
Firestone, Harvey 155
Flandin, Pierre-Etienne 198
Foch, Ferdinand (Maréchal) 47, 211
Ford, Edsel 141

Ford, Henry 22, 33, 44, 61, 63, 137, 142, 151, 152, 179, 184, 191
Franchiset, Pierre 172, 181
Frantzen, Paul 192, 200

Gabriel, Sir Vivian (Colonel) 118, 121
Galliéni, Joseph (General) 37
Gaston Ltd 68
George VI (as Duke of York) 110
Goebbels, Joseph (Doctor) 154
Goldfeder, Bronislaus 21
Grégoire, Jean-Albert 172
Grosvenor, Hugh (2nd Duke of Westminster) 84
Guillot, Louis 33

Haardt, Georges-Marie 33, 39, 65, 67, 94, 116, 133, 156, 192, 194
Hackin, Joseph 119
Harbleicher, André (and daughter Suzanne) 32
Herrick, Myron T. 79
Hermet, Antoine 198
Hinstin, Jacques 28, 31
Highland Park (Ford factory at Dearborn, USA) 33
Hitler, Adolf 63, 178, 211
Hoover, Herbert 44, 148
Hylton, Jack 84

Jacovleff, Alexandre 105, 119
Jacopozzi, Fernand 76
Julien, Maurice 172

Kegresse, Adolphe 61, 85, 99
Kendal, Denis 181
King, Benjamin xxx
King Su-Jen (Marshal) 129, 131
Knight, Charles (and Silent Knight engines) 32

Lapperine, Henri (General) 92, 93
Laval, Pierre 149
Lazard Frères (merchant bankers) 191, 193
Lecot, Francois 182, 205-6
Ledwinka, Joseph 172
Lefebvre, André 173, 174
Lefevre, Georges 119
Lehideux, Francois 176
Lemaire, Pierre 144
Lindbergh, Charles 78
Loucheur, Louis 38
Lourde, Marcel 89
Louys, Pierre 114, 158

Manheimer, Charles 34, 193
Marchand, Cesar 160
Mattern, Ernest 34
Maxim's (restaurant) 30, 52, 175
Menuhin, Yehudi 83

Mercedes-Benz (diesel engines) 162
Metz, Daniel 28, 67, 69, 72, 73, 89, 180, 204
Michelat, Arthur-Leon 113
Michelin, Edouard (and brother André) 72, 196
Michelin, Marcel 180
Michelin, Pierre 197, 200-1
Minerva (automobiles) 32
Moch, Jules 198
Mole, Raymond 180
Mors (automobiles) 31, 33, 172
Moyet, Edmond 55
Muller, William J. 172

National Geographical Society 116, 148
Nicholas II (Tsar of Russia) 85

Ostheimer, Jean 200

Perry, Sir Perceval (later Lord Perry) 44, 73, 152, 210
Pershing (General) 44
Petain, Phillippe (Maréchal) 45, 103, 211
Petropavlosky, Vladimir 120
Peugeot/PSA (automobiles) 209
Pitchford, Jack 164
Point, Victor (Lieutenant-Commander) 119, 126, 128
Poirer, Leon 105
Pommier, Alfred 193
Prud'homme, Roger 178

Quai de Javel, Paris (Citroën factory) 40-2, 176-7, 207
Queen Mary (consort of King George V) 110

Reiner, Sylvain 134
Renault, Louis 11, 23, 103, 155, 174, 179, 180, 186, 198, 212
Ricardo, Sir Harry 163
Rocherand, Charles 62, 114, 156
Rockefeller, John D. 64, 137
Rolls, Hon C.S 32
Rouge River (Ford factory at Detroit) 61
Rothschild (family) 8, 204
Royal National Lifeboat Institution 110

de Saint-Sauveur, Armand 192, 213
de Saint-Sauveur, Paul-André 192, 213
Sainturat, Maurice 163
Salomon, Jules 54
Sartre, Jean-Paul 11
Schwab, Felix 33, 67, 73, 193
Schwob de Héricourt, Jacques 28, 86
Sensaud de Lavaud, Dimitri 173
Simenon, Georges 80
Sizair & Naudin (automobiles) 31
Slough Works (Citroën Cars Ltd factory) 73, 208

Slough Estates 88
Smith, F.E (as 1st Earl of Birkenhead) 111
Sorenson, Charles E. 191
Stavisky, Serge 196
Swinton, Sir Ernest (General) 89, 118, 180, 204

Taylor, Frederick Winslow 22, 39

Teilhard de Chardin, Pierre (pere) 120
Thyssen, Heinrich 150

Voisin, Gabriel 51, 81, 114, 162, 173

Williams, Maynard Owen 119, 132, 149
Wisner, Rene 164